Learning Scala

Jason Swartz

Beijing · Cambridge · Farnham · Köln · Sebastopol · Tokyo

Learning Scala

by Jason Swartz

Copyright © 2015 Jason Swartz. All rights reserved.

Printed in the United States of America.

Published by O'Reilly Media, Inc., 1005 Gravenstein Highway North, Sebastopol, CA 95472.

O'Reilly books may be purchased for educational, business, or sales promotional use. Online editions are also available for most titles (*http://safaribooksonline.com*). For more information, contact our corporate/institutional sales department: 800-998-9938 or *corporate@oreilly.com*.

Editors: Simon St. Laurent and Meghan Blanchette	**Indexer:** Ellen Troutman
Production Editor: Colleen Lobner	**Cover Designer:** Ellie Volckhausen
Copyeditor: Kim Cofer	**Interior Designer:** David Futato
Proofreader: Charles Roumeliotis	**Illustrator:** Rebecca Demarest

December 2014:   First Edition

Revision History for the First Edition:

2014-12-08:   First release

See *http://oreilly.com/catalog/errata.csp?isbn=9781449367930* for release details.

ISBN: 978-1-449-36793-0

[LSI]

For my loving wife, who foresees great prospects; and for my loving daughter, who also foresees the first printed copy coming her way.

Table of Contents

Part II. Object-Oriented Scala

Preface

Welcome to *Learning Scala*. In this book I will provide you with a comprehensive yet approachable introduction to the Scala programming language.

Who This Book Is For

This book is meant for developers who have worked in object-oriented languages such as Java, Ruby, or Python and are interested in improving their craft by learning Scala. Java developers will recognize the core object-oriented, static typing and generic collections in Scala. However, they may be challenged to switch to Scala's more expressive and flexible syntax, and the use of immutable data and function literals to solve problems. Ruby and Python developers will be familiar with the use of function literals (aka closures or blocks) to work with collections, but may be challenged with its static, generic-supporting type system.

For these and any other developers who want to learn how to develop in the Scala programming language, this book provides an organized and examples-based guide that follows a gradual learning curve.

Why Write "Learning Scala"?

When I picked up Scala in early 2012, I found the process of learning the language was longer and more challenging than it ought to be. The available books on Scala did cover the core features of the language. However, I found it difficult to switch from Java to Scala's unfamiliar syntax, its preference for immutable data structures, and its sheer extensibility. It took me several weeks to become comfortable writing new code, several months to fully understand other developers' code, and up to a year to figure out the more advanced features of the language.

I chose to write this book so that future developers will have an easier time learning the language. Now, even using this book the process of learning Scala won't be *easy*; picking up new skills is always going to be challenging, and learning a new language with an unfamiliar syntax and new methodologies is going to take dedication and lots of work. However, this book at least should make the process easier. Hopefully it will ensure that more developers than before will pick up Scala, and also become capable enough to work with it as their main language.

Why Learn Scala (or, Why Should You Read "Learning Scala")?

I enjoy developing with Scala and highly recommend it to anyone writing server applications and other types of programs suitable for Java-like languages. If you are working in domains suitable for running the Java Virtual Machine such as web applications, services, jobs, or data processing, then I'll certainly recommend that you try using Scala.

Here's *why* you should take this advice and learn to develop in Scala.

Reason 1—Your Code Will Be Better

You will be able to start using functional programming techniques to stabilize your applications and reduce issues that arise from unintended side effects. By switching from mutable data structures to immutable data structures and from regular methods to pure functions that have no effect on their environment, your code will be safer, more stable, and much easier to comprehend.

Your code will also be simpler and more expressive. If you currently work in a dynamic language such as Python, Ruby, or JavaScript, you already are familiar with the benefits of using a short, expressive syntax, avoiding unnecessary punctuation, and condensing map, filter, and reduce operations to simple one-liners. If you are more familiar with statically typed languages like Java, C#, or C++, you'll be able to shed explicit types, punctuation, and boilerplate code. You will also be able to pick up an expressive syntax rarely seen in other compiled languages.

Finally, your code will be strongly typed (even without specifying explicit types) and support both multiple inheritance and mixin capabilities. Also, any type incompatibilities will be caught before your code ever runs. Developers in statically typed languages will be familiar with the type safety and performance available in Scala. Those using dynamic languages will be able to drastically increase safety and performance while staying with an expressive language.

Reason 2—You'll Be a Better Engineer

An engineer who can write short and expressive code (as one expects in Ruby or Python) while also delivering a type-safe and high-performance application (as one expects from Java or C++) would be considered both impressive and valuable. I am assuming that if you read this book and take up Scala programming you will be writing programs that have all of these benefits. You'll be able to take full advantage of Scala's functional programming features, deliver type-safe and expressive code, and be more productive than you have ever been.

Learning any new programming language is a worthwhile endeavor, because you'll pick up new and different ways to approach problem solving and algorithm and data structure design, along with ways to express these new techniques in a foreign syntax. On top of this, taking up a functional programming language like Scala will help to shape how you view the concepts of data mutability, higher-order functions, and side effects, not only as new ideas but how they apply to your current coding work and designs. You may find that working with inline functions and static types are unnecessary for your current needs, but you'll have some experience with their benefits and drawbacks. Plus, if it becomes possible to apply these features in a partial manner to your current language, such as the new lambda expression support in Java 8, you'll be ready to handle them appropriately.

Reason 3—You'll Be a Happier Engineer

This is admittedly a bold statement from someone you haven't met and who shouldn't presume to know what effect Scala development will have on your brain. I'll only state that if your code proficiency improves to the point that you are easily writing code that works better, reads better, debugs better, and runs faster than before, and on top of all this takes less time to write, you're going to be happier doing so.

Not that life is all about coding, of course. Nor does the work schedule of average software engineers involve more than half of their time spent actually writing code.

But that time spent writing code will be more fun, and you'll be able to take more pride in your work. That should be reason enough to learn something new.

Why Learning Scala May Not Be for You

You should know that Scala has a reputation for being difficult to learn. The language combines two apparently conflicting software engineering paradigms: object-oriented programming and functional programming. This synergy will be surprising to newcomers and the resulting syntax takes some practice to pick up. Scala also has a sophisticated type system that enables custom typing declarations at a level rarely seen outside of academic languages. Ascertaining the syntax and utility of this type system will be challenging, especially if you do not have academic experience with abstract algebra or type theory.

If you do not have enough time to spend on reading this book and going through its exercises, or alternately prefer more challenging or theoretical routes to learning the language, then this book may not be suitable for you.

About the Syntax Notation in This Book

Here is an example of the syntax notation you'll encounter in this book:

```
val <identifier>[: <type>] = <data>
```

This specific example is the definition of a *value*, a type of variable in Scala that cannot be reassigned. It uses my own informal notation for defining the Scala language's syntax, one that can be easier to read than the traditional notations used to define languages but that comes at the cost of being less formal and precise.

Here is how this notation works:

- Keywords and punctuation are printed normally as they would appear in source code.

- Variable items, such as values, types, and literals, are surrounded by angular brackets ("<" and ">").

- Optional segments are surrounded by square brackets ("[" and "]").

For example, in the preceding example "val" is a keyword, "identifier" and "data" are variable items that change with the context, and "type" is an optional item that (if specified) must be separated from the identifier by a colon (":").

I do suggest reading the formal Scala language specification in addition to this book. Although it uses a traditional syntax notation that may be difficult to learn, it is still invaluable for determining the exact syntax requirements of any given feature. The official title is *The Scala Language Specification* (Odersky, 2011), and you can find it either on the official Scala site or with a quick web search.

Conventions Used in This Book

The following typographical conventions are used in this book:

Italic
> Indicates new terms, URLs, email addresses, filenames, and file extensions.

`Constant width`
> Used for program listings, as well as within paragraphs to refer to program elements such as variable or function names, databases, data types, environment variables, statements, and keywords.

`Constant width bold`
> Shows commands or other text that should be typed literally by the user.

Constant width italic

Shows text that should be replaced with user-supplied values or by values determined by context.

This element signifies a tip or suggestion.

This element signifies a general note.

This element indicates a warning or caution.

Using Code Examples

Supplemental material (code examples, exercises, etc.) is available for download at *http://bit.ly/Learning-Scala-materials*.

This book is here to help you get your job done. In general, if example code is offered with this book, you may use it in your programs and documentation. You do not need to contact us for permission unless you're reproducing a significant portion of the code. For example, writing a program that uses several chunks of code from this book does not require permission. Selling or distributing a CD-ROM of examples from O'Reilly books does require permission. Answering a question by citing this book and quoting example code does not require permission. Incorporating a significant amount of example code from this book into your product's documentation does require permission.

We appreciate, but do not require, attribution. An attribution usually includes the title, author, publisher, and ISBN. For example: "*Learning Scala* by Jason Swartz (O'Reilly). Copyright 2015 Jason Swartz, 978-1-449-36793-0."

If you feel your use of code examples falls outside fair use or the permission given above, feel free to contact us at *permissions@oreilly.com*.

Safari® Books Online

 *Safari Books Online* is an on-demand digital library that delivers expert content in both book and video form from the world's leading authors in technology and business.

Technology professionals, software developers, web designers, and business and creative professionals use Safari Books Online as their primary resource for research, problem solving, learning, and certification training.

Safari Books Online offers a range of plans and pricing for enterprise, government, education, and individuals.

Members have access to thousands of books, training videos, and prepublication manuscripts in one fully searchable database from publishers like O'Reilly Media, Prentice Hall Professional, Addison-Wesley Professional, Microsoft Press, Sams, Que, Peachpit Press, Focal Press, Cisco Press, John Wiley & Sons, Syngress, Morgan Kaufmann, IBM Redbooks, Packt, Adobe Press, FT Press, Apress, Manning, New Riders, McGraw-Hill, Jones & Bartlett, Course Technology, and hundreds more. For more information about Safari Books Online, please visit us online.

How to Contact Us

Please address comments and questions concerning this book to the publisher:

O'Reilly Media, Inc.
1005 Gravenstein Highway North
Sebastopol, CA 95472
800-998-9938 (in the United States or Canada)
707-829-0515 (international or local)
707-829-0104 (fax)

We have a web page for this book, where we list errata, examples, and any additional information. You can access this page at *http://bit.ly/learning-scala*.

To comment or ask technical questions about this book, send email to *bookquestions@oreilly.com*.

For more information about our books, courses, conferences, and news, see our website at *http://www.oreilly.com*.

Find us on Facebook: *http://facebook.com/oreilly*

Follow us on Twitter: *http://twitter.com/oreillymedia*

Watch us on YouTube: *http://www.youtube.com/oreillymedia*

Acknowledgments

I would like to thank my editor, Meghan Blanchette, for all her efforts to improve the quality of the book and to make its delivery possible. I would also like to thank Simon St. Laurent for his help and encouragement in proposing the book and launching the entire process.

This book would also not have been possible without the many excellent reviewers who spent their own time reading and reviewing its many revisions. Thank you so much, Edward Yue Shung Wong, Shannon "JJ" Behrens, Manish Pandit, Devendra Jaisinghani, Art Peel, Ryan Delucchi, Semmy Purewal, Luc Perkins, Robert Geist, and Alexander Trauzzi! I've learned so much from you and really appreciate everything you have done.

I would like to thank Professor Martin Odersky, the fine folks at EPFL and Typesafe, and the members of the Scala community for creating and improving such an amazing language.

I'd also like to thank my wife, Jeanne, and daughter, Oona, for making their sacrifices and providing moral support so I could write this book.

Finally, I'd like to thank my brother, Joshua, for suggesting that I just go ahead and write a book. Josh, I don't know what you were expecting when you said that, but here it is.

PART I

Core Scala

CHAPTER 1

Getting Started with the Scalable Language

The Scala programming language has a wonderfully continental ring to its name, as befits its origins at the École polytechnique fédérale de Lausanne (EPFL) in Lausanne, Switzerland. The Scala logo represents a circular stairway, which may lead you to believe its origin is the term *La Scala*, meaning a staircase or ladder in Italian, or that it derives from the famous Italian opera house *Teatro alla Scala*. In fact the name *Scala* is an abbreviation of the term *SCAlable LAnguage*, a fitting description of its intention. Professor Martin Odersky and his group at EPFL created the language in 2003 to provide a high-performance, concurrent-ready environment for functional programming *and* object-oriented programming on the Java Virtual Machine (JVM) platform.

Now that you have the background story, let's install Scala and try it out.

Installing Scala

As a JVM language, Scala requires the use of a Java runtime. Scala 2.11, the version you'll be using, needs at least Java 6. However, I recommend installing the Java 8 JDK (aka Java SE for Standard Environment) instead for optimal performance. You can download the Java 8 JDK (or a later version, if available) for most platforms directly from Oracle's website. Installers are available, so you shouldn't need to manually configure your PATH variable to get the applications installed.

When finished, verify your Java version by running `java -version` from the command line. Here is an example of running this command for Java 8:

```
$ java -version
java version "1.8.0_05"
Java(TM) SE Runtime Environment (build 1.8.0_05-b13)
Java HotSpot(TM) 64-Bit Server VM (build 25.5-b02, mixed mode)
```

Now that Java is installed, it's time to install Scala. There are two ways to install Scala (or any other fine programming tool): the manual approach, suitable for command-line heroes who like to modify their system's environment variables, and the automatic approach, for the rest of us.

To install Scala manually, download the Scala 2.11 distribution from *http://www.scala-lang.org* and add its "bin" directory to your path. The distribution includes the Scala runtimes, tools, compiled libraries, and source, but the most important item we'll need is the `scala` command. This command provides (among other features) the REPL (Read-Eval-Print-Loop) shell we will use to learn and experiment with the Scala language.

To install Scala automatically, use a package manager such as Homebrew (*http://brew.sh/*) for OS X, Chocolatey (*https://chocolatey.org/*) for Windows, or apt-get/Yum (*http://bit.ly/ls-aptget*) for Linux systems. These are freely available and will handle finding the package, downloading and extracting it, and installing it so you can access it from the command line. The scala package is available in all of these package managers as "scala," so you can install it with (`brew/choco/apt-get-yum`) `install scala`.

When installed, execute the `scala` command from the command line. You should see a welcome message like the following (although your Scala and Java version messages may be different):

```
$ scala
Welcome to Scala version 2.11.0 (Java HotSpot(TM) 64-Bit Server VM,
  Java 1.8.0_05).
Type in expressions to have them evaluated.
Type :help for more information.

scala>
```

When you see the *Welcome to Scala* message and the `scala>` prompt you are now in the Scala REPL and are ready to start coding.

If the command is found but there are problems launching it, make sure your Java command is installed correctly and that your system path points to the correct Java version.

Using the Scala REPL

If you have used other REPL shells like Python's python, Ruby's irb, or Groovy's groovysh you'll find the Scala REPL familiar. As with the REPL's provided with the Python, Ruby, and Groovy runtimes, Scala's REPL provides support for evaluating and executing code one line at a time with helpful feedback.

If you haven't used a REPL, or are just unaccustomed to writing code outside an IDE or editor, it will take some practice to learn how to develop in the Scala REPL. However, it provides an unsurpassed way to learn and experiment quickly and responsively with the Scala language and libraries. You can enter single lines of code to evaluate and compile, and any variables you create are available for the lifetime of your session. A multiline paste mode supports entering multiple lines of code to be compiled together (instead of individually), and external source code and libraries can be loaded at any time. A help system is available and can be started by entering the :help command.

Let's get started using the REPL by implementing the classic first exercise of all serious programming books, the "Hello World" application. Start up the REPL and make sure you see the scala> prompt on your screen:

```
scala>
```

After the prompt type **println("Hello, World!")** and press Return. The REPL will run your println() command and print the output on a line below your command. Following the printout will be another scala> prompt, waiting for a new command to run. This is the Read, Evaluate, Print, Loop behavior from which the REPL derives its name.

Here is how the input and response should appear in the REPL:

```
scala> println("Hello, World")
Hello, World

scala>
```

Congratulations, you have now written and executed Scala code.

The println() function, universally available to all Scala code, prints a message to the JVM's *stdout* stream. When used in application servers that *stdout* stream is typically logged to a file (e.g., Tomcat's *catalina.out*), but in the Scala REPL the println() function's messages appear directly in the REPL.

You can use standard readline-style up-arrow and down-arrow keys to navigate to the previous and next input lines. For example, press the up-arrow key and hit Return to rerun the previous command, or press up arrow and enter a new message to print. REPL history is stored between sessions, so you can quit, run the scala command again, and press up arrow to access your previous commands.

Let's try performing a simple arithmetic operation. At a new prompt type **5 * 7** and press Return. Your display should look like this:

```
scala> 5 * 7
res0: Int = 35

scala>
```

This time your Scala command did not print output, but instead returned a value, the product of 5 and 7. When your commands return (or are themselves) values, the REPL will assign them to a new, constant variable so that you can refer to the value in later operations. These "res" variables (a shortened version of "result," perhaps) are sequentially numbered so that there will always be a unique container for your command's result.

Now that res0 contains the output of the multiplication command, lets make use of it. Type **2 * res0** at a fresh prompt and press Return. You should see something like this:

```scala
scala> 2 * res0
res1: Int = 70

scala>
```

As expected, the REPL recognized the res0 variable it previously created in your arithmetic expression, and generated a new variable res1 to store the result of the new expression.

Summary

I hope you've seen how using the Scala REPL to evaluate and experiment with code provides an enriched learning environment for this programming language. As you continue through this book, keep the REPL open and use it to validate everything you learn. The code samples throughout the book are presented as raw captures of REPL sessions to both validate that they work and what they print out, and also to make it easier for you to replicate them in your own REPL session.

Even better, modify and rework code examples until they break. Scala is a compiled, statically typed language, so the REPL (which compiles a line after you hit Return) will let you know immediately if you have entered incorrect Scala code or not. This will help you pick up the language more quickly and better understand the limits of its syntax and features.

Exercises

1. Although println() is a good way to print a string, can you find a way to print a string without println? Also, what kinds of numbers, strings, and other data does the REPL support?

2. In the Scala REPL, convert the temperature value of 22.5 Centigrade to Fahrenheit. The conversion formula is $cToF(x) = (x * 9/5) + 32$.

3. Take the result from exercise 2, halve it, and convert it back to Centigrade. You can use the generated constant variable (e.g., "res0") instead of copying and pasting the value yourself.

4. The REPL can load and interpret Scala code from an external file with the `:load <file>` command. Create a new file named *Hello.scala* and add a command that will print a greeting, then execute it from the REPL.

5. Another way to load external Scala code is to paste it into the REPL in "raw" mode, where the code is compiled as if it were actually in a proper source file. To do this, type `:paste -raw`, hit Return, and then paste the contents of your source file from exercise 4. After exiting "paste" mode you should see the greeting.

CHAPTER 2

Working with Data: Literals, Values, Variables, and Types

In this chapter we will cover the core data and variable types in Scala. Let's start with the definitions of the terms *literal*, *value*, *variable*, and *type*:

- A *literal* (or literal data) is data that appears directly in the source code, like the number 5, the character *A*, and the text "Hello, World."
- A *value* is an immutable, typed storage unit. A value can be assigned data when it is defined, but can never be reassigned.
- A *variable* is a mutable, typed storage unit. A variable can be assigned data when it is defined and can also be reassigned data at any time.
- A *type* is the *kind* of data you are working with, a definition or classification of data. All data in Scala corresponds to a specific type, and all Scala types are defined as classes with methods that operate on the data.

The data stored in values and variables in Scala will get automatically deallocated by the Java Virtual Machine's garbage collection when they are no longer used. There is no ability, or need, to deallocate them manually.

Let's try exercising these terms by working with data in the Scala REPL. Scala values are defined with the syntax val `<name>`: `<type>` = `<literal>`, so we will create a value with the name x, type Int (short for "integer"), and assigned it the literal number 5:

```
scala> val x: Int = 5
x: Int = 5
```

What happened here? The REPL (again, a Read-Evaluate-Print-Loop shell) read the value definition, evaluated it, and reprinted it as a confirmation. The new value, named x, is now defined and available to use. So let's use it:

```
scala> x
res0: Int = 5

scala> x * 2
res1: Int = 10

scala> x / 5
res2: Int = 1
```

Each of these three input lines are valid Scala syntax and return an integer value. In each case, because a value is returned, the REPL repeats the value and its type and also assigns a unique, sequentially named value starting with res0 (short for "result"). You can choose to make use of these "result" values just like any value you explicitly define:

```
scala> res0 * res1
res3: Int = 50
```

Here the values res0 and res1 are multiplied, resulting in the value 50 being returned and stored in the new value named res3.

Let's try working with variables now. Variables, which unlike values are mutable and can be reassigned new values, are defined with the syntax var <name>: <type> = <literal>.

Here is an example of working with variables:

```
scala> var a: Double = 2.72
a: Double = 2.72

scala> a = 355.0 / 113.0
a: Double = 3.1415929203539825

scala> a = 5
a: Double = 5.0
```

In this example we defined the variable a to have the type Double, a double-precision floating-point number. And then, because it is a variable, we reassigned it to a different value.

This has been a short introduction to using values, variables, types, and literals in Scala. In the rest of this chapter we will cover each of these subject areas in depth.

Values

Values are immutable, typed storage units, and by convention are the default method for storing data. You can define a new value using the val keyword.

Syntax: Defining a Value

```
val <identifier>[: <type>] = <data>
```

Values require both a name and assigned data, but they do not require an explicit type. If the type is not specified (i.e., the ": <type>" syntax is not included), the Scala compiler will infer the type based on the assigned data.

Here are some examples of defining values with their type in the Scala REPL:

```scala
scala> val x: Int = 20
x: Int = 20

scala> val greeting: String = "Hello, World"
greeting: String = Hello, World

scala> val atSymbol: Char = '@'
atSymbol: Char = @
```

You may have noticed from the syntax diagram that specifying the type in value definitions is optional. In situations where it is possible to deduce the type of the value based on its assignment (for example, the literal 20 in the first example is obviously an integer), you can leave off the type from a value definition. The Scala compiler will then discern the type of the value from its assignment, a process known as *type inference*. Values defined without a type are not typeless; they are assigned the proper type just as if the type had been included in the definition.

Let's try the examples again without specifying their types:

```scala
scala> val x = 20
x: Int = 20

scala> val greeting = "Hello, World"
greeting: String = Hello, World

scala> val atSymbol = '@'
atSymbol: Char = @
```

In this example the values end up having the same types (Int, String, and Char) as they did when the types were explicitly stated. The Scala compiler, via the REPL, was able to deduce that the literal 20 corresponds to the type Int, the literal "Hello, World" to the type String, and the literal @ to the type Char.

Using Scala's type inference is a helpful shortcut when writing code because it removes the need to explicitly write the type of a value. As a guideline it should only be used when it does not reduce the readability of your code. In the case that someone reading your code would not be able to figure out what the type of the value is, it would be better to include the explicit type in the value definition.

Although type inference will deduce the correct type to use to store data, it will not override an explicit type that you set. If you define a value with a type that is incompatible with the initial value you will get a compilation error:

```
scala> val x: Int = "Hello"
<console>:7: error: type mismatch;
 found    : String("Hello")
 required: Int
       val x: Int = "Hello"
```

The error here affirms that an Int type cannot be used to store a String.

Variables

In computer science the term *variable* typically refers to a unique identifier corresponding to an allocated or reserved memory space, into which values can be stored and from which values can be retrieved. As long as the memory space is reserved, it can be assigned new values over and over again. Thus, the contents of the memory space are dynamic, or *variable*.

In most languages, such as C, Java, PHP, Python, and Ruby, this is the typical pattern for working with named, assignable memory storage. Variables are dynamic, mutable, and reassignable (with the exception of those defined with special restrictions such as Java's final keyword).

In Scala, values are preferred over variables by convention, due to the stability and predictability they bring to source code. When you define a value you can be assured that it will retain the same value regardless of any other code that may access it. Reading and debugging code is easier when a value assigned at the beginning of a code segment is unchanged through the end of the code segment. Finally, when working with data that may be available for the life span of an application, or accessible from concurrent or multithreaded code, an immutable value will be more stable and less prone to errors than mutable data that may be modified at unexpected times.

The example code and exercises in this book prefer the use of values over variables. However, in those places where variables are more suitable, such as local variables that store temporary data or accumulate values in loops, variables will certainly be used.

Now that the preference for values over variables has been explained in detail, we can put that aside and cover how to use variables in Scala.

The var keyword is used to define a variable with a given name, type, and assignment.

Syntax: Defining a Variable

```
var <identifier>[: <type>] = <data>
```

Like values, variables can be defined with or without an explicit type. If no type is specified the Scala compiler will use type inference to determine the correct type to assign to your variable. Unlike values, variables can be reassigned new data at any time.

Here is an example of defining a variable and then reassigning it, in this case to the product of itself and another number:

```
scala> var x = 5
x: Int = 5

scala> x = x * 4
x: Int = 20
```

Although a variable can be reassigned, its designated type cannot, and so a variable cannot be reassigned data that has an incompatible type. For example, defining a variable of type Int and then assigning it a String value will result in a compiler error:

```
scala> var x = 5
x: Int = 5

scala> x = "what's up?"
<console>:8: error: type mismatch;
 found   : String("what\'s up?")
 required: Int
       x = "what's up?"
           ^
```

However, defining a variable of type Double and assigning it an Int value will work because Int numbers can be converted to Double numbers automatically:

```
scala> var y = 1.5
y: Double = 1.5

scala> y = 42
y: Double = 42.0
```

Naming

Scala names can use letters, numbers, and a range of special *operator* characters. This makes it possible to use standard mathematical operators (e.g., * and :+) and constants (e.g., π and φ) in place of longer names to make the code more expressive.

The Scala Language Specification (*http://bit.ly/ls-scalaref*) defines these operator characters as "all other characters in \u0020-007F and Unicode categories Sm [Symbol/ Math] ... except parentheses ([]) and periods." Square brackets (referred to in the text as parentheses) are reserved for use in type parameterization, while periods are reserved for access to the fields and methods of objects (instantiated types).

Here are the rules for combining letters, numbers, and characters into valid identifiers in Scala.

1. A letter followed by zero or more letters and digits.

2. A letter followed by zero or more letters and digits, then an underscore (_), and then one or more of *either* letters and digits *or* operator characters.

3. One or more operator characters.

4. One or more of *any* character except a backquote, all enclosed in a pair of backquotes.

 Names enclosed in backquotes can, unlike the other names, be reserved keywords in Scala such as true, while, =, and var.

Let's try out some of these naming rules in the REPL:

```
scala> val π = 3.14159                                              ❶
π: Double = 3.14159

scala> val $ = "USD currency symbol"
$: String = USD currency symbol

scala> val o_O = "Hmm"
o_O: String = Hmm

scala> val 50cent = "$0.50"                                          ❷
<console>:1: error: Invalid literal number
       val 50cent = "$0.50"
             ^

scala> val a.b = 25                                                  ❸
<console>:7: error: not found: value a
       val a.b = 25

scala> val `a.b` = 4                                                 ❹
a.b: Int = 4
```

❶ The special character "π" is a valid Scala identifier.

❷ The value name "50cent" is invalid because names cannot start with numbers. In this case the compiler started parsing the name as a literal number and ran into problems at the letter "c".

❸ The value name "a.b" is invalid because a period isn't an operator character.

❹ Rewriting this value with backquotes fixes the problem, although the aesthetics of using backquotes isn't that great.

Value and variable names, by convention, should start with a lowercase letter and then capitalize additional words. This is popularly known as *camel case*, and though not required it is recommended for all Scala developers. This helps to distinguish them from types and classes which (also by convention, not by rule) follow camel case but start with an uppercase letter.

Types

Scala has both numeric (e.g., Int and Double) and nonnumeric types (e.g., String) that can be used to define values and variables. These core types are the building blocks for all other types including objects and collections, and are themselves objects that have methods and operators that act on their data.

Unlike Java and C there is no concept of a primitive type in Scala. While the Java Virtual Machine supports the primitive integer type int and the integer class Integer, Scala only supports its own integer class, Int.

Numeric Data Types

Table 2-1 displays Scala's numeric data types.

Table 2-1. Core numeric types

Name	Description	Size	Min	Max
Byte	Signed integer	1 byte	−127	128
Short	Signed integer	2 bytes	−32768	32767
Int	Signed integer	4 bytes	-2^{31}	$2^{31}-1$
Long	Signed integer	8 bytes	-2^{63}	$2^{63}-1$
Float	Signed floating point	4 bytes	n/a	n/a
Double	Signed floating point	8 bytes	n/a	n/a

> See the API documentation for java.lang.Float and java.lang.Dou ble for a description of the calculated maximum and minimum values for these floating-point numbers.

Scala supports the ability to automatically convert numbers from one type to another based on the rank of the type. The numeric types in Table 2-1 are sorted by their automatic conversion rank, where the Byte type is the lowest and can be converted to any other type.

Let's try this out by creating values of different types and automatically converting them to higher-ranked types:

```
scala> val b: Byte = 10
b: Byte = 10
```

```
scala> val s: Short = b
s: Short = 10

scala> val d: Double = s
d: Double = 10.0
```

The b and s values here were assigned to new values that had a higher rank, and so were automatically converted (or "upconverted" as some say) to the higher ranks.

 Java developers will recognize the names of these types, which are wrappers around the core JVM types of the same names (except the JVM's Integer is Scala's Int). Wrapping JVM types ensures that Scala and Java are interoperable, and that Scala can make use of every Java library.

Scala does not allow automatic conversion from higher ranked types to lower ranked types. This makes sense, because you could otherwise lose data if you convert to a type with less storage. Here is an example of trying to automatically convert a higher ranked type to a lower ranked type and the ensuing error:

```
scala> val l: Long = 20
l: Long = 20

scala> val i: Int = l
<console>:8: error: type mismatch;
 found    : Long
 required: Int
        val i: Int = l
```

You can choose to manually convert between types using the *toType* methods available on all numeric types. Although this makes it possible to lose data by converting to a lesser ranked type, it is useful when you know that the data is compatible with the lower ranked type.

For example, here is a Long value that can be safely converted to type Int using the toInt method, because its data is within the storage bounds of an Int:

```
scala> val l: Long = 20
l: Long = 20

scala> val i: Int = l.toInt
i: Int = 20
```

An alternative to using explicit types is to specify the type of your literal data directly, using Scala's notation for literal types. See Table 2-2 for the full list of notations for specifying the types of literals.

Table 2-2. Numeric literals

Literal	Type	Description
5	Int	Unadorned integer literals are Int by default
0x0f	Int	The "0x" prefix denotes hexadecimal notation
5l	Long	The "l" suffix denotes a Long type
5.0	Double	Unadorned decimal literals are Double by default
5f	Float	The "f" suffix denotes a Float type
5d	Double	The "d suffix denotes a Double type

 Literal Characters Are Case-Insensitive
You can use either lowercase or uppercase letters in Scala's literal types.
The literal number 5L is the same as the literal number 5l.

Let's try out these literals by assigning them to new values without stating the type. The Scala REPL will use type inference to calculate the appropriate types for each value:

```scala
scala> val anInt = 5
anInt: Int = 5

scala> val yellowRgb = 0xffff00
yellowRgb: Int = 16776960

scala> val id = 100l
id: Long = 100

scala> val pi = 3.1416
pi: Double = 3.1416
```

Strings

The String type represents "strings" of text, one of the most common core types in any programming language. Scala's String is built on Java's String and adds unique features like multiline literals and string interpolation.

Write String literals using double quotes, with special characters escaped with backslashes:

```scala
scala> val hello = "Hello There"
hello: String = Hello There

scala> val signature = "With Regards, \nYour friend"
signature: String =
With Regards,
Your friend
```

Like numeric types, the String type supports the use of math operators. For example, use the equals operator (==) to compare two String values. Unlike Java, the equals operator (==) checks for true equality, not object reference equality:

```
scala> val greeting = "Hello, " + "World"
greeting: String = Hello, World

scala> val matched = (greeting == "Hello, World")
matched: Boolean = true

scala> val theme = "Na " * 16 + "Batman!" // what do you expect this to print?
```

A multiline String can be created using triple-quotes. Multiline strings are literal, and so do not recognize the use of backslashes as the start of special characters:

```
scala> val greeting = """She suggested reformatting the file
     | by replacing tabs (\t) with newlines (\n);
     | "Why do that?", he asked. """
greeting: String =
She suggested reformatting the file
by replacing tabs (\t) with newlines (\n);
"Why do that?", he asked.
```

String interpolation

Building a String based on other values is reasonably easy to do with string addition. Here is a String built by adding text before and after the Float value:

```
scala> val approx = 355/113f
approx: Float = 3.141593

scala> println("Pi, using 355/113, is about " + approx + "." )
Pi, using 355/113, is about 3.141593.
```

A more direct way to combine your values or variables inside a String is with *string interpolation*, a special mode where external value and variable names are recognized and resolved. The Scala notation for string interpolation is an "s" prefix added before the first double quote of the string. Then dollar sign operators ($) (with optional braces) can be used to note references to external data.

Here is the example again using string interpolation:

```
scala> println(s"Pi, using 355/113, is about $approx." )
Pi, using 355/113, is about 3.141593.
```

You will need the optional braces if you have any nonword characters in your reference (such as a calculation), or if your reference can't be distinguished from the surrounding text:

```
scala> val item = "apple"
item: String = apple
```

```
scala> s"How do you like them ${item}s?"
res0: String = How do you like them apples?

scala> s"Fish n chips n vinegar, ${"pepper "*3}salt"
res1: String = Fish n chips n vinegar, pepper pepper pepper salt
```

An alternate format for string interpolation uses printf notation, very useful when you want to control the data formatting such as the character count or display of decimal values. To use printf notation change the prefix to an "f" and follow the end of the reference immediately with the printf notation:

 If you are unfamiliar with printf there are numerous online references for the format, including the official Javadoc (*http://bit.ly/ls-javadoc*) for java.util.Formatter, the underlying engine used by Scala to format these strings.

```
scala> val item = "apple"
item: String = apple

scala> f"I wrote a new $item%.3s today"
res2: String = I wrote a new app today

scala> f"Enjoying this $item ${355/113.0}%.5f times today"
res3: String = Enjoying this apple 3.14159 times today
```

These printf notations make the references a little harder to read than in the previous examples, but do provide essential control over the output.

Now that we have learned how to control data output with strings, let's find out how to do the opposite with regular expressions.

Regular expressions

A *regular expression* is a string of characters and punctuation that represents a search pattern. Popularized by Perl and command-line utilities like Grep, regular expressions are a standard feature in the libraries of most programming languages including Scala.

The format for Scala's regular expressions is based on the Java class java.util.regex.Pattern. I recommend reading the Javadoc (the Java API documentation) for java.util.regex.Pattern if you are unfamiliar with this type, because Java's (and thus Scala's) regular expressions may be different from the format you have used with other languages and tools.

The String type provides a number of built-in operations that support regular expressions. Table 2-3 displays a selection of these operations.

Table 2-3. Regular expression operations

Name	Example	Description
matches	`"Froggy went a' courting" matches ".*` `courting"`	Returns true if the regular expression matches the entire string.
replaceAll	`"milk, tea, muck" replaceAll ("m[^ ]` `+k", "coffee")`	Replaces all matches with replacement text.
replaceFirst	`"milk, tea, muck" replaceFirst ("m[^ ]` `+k", "coffee")`	Replaces the first match with replacement text.

For more advanced handling of regular expressions, convert a string to a regular expression type by invoking its r operator. This will return a Regex instance that can handle additional search and replace operations as well as capture group support. A *capture group* makes it possible to select items in a given string and convert them to local values based on the regular expression pattern. The pattern must include at least one capture group defined by parentheses, and the input must include at least one of the captured patterns to return the value.

Syntax: Capturing Values with Regular Expressions

```
val <Regex value>(<identifier>) = <input string>
```

Let's try this out by capturing the numeric value from the output of the previous example (see "String interpolation" on page 18). We'll use multiline strings to store our regular expression pattern, because they are literal and allow us to write a backslash without a second, escaping backslash:

```
scala> val input = "Enjoying this apple 3.14159 times today"
input: String = Enjoying this apple 3.14159 times today

scala> val pattern = """.* apple ([\d.]+) times .*""".r          ❶
pattern: scala.util.matching.Regex = .* apple ([\d.]+) times .*   ❷

scala> val pattern(amountText) = input                           ❸
amountText: String = 3.14159

scala> val amount = amountText.toDouble                          ❹
amount: Double = 3.14159
```

❶ The capture group is the series of digits and a period between the words apple and times.

❷ The full regular expression type is scala.util.matching.Regex, or just util.matching.Regex.

❸ The format is admittedly a bit odd. The name of the new value containing the capture group match, amountText, does not directly follow the val identifier.

❹ After converting the amount in text form to a Double we have our numeric value.

Regular expressions serve as a compact and efficient means to process text, with operations such as matching, replacing, and capturing. If you are still new to regular expressions, it is worth investing time to study them because they are widely applicable in modern software development.

An Overview of Scala Types

In this section we will move on from numbers and strings to a broader look at the range of core types. All of Scala's types, from numbers to strings to collections, exist as part of a type hierarchy. Every class that you define in Scala will also belong to this hierarchy automatically.

Figure 2-1 shows the hierarchy of Scala's core (numeric and nonnumeric) types.

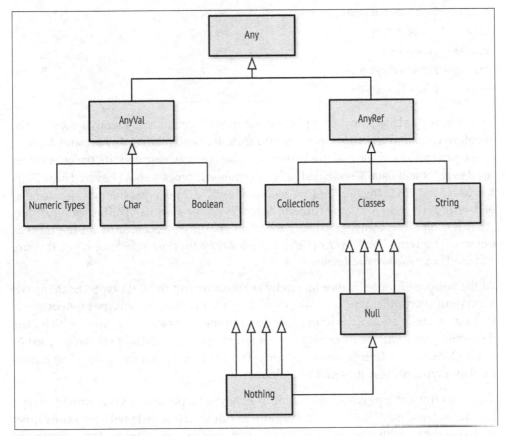

Figure 2-1. The Scala type hierarchy

The open-headed arrows in the diagram indicate supertypes, a common notation in object-oriented diagrams. The multiple-arrow types at the bottom indicate that they are subtypes of every type in the system, including classes you define on your own.

In Table 2-4 you can see a full listing of the specific types mentioned in this diagram, followed by more complete descriptions.

Table 2-4. Core nonnumeric types

Name	Description	Instantiable
Any	The root of all types in Scala	No
AnyVal	The root of all value types	No
AnyRef	The root of all reference (nonvalue) types	No
Nothing	The subclass of all types	No
Null	The subclass of all AnyRef types signifying a null value	No
Char	Unicode character	Yes
Boolean	true or false	Yes
String	A string of characters (i.e., text)	Yes
Unit	Denotes the lack of a value	No

The Any, AnyVal, and AnyRef types are the root of Scala's type hierarchy. Any is the absolute root, and all other types descend from its two children, AnyVal and AnyRef. The types that extend AnyVal are known as *value types* because they are the core values used to represent data. They include all of the numeric types we have covered plus Char, Boolean, and Unit. AnyVal types are accessed just like other types but may be allocated at runtime either on the heap as objects or locally on the stack as a JVM primitive value. All other types have AnyRef as their root and are only ever allocated on the heap as objects. The term "Ref" in "AnyRef" indicates they they are reference types that are accessed via a memory reference.

At the bottom of the Scala type hierarchy are the Nothing and Null types. Nothing is a subtype of every other type and exists to provide a compatible return type for operations that significantly affect a program's flow. For example, the return keyword, which exits a function early with a return value, has a return type of Nothing so it can be used in the middle of initializing a value and not affect the type of that value. Nothing is only used as a type, because it cannot be instantiated.

The other bottom type is Null, a subtype of all AnyRef types that exists to provide a type for the keyword null. A String variable, for example, can be assigned null at any time, such that the variable does not point to any string instance in memory. This assignment of null to a variable declared as type String is acceptable because null is a compatible type for String. Defining a type for null is an example of how Scala's syntax prefers the use of real types and instances to reserved keywords.

Char is the only type that could also appear in "Numeric Data Types" on page 15. As the basis of the String type it contains a single character and so is sometimes considered to be a unit of text. Essentially it is a scalar type that can be converted to and from other numbers.

Char literals are written with single quotes, distinguishing them from String literals, which are written with double quotes. If you're familiar with the ASCII character numbering system, this example should be obvious:

```scala
scala> val c = 'A'
c: Char = A

scala> val i: Int = c
i: Int = 65

scala> val t: Char = 116
t: Char = t
```

The Boolean type is limited to the values true and false. In addition to using true and false, you can also obtain Boolean values from comparison and Boolean logic operators:

```scala
scala> val isTrue = !true
isTrue: Boolean = false

scala> val isFalse = !true
isFalse: Boolean = false

scala> val unequal = (5 != 6)
unequal: Boolean = true

scala> val isLess = (5 < 6)
isLess: Boolean = true

scala> val unequalAndLess = unequal & isLess
unequalAndLess: Boolean = true

scala> val definitelyFalse = false && unequal
definitelyFalse: Boolean = false
```

What is the Difference Between & and && ?

The Boolean comparison operators && and || are *lazy* in that they will not bother evaluating the second argument if the first argument is sufficient. The operators & and | will always check both arguments before returning a result.

Unlike many dynamic languages, Scala does not support automatic conversion of other types to Booleans. A nonnull string cannot be evaluated as true, and the number zero does not equal `false`. If you need to evaluate a value's state to a Boolean, use an explicit comparison:

```
scala> val zero = 0
zero: Int = 0

scala> val isValid = zero > 0
isValid: Boolean = false
```

The `Unit` type is unlike the other core types here (numeric and nonnumeric) in that instead of denoting a type of data it denotes the lack of data. In a way it is similar to the `void` keyword used in Java and C, which is used to define a function that doesn't return data. The `Unit` type is similarly used in Scala as the return type for functions or expressions that don't return anything. For example, the common `println` function could be said to return a `Unit` type because it returns nothing.

The `Unit` literal is an empty pair of parentheses, (), which if you consider it is a fine representation of not having a value. If you want you can define a value or variable with the `Unit` type, but again its common usage is for defining functions and expressions:

```
scala> val nada = ()
nada: Unit = ()
```

Now that we have covered the core types, let's have a look at the operations they all have in common.

Type operations

Table 2-5 displays the operations available on all types in Scala. The `toString` and `hashCode` methods are required on all JVM instances.

Table 2-5. Common type operations

Name	Example	Description
asInstanceOf[<type>]	5.asInstanceOf[Long]	Converts the value to a value of the desired type. Causes an error if the value is not compatible with the new type.
getClass	(7.0 / 5).getClass	Returns the type (i.e., the class) of a value.
isInstanceOf	(5.0).isInstanceOf[Float]	Returns true if the value has the given type.
hashCode	"A".hashCode	Returns the hash code of the value, useful for hash-based collections.
to<type>	20.toByte; 47.toFloat	Conversion functions to convert a value to a compatible value.
toString	(3.0 / 4.0).toString	Renders the value to a `String`.

Avoid asInstanceOf

The `asInstanceOf` operation will cause an error if the value cannot be converted to the requested type. To avoid runtime errors with this operation, prefer the `to<type>` typed conversion operations when possible.

The types we have covered so far in this chapter are all (with the possible exception of `String`) *scalar* values, which represent a single element (or, of course with `Unit`, the lack of any element). As a complement to these scalar values, we will finish the chapter with the `Tuple` type, which can collect two or more of these values into a new, ordered element.

Tuples

A *tuple* is an ordered container of two or more values, all of which may have different types. You may be familiar with this term from working with relational databases, where a single row of a table is considered its own tuple. Tuples can be useful when you need to logically group values, representing them as a coherent unit. Unlike lists and arrays, however, there is no way to iterate through elements in a tuple. Its purpose is only as a container for more than one value.

You can create a tuple by writing your values separated by a comma and surrounded by a pair of parentheses.

Syntax: Create a Tuple

```
( <value 1>, <value 2>[, <value 3>...] )
```

For example, here is a tuple containing `Int`, `String`, and `Boolean` values:

```
scala> val info = (5, "Korben", true)
info: (Int, String, Boolean) = (5,Korben,true)
```

You can access an individual element from a tuple by its 1-based index (e.g., where the first element is 1, second is 2, etc.):

```
scala> val name = info._2
name: String = Korben
```

An alternate form of creating a 2-sized tuple is with the relation operator (`->`). This is a popular shortcut for representing key-value pairs in tuples:

```
scala> val red = "red" -> "0xff0000"
red: (String, String) = (red,0xff0000)

scala> val reversed = red._2 -> red._1
reversed: (String, String) = (0xff0000,red)
```

Tuples provide a generic means to structure data, and are useful when you need to group discrete elements for handling.

Summary

This may be a challenging chapter to see through to the end, because you had to read all about types and data without learning how to do real *programming* in Scala yet. I'm glad you did.

What was the oddest or most-unexpected part of this chapter? The use of keywords to announce value and variable definition? The reversed manner (if you're coming from Java) of defining a variable's name before its type? The idea that much of your code can use fixed, nonreassignable values instead of (variable) variables?

If these ideas were hard to take, the good news is that, as you gain experience in Scala developemnt, they will become quite normal. Eventually they may even seem to be obvious choices for a well-designed functional programming language.

At this point you should know how to define your own values and variables, although we haven't yet learned where to come up with useful data to store in them. In the next chapter you will study ways to derive and calculate this data using logical structures known as *expressions*.

Exercises

1. Write a new Centigrade-to-Fahrenheit conversion (using the formula (x * 9/5) + 32), saving each step of the conversion into separate values. What do you expect the type of each value will be?

2. Modify the Centigrade-to-Fahrenheit formula to return an integer instead of a floating-point number.

3. Using the input value 2.7255, generate the string "You owe $2.73." Is this doable with string interpolation?

4. Is there a simpler way to write the following?

   ```
   val flag: Boolean = false
   val result: Boolean = (flag == false)
   ```

5. Convert the number 128 to a Char, a String, a Double, and then back to an Int. Do you expect the original amount to be retained? Do you need any special conversion functions for this?

6. Using the input string "Frank,123 Main,925-555-1943,95122" and regular expression matching, retrieve the telephone number. Can you convert each part of the telephone number to its own integer value? How would you store this in a tuple?

CHAPTER 3

Expressions and Conditionals

This chapter focuses on Scala's expressions, statements, and conditionals. The term *expression* as used in this book indicates a unit of code that returns a value after it has been executed. One or more lines of code can be considered an expression if they are collected together using curly braces ({ and }). This is known as an *expression block*.

Expressions provide a foundation for functional programming because they make it possible to return data instead of modifying existing data (such as a variable). This enables the use of immutable data, a key functional programming concept where new data is stored in new values instead of in existing variables. Functions, of course, can be used to return new data, but they are in a way just another type of expression.

When all of your code can be organized (or conceptualized) into a collection of one or more hierarchical expressions that return values using immutable data will be straightforward. The return values of expressions will be passed to other expressions or stored into values. As you migrate from using variables, your functions and expressions will have fewer *side effects*. In other words, they will purely act on the input you give them without affecting any data other than their return value. This is one of the main goals and benefits of functional programming.

Expressions

As noted earlier, an *expression* is a single unit of code that returns a value.

Let's start out with an example of a simple expression in Scala, just a `String` literal on its own:

```
scala> "hello"
res0: String = hello
```

OK, that's not a very impressive expression. Here's a more complicated one:

```
scala> "hel" + 'l' + "o"
res1: String = hello
```

This example and the previous example are valid expressions that, while implemented differently, generate the same result. What's important about expressions is the value they return. The entire point of them is to return a value that gets captured and used.

Defining Values and Variables with Expressions

We have seen that expressions cover both literal values ("hello") and calculated values. Previously we have defined values and variables as being assigned literal values. However, it is more accurate to say that they are assigned the return value of expressions. This is true whether the expression is a literal (e.g., 5), a calculation, or a function call.

Given this, let's redefine the syntax for defining values and variables based on expressions.

Syntax: Defining Values and Variables, Using Expressions

```
val <identifier>[: <type>] = <expression>
var <identifier>[: <type>] = <expression>
```

Because literal values are also a kind of expression, these definitions are more encompassing and accurate. It turns out that expressions are also a good foundation for defining most of Scala's syntax. Look for the term "<expression>" in future syntax notations to indicate where any expression may be used.

Expression Blocks

Multiple expressions can be combined using curly braces ({ and }) to create a single *expression block*. An expression has its own scope, and may contain values and variables local to the expression block. The last expression in the block is the return value for the entire block.

As an example, here is a line with two expressions that would work better as a block:

```
scala> val x = 5 * 20; val amount = x + 10
x: Int = 100
amount: Int = 110
```

The only value we really care about keeping is "amount," so let's combine the expressions including the "x" value into a block. We'll use its return value to define the "amount" value:

```
scala> val amount = { val x = 5 * 20; x + 10 }
amount: Int = 110
```

The last expression in the block, "x + 10," determines the block's return value. The "x" value, previously defined at the same level of "amount," is now defined locally to the block. The code is now cleaner, because the intent of using "x" to define "amount" is now obvious.

Expression blocks can span as many lines as you need. The preceding example could have been rewritten without the semicolons as follows:

```scala
scala> val amount = {
     |    val x = 5 * 20
     |    x + 10
     | }
amount: Int = 110
```

Expression blocks are also nestable, with each level of expression block having its own scoped values and variables.

Here is a short example demonstrating a three-deep nested expression block:

```scala
scala> { val a = 1; { val b = a * 2; { val c = b + 4; c } } }
res5: Int = 6
```

These examples may not indicate compelling reasons to use expression blocks on their own. However, it is important to understand their syntax and compositional nature because we will revisit them when we cover control structures later in this chapter.

Statements

A *statement* is just an expression that doesn't return a value. Statements have a return type of Unit, the type that indicates the lack of a value. Some common statements used in Scala programming include calls to println() and value and variable definitions.

For example, the following value definition is a statement because it doesn't return anything:

```scala
scala> val x = 1
x: Int = 1
```

The REPL repeats the definition of x but there is not actual data returned that can be used to create a new value.

A statement block, unlike an expression block, does not return a value. Because a statement block has no output, it is commonly used to modify existing data or make changes outside the scope of the application (e.g., writing to the console, updating a database, connecting to an external server).

If..Else Expression Blocks

The If..Else conditional expression is a classic programming construct for choosing a branch of code based on whether an expression resolves to true or false. In many languages this takes the form of an "if .. else if .. else" block, which starts with an "if," continues with zero to many "else if" sections, and ends with a final "else" catch-all statement.

As a matter of practice you can write these same "if .. else if .. else" blocks in Scala and they will work just as you have experienced them in Java and other languages. As a matter of formal syntax, however, Scala only supports a single "if" and optional "else" block, and does not recognize the "else if" block as a single construct.

So how do "else if" blocks still work correctly in Scala? Because "if .. else" blocks are based on expression blocks, and expression blocks can be easily nested, an "if .. else if .. else" expression is equivalent to a nested "if .. else { if .. else }" expression. Logically this is exactly the same as an "if .. else if .. else" block, and as a matter of syntax Scala recognizes the second "if else" as a nested expression of the outer "if .. else" block.

Let's start exploring actual "if" and "if .. else" blocks by looking at the syntax for the simple "if" block.

If Expressions

Syntax: Using an If Expression

```
if (<Boolean expression>) <expression>
```

The term *Boolean expression* here indicates an expression that will return either true or false.

Here is a simple if block that prints a notice if the Boolean expression is true:

```
scala> if ( 47 % 3 > 0 ) println("Not a multiple of 3")
Not a multiple of 3
```

Of course 47 isn't a multiple of 3, so the Boolean expression was true and the println was trigggered.

Although an if block can act as an expression, it is better suited for statements like this one. The problem with using if blocks as expressions is that they only conditionally return a value. If the Boolean expression returns false, what do you expect the if block to return?

```
scala> val result = if ( false ) "what does this return?"
result: Any = ()
```

The type of the result value in this example is unspecified so the compiler used type inference to determine the most appropriate type. Either a String or Unit could have been returned, so the compiler chose the root class Any. This is the one class common to both String (which extends AnyRef) and to Unit (which extends AnyVal).

Unlike the solitary "if" block, the "if .. else" block is well suited to working with expressions.

If-Else Expressions

Syntax: If .. Else Expressions

```
if (<Boolean expression>) <expression>
else <expression>
```

Here is an example:

```
scala> val x = 10; val y = 20
x: Int = 10
y: Int = 20

scala> val max = if (x > y) x else y
max: Int = 20
```

You can see that the x and y values make up the entirety of the if and else expressions. The resulting value is assigned to max, which we and the Scala compiler know will be an Int because both expressions have return values of type Int.

Some wonder why Scala doesn't have a ternary expression (popular in C and Java) where the punctuation characters ? and : act as a one-line if and else expression. It should be clear from this example that Scala doesn't really need it because its if and else blocks can fit compactly on a single line (and, unlike in C and Java, they are already an expression).

Using a single expression without an expression block in if..else expressions works well if everything fits on one line. When your if..else expression doesn't easily fit on a single line, however, consider using expression blocks to make your code more readable. if expressions without an else should always use curly braces, because they tend to be statements that create side effects.

if..else blocks are a simple and common way to write conditional logic. There are other, more elegant ways to do so in Scala, however, using *match expressions*.

Match Expressions

Match expressions are akin to C's and Java's "switch" statements, where a single input item is evaluated and the first pattern that is "matched" is executed and its value returned. Like C's and Java's "switch" statements, Scala's match expressions support a default or wildcard "catch-all" pattern. Unlike them, only zero or one patterns can match;

there is no "fall-through" from one pattern to the next one in line, nor is there a "break" statement that would prevent this fall-through.

The traditional "switch" statement is limited to matching by value, but Scala's match expressions are an amazingly flexible device that also enables matching such diverse items as types, regular expressions, numeric ranges, and data structure contents. Although many match expressions could be replaced with simple "if .. else if .. else" blocks, doing so would result in a loss of the concise syntax that match expressions offer.

In fact, most Scala developers prefer match expressions over "if .. else" blocks because of their expressiveness and concise syntax.

In this section we will cover the basic syntax and uses of match expressions. As you read through the book, you will pick up new features that may be applicable to match expressions. Try experimenting with them to find new ways to express relationships or equivalence through match expressions.

Syntax: Using a Match Expression

```
<expression> match {
  case <pattern match> => <expression>
  [case...]
}
```

Multiple Expressions Allowed but Not Recommended
Scala officially supports having multiple expressions follow the arrow (=>), but this is not recommended because it may reduce readability. If you have multiple expressions in a case block, convert them to an expression block by wrapping them with curly braces.

Let's try this out by converting the "if .. else" example from the previous section into a match expression. In this version the Boolean expression is handled first, and then the result is matched to either `true` or `false`:

```
scala> val x = 10; val y = 20
x: Int = 10
y: Int = 20

scala> val max = x > y match {
     |   case true => x
     |   case false => y
     | }
max: Int = 20
```

The logic works out to the same as in the "if .. else" block but is implemented differently.

Here is another example of a match expression, one that takes an integer status code and tries to return the most appropriate message for it. Depending on the input to the expression, additional actions may be taken besides just returning a value:

```
scala> val status = 500
status: Int = 500

scala> val message = status match {
     |      case 200 =>
     |          "ok"
     |      case 400 => {
     |          println("ERROR - we called the service incorrectly")
     |          "error"
     |      }
     |      case 500 => {
     |          println("ERROR - the service encountered an error")
     |          "error"
     |      }
     | }
ERROR - the service encountered an error
message: String = error
```

This match expression prints error messages in case the status is 400 or 500 in addition to returning the message "error." The `println` statement is a good example of including more than one expression in a `case` block. There is no limit to the number of statements and expressions you can have inside a case block, although only the last expression will be used for the match expression's return value.

You can combine multiple patterns together with a *pattern alternative*, where the `case` block will be triggered if any one of the patterns match.

Syntax: A Pattern Alternative

```
case <pattern 1> | <pattern 2> .. => <one or more expressions>
```

The *pattern alternative* makes it possible to prevent duplicated code by reusing the same `case` block for multiple patterns. Here is an example showing the uses of these pipes (|) to collapse a 7-pattern match expression down to only two patterns:

```
scala> val day = "MON"
day: String = MON

scala> val kind = day match {
     |      case "MON" | "TUE" | "WED" | "THU" | "FRI" =>
     |          "weekday"
     |      case "SAT" | "SUN" =>
     |          "weekend"
     | }
kind: String = weekday
```

So far the examples have left open the possibility that a pattern may not be found that matches the input expression. In case this event does occur, for example if the input to the previous example was "MONDAY," what do you think would happen?

Well, it's more fun to try it out than to explain, so here is an example of a match expression that fails to provide a matching pattern for the input expression:

```scala
scala> "match me" match { case "nope" => "sorry" }
scala.MatchError: match me (of class java.lang.String)
  ... 32 elided
```

The input of "match me" didn't match the only given pattern, "nope," so the Scala compiler treated this as a runtime error. The error type, `scala.MatchError`, indicates that this is a failure of the match expression to handle its input.

 The message "... 32 elided" in the preceding example indicates that the error's stack trace (a list of all the nested function calls down to the one that caused the error) was reduced for readability.

To prevent errors from disrupting your match expression, use a wildcard match-all pattern or else add enough patterns to cover all possible inputs. A wildcard pattern placed as the final pattern in a match expression will match all possible input patterns and prevent a `scala.MatchError` from occurring.

Matching with Wildcard Patterns

There are two kinds of wildcard patterns you can use in a match expression: value binding and wildcard (aka "underscore") operators.

With *value binding* (aka *variable binding*) the input to a match expression is bound to a local value, which can then be used in the body of the `case` block. Because the pattern contains the name of the value to be bound there is no actual pattern to match against, and thus value binding is a wildcard pattern because it will match any input value.

Syntax: A Value Binding Pattern

```scala
case <identifier> => <one or more expressions>
```

Here is an example that tries to match a specific literal and otherwises uses value binding to ensure all other possible values are matched:

```scala
scala> val message = "Ok"
message: String = Ok

scala> val status = message match {
     |   case "Ok" => 200
     |   case other => {
     |     println(s"Couldn't parse $other")
     |     -1
     |   }
```

```
  | }
status: Int = 200
```

The value `other` is defined for the duration of the `case` block and is assigned the value of `message`, the input to the match expression.

The other type of wildcard pattern is the use of the wildcard operator. This is an underscore (_) character that acts as an unnamed placeholder for the eventual value of an expression at runtime. As with value binding, the underscore operator doesn't provide a pattern to match against, and thus it is a wildcard pattern that will match any input value.

Syntax: A Wildcard Operator Pattern

```
case _ => <one or more expressions>
```

The wildcard cannot be accessed on the right side of the arrow, unlike with value binding. If you need to access the value of the wildcard in the case block, consider using a value binding, or just accessing the input to the match expression (if available).

Why an Underscore as a wildcard?
Using underscores to indicate unknown values comes from the field of mathematics, arithmetic in particular, where missing amounts are denoted in problems with one or more underscores. For example, the equation 5 * _ = 15 is a problem that must be solved for _, the missing value.

Here is a similar example to the one earlier only with a wildcard operator instead of a bound value:

```
scala> val message = "Unauthorized"
message: String = Unauthorized

scala> val status = message match {
     |   case "Ok" => 200
     |   case _ => {
     |     println(s"Couldn't parse $message")
     |     -1
     |   }
     | }
Couldn't parse Unauthorized
status: Int = -1
```

In this case the underscore operator matches the runtime value of the input to the match expression. However, it can't be accessed inside the case block as a bound value would, and thus the input to the match expression is used to create an informative `println` statement.

Matching with Pattern Guards

A *pattern guard* adds an if expression to a value-binding pattern, making it possible to mix conditional logic into match expressions. When a pattern guard is used the pattern will only be matched when the if expression returns true.

Syntax: A Pattern Guard

```
case <pattern> if <Boolean expression> => <one or more expressions>
```

Unlike regular if expressions, the if expression here doesn't require parentheses ((and)) around its Boolean expression. Regular if expressions require the parentheses in order to simplify the job of parsing the full command and delineate the Boolean expression from the conditional expression. In this case the arrow (=>) handles that task and simplifies parsing. You can, however, add the parentheses around the Boolean expression if you wish.

Let's use a pattern guard to differentiate between a nonnull and a null response and report the correct message:

```
scala> val response: String = null
response: String = null

scala> response match {
     |    case s if s != null => println(s"Received '$s'")
     |    case s => println("Error! Received a null response")
     | }
Error! Received a null response
```

Matching Types with Pattern Variables

Another way to do pattern matching in a match expression is to match the *type* of the input expression. *Pattern variables*, if matched, may convert the input value to a value with a different type. This new value and type can then be used inside the case block.

Syntax: Specifying a Pattern Variable

```
case <identifier>: <type> => <one or more expressions>
```

The only restriction for pattern variable naming, other than the naming requirements already in place for values and variables, is that they must start with a lowercase letter.

You might be considering the utility of using a match expression to determine a value's type, given that all values have types and they are typically rather descriptive. The support of *polymorphic* types in Scala should be a clue to a match expression's utility. A value of type Int may get assigned to another value of type Any, or it may be returned as Any from a Java or Scala library call. Although the data is indeed an Int, the value will have the higher type Any.

Let's reproduce this situation by creating an Int, assigning it to an Any, and using a match expression to resolve its true type:

```
scala> val x: Int = 12180
x: Int = 12180

scala> val y: Any = x
y: Any = 12180

scala> y match {
     |     case x: String => s"'x'"
     |     case x: Double => f"$x%.2f"
     |     case x: Float => f"$x%.2f"
     |     case x: Long => s"${x}l"
     |     case x: Int => s"${x}i"
     | }
res9: String = 12180i
```

Even though the value given to the match expression has the type Any, the data it is storing was created as an Int. The match expression was able to match based on the actual type of the value, not just on the type that it was given. Thus, the integer 12180, even when given as type Any, could be correctly recognized as an integer and formatted as such.

Loops

Loops are the last expression-based control structure we'll examine in this chapter. A *loop* is a term for exercising a task repeatedly, and may include iterating through a range of data or repeating until a Boolean expression returns false.

The most important looping structure in Scala is the *for-loop*, also known as a *for-comprehension*. For-loops can iterate over a range of data executing an expression every time and optionally return a collection of all the expression's return values. These for-loops are highly customizable, supporting nested iterating, filtering, and value binding.

To get started we will introduce a new data structure called a Range, which iterates over a series of numbers. Ranges are created using the to or until operator with starting and ending integers, where the to operator creates an inclusive list and the until operator creates an exclusive list.

Syntax: Defining a Numeric Range

```
<starting integer> [to|until] <ending integer> [by increment]
```

Next is the basic definition of a for-loop.

Syntax: Iterating with a Basic For-Loop

```
for (<identifier> <- <iterator>) [yield] [<expression>]
```

The `yield` keyword is optional. If it is specified along with an expression, the return value of every expression that gets invoked will be returned as a collection. If it isn't specified, but the expression is still specified, the expression will be invoked but its return values will not be accessible.

You can define for-loops with parentheses or curly braces. The difference between the two styles comes when using multiple iterators (or other valid for-loop items, as we'll see), one on each line. With parentheses-based for-loops, each iterator line before the final one must end with a semicolon. With curly-braces-based for-loops, the semicolon after an iterator line is optional.

Let's start out printing a simple week planner by iterating over the days of a week, from 1 to 7 (inclusive), and printing out a header for each one:

```scala
scala> for (x <- 1 to 7) { println(s"Day $x:") }
Day 1:
Day 2:
Day 3:
Day 4:
Day 5:
Day 6:
Day 7:
```

The curly braces in the loop's expression (really a statement here because there isn't a `yield` keyword) are optional because there is only a single command, but I added them to make this look more like a traditional Java/C "for" loop.

However, what if what I really need is a collection of these "Day X:" messages? Then I can reuse them in other ways, or print them out as many times as I need. The `yield` keyword is the solution. I can convert the iterated statement into an expression that returns each message instead of printing it out, and add the `yield` keyword to convert the entire loop into an expression that returns the collection:

```scala
scala> for (x <- 1 to 7) yield { s"Day $x:" }
res10: scala.collection.immutable.IndexedSeq[String] = Vector(Day 1:,
Day 2:, Day 3:, Day 4:, Day 5:, Day 6:, Day 7:)
```

The Scala REPL's printout is more complicated than we have seen. This one is reporting that `res10` has the type `IndexedSeq[String]`, an indexed sequence of `String`, and is assigned a `Vector`, one of the implementations of `IndexedSeq`. Because of Scala's support for object-oriented polymorphism, a `Vector` (a subtype of `IndexedSeq`) can be assigned to an `IndexedSeq`-typed value.

In a way you can consider this for-loop to be a *map*, because it takes the expression of rendering the day to a `String` and applies it for every member of the input range. We have used this to map the range of numbers from 1 to 7 into a collection of messages of the same size. Like other sequences, this collection can now be used as an iterator in other for-loops.

Let's try it out by creating a for-loop that iterates over the sequence we built and printing each message, this time all on the same line instead of on their own lines. Again we only have a single command in the iterated expression, so this time we will leave off the curly braces because they are not necessary here:

```
scala> for (day <- res0) print(day + ", ")
Day 1:, Day 2:, Day 3:, Day 4:, Day 5:, Day 6:, Day 7:,
```

Iterator Guards

Like a pattern guard in a match expression, an *iterator guard* (also known as a *filter*) adds an `if` expression to an iterator. When an iterator guard is used, an iteration will be skipped unless the `if` expression returns `true`.

Syntax: An Iterator Guard

```
for (<identifier> <- <iterator> if <Boolean expression>) ...
```

Here is an example of using iterator guards to create a collection of numbers that are multiples of 3:

```
scala> val threes = for (i <- 1 to 20 if i % 3 == 0) yield i
threes: scala.collection.immutable.IndexedSeq[Int] = Vector(3, 6, 9, 12, 15, 18)
```

An iterator guard can also appear on its own line, separate from the iterator. Here's another example for-loop with separate iterator and iterator guards:

```
scala> val quote = "Faith,Hope,,Charity"
quote: String = Faith,Hope,,Charity

scala> for {
     |    t <- quote.split(",")
     |    if t != null
     |    if t.size > 0
     | }
     | { println(t) }
Faith
Hope
Charity
```

Nested Iterators

Nested iterators are extra iterators added to a for-loop, multiplying the total number of iterations by their iterator count. They are called *nested* iterators because adding them to an existing loop has the same effect as if they were written as a separate nested loop. Because the total number of iterations is the product of all of the iterators, adding a nested loop that will iterate once will not change the number of iterations, whereas a nested loop that does not iterate will cancel all iterations.

Here is an example of a for-loop with two iterators:

```
scala> for { x <- 1 to 2
     |         y <- 1 to 3 }
     | { print(s"($x,$y) ") }
(1,1) (1,2) (1,3) (2,1) (2,2) (2,3)
scala>
```

Because the product of the two iterators is six iterations, the print statement is called six times.

Value Binding

A common tactic in for-loops is to define temporary values or variables inside the expression block based on the current iteration. An alternate way to do this in Scala is to use *value binding* in the for-loop's definition, which works the same but can help to minimize the size and complexity of the expression block. Bound values can be used for nested iterators, iterator guards, and other bound values.

Syntax: Value Binding in For-Loops

```
for (<identifier> <- <iterator>; <identifier> = <expression>) ...
```

In this example I will use the "left-shift" binary operator (<<) on an Int to compute the powers of two from zero to eight. The argument to the operator is the number of times to "shift" the number leftwards by one bit, effectively mupltiplying it by two. The result of each operation is bound to the value "pow" in the current iteration:

```
scala> val powersOf2 = for (i <- 0 to 8; pow = 1 << i) yield pow
powersOf2: scala.collection.immutable.IndexedSeq[Int] = Vector(1, 2, 4, 8,
16, 32, 64, 128, 256)
```

The "pow" value is defined and assigned for each iteration in the loop. Because that value is yielded by the for-loop, the result is a collection of the "pow" value from each iteration.

Value binding within the definition of a for-loop makes it possible to centralize most of the loop's logic inside the definition. The result is a more compact for-loop with an even more compact yield expression (if used).

While and Do/While Loops

In addition to for-loops Scala also supports "while" and "do/while" loops, which repeat a statement until a Boolean expression returns false. These are not as commonly used as for-loops in Scala, however, because they are not expressions and cannot be used to yield values.

Syntax: A While Loop

```
while (<Boolean expression>) statement
```

As a very simple example here is a while loop that decrements a number repeatedly until it is no longer greater than zero:

```
scala> var x = 10; while (x > 0) x -= 1
x: Int = 0
```

The "do/while" loop is similar but the statement is executed *before* the Boolean expression is first evaluated. In this example I have a Boolean expression that will return false, but is only checked after the statement has had a chance to run:

```
scala> val x = 0
x: Int = 0

scala> do println(s"Here I am, x = $x") while (x > 0)
Here I am, x = 0
```

The while and do/while loops may have their uses, for example if you're reading from a socket and need to continue iterating until there is no more content to read. However, Scala offers a number of more expressive *and* more functional ways to handle loops than while and do/while loops. These include the for-loops we already covered as well as some new ones we'll study in Chapter 6.

Summary

We covered if/else conditions, pattern matching, and loops in detail in this chapter. These structures provide a solid basis for writing core logic in Scala.

However, these three (or two) structures are just as important to learning Scala development as learning about the fundamentals of expressions. The namesake of this chapter —expressions and their return values—are the real core building block of any application. Expressions themselves may seem to be an obvious concept, and devoting an entire chapter to them has the appearance of being overly generous to the topic. The reason I have devoted a chapter to them is that learning to work in terms of expressions is a useful and valuable skill. You should consider expressions when writing code, and even structure your applications around them. Some important principles to keep in mind when writing expressions are (1) how you will organize your code as expressions, (2) how your expressions will derive a return value, and (3) what you will do with that return value.

Expressions, in addition to being a foundation for your code organization, are also a foundation for Scala's syntax. In this chapter we have defined if/else conditions, pattern matching, and loops in terms of how they are structured around expressions. In the next chapter we will continue this practice by introducing functions as named, reusable expressions and defining them as such. Future chapters will continue this trend of defining concepts and structures in terms of expressions. Thus, understanding the basic nature and syntax of expressions and expression blocks is a crucial key to picking up the syntax for the rest of the language.

Exercises

While the Scala REPL provides an excellent venue for experimenting with the language's features, writing more than a line or two of code in it can be challenging. Because you'll need to start working with more than a few lines of code, it's time to start working in standalone Scala source files.

The `scala` command, which launches the Scala REPL, can also be used to evaluate and execute Scala source files:

```
$ scala <source file>
```

To test this out, create a new file titled *Hello.scala* with the following contents:

```
println("Hello, World")
```

Then execute it with the `scala` command:

```
$ scala Hello.scala
Hello, World

$
```

You should see the result ("Hello, World") printed on the next line.

An alternate way to execute external Scala files is with the `:load` command in the Scala REPL. This is useful if you want to stay in the Scala REPL while still using a text editor or IDE to edit your code.

To test this out, in the same directory you created the *Hello.scala* file, start the Scala REPL and run `:load Hello.scala`:

```
scala> :load Hello.scala
Loading Hello.scala...
Hello, World

scala>
```

The `:load` command is a Scala REPL feature and not actually part of the Scala language. Scala REPL commands are distinguished from regular Scala syntax by their ":" prefix.

Now that you have the option of developing within the Scala REPL or in a separate text editor or IDE, you can get started with the exercises for this chapter.

1. Given a string `name`, write a match expression that will return the same string if nonempty, or else the string "n/a" if it is empty.

2. Given a double `amount`, write an expression to return "greater" if it is more than zero, "same" if it equals zero, and "less" if it is less than zero. Can you write this with if..else blocks? How about with match expressions?

3. Write an expression to convert one of the input values `cyan`, `magenta`, `yellow` to their six-char hexadecimal equivalents in string form. What can you do to handle error conditions?

4. Print the numbers 1 to 100, with each line containing a group of five numbers. For example:

```
1, 2, 3, 4, 5,
6, 7, 8, 9, 10
. . . .
```

5. Write an expression to print the numbers from 1 to 100, except that for multiples of 3, print "type," and for multiples of 5, print "safe." For multiples of both 3 and 5, print "typesafe."

6. Can you rewrite the answer to exercise 5 to fit on one line? It probably won't be easier to read, but reducing code to its shortest form is an art, and a good exercise to learn the language.

CHAPTER 4

Functions

Functions are the core building blocks of reusable logic. Of course, you probably already knew that, because nearly all other languages also have functions (or methods, the object-oriented version of functions). Devoting an entire chapter to a concept common across languages may thus seem odd, but to Scala and other functional programming languages functions are very important.

Functional programming languages are geared to support the creation of highly reusable and composable functions and to help developers organize their code base around them. Much like a Unix power user will compose multiple single-purpose tools into a complex piped command, a functional programmer will combine single-purpose function invocations into chains of operations (think Map/Reduce). A function that was written with a simple purpose (e.g., to double a number) may be picked up and applied across a 50,000-node list, or given to an actor to be executed locally or in a remote server.

In Scala, *functions* are named, reusable expressions. They may be parameterized and they may return a value, but neither of these features are required. These features are, however, useful for ensuring maximum reusability and composability. They will also help you write shorter, more readable, and more stable applications. Using parameterized functions you can normalize duplicated code, simplifying your logic and making it more discoverable. Testing your code becomes easier, because normalized and parameterized logic is easier to test than denormalized logic repeated throughout your code.

Even greater benefits may come from following standard functional programming methodology and building *pure* functions when possible. In functional programming a *pure* function is one that:

- Has one or more input parameters
- Performs calculations using only the input parameters
- Returns a value

- Always returns the same value for the same input
- Does not use or affect any data outside the function
- Is not affected by any data outside the function

Pure functions are essentially equivalent to functions in mathematics, where the definition is a calculation derived only from the input parameters, and are the building blocks for programs in functional programming. They are more stable than functions that do not meet these requirements because they are stateless and orthogonal to external data such as files, databases, sockets, global variables, or other shared data. In essence, they are uncorruptible and noncorrupting expressions of pure logic.

On the other hand, it can be really hard to write useful applications that don't affect files, databases, or sockets, so it is rare to write one that only contains pure functions. Instead of trying to find a way to exlusively use pure functions in their applications, Scala developers will generally compromise and seek ways to reduce the number of unpure functions. Keeping unpure functions clearly named and organized in such a way that they can be easily identified versus pure functions is a common goal of modularizing and organizing Scala applications.

With this in mind, let's learn how to write functions in Scala. Because Scala's function definitions are flexible, with several optional components, we'll start with the most basic type first.

Syntax: Defining an Input-less Function

```
def <identifier> = <expression>
```

At its most basic, a Scala function is a named wrapper for an expression. When you need a function to format the current data, check a remote service for new data, or just to return a fixed value, this is the format for you. Here is an example of defining and invoking input-less functions:

```
scala> def hi = "hi"
hi: String

scala> hi
res0: String = hi
```

The return type of functions, as with values and variables, are present even if they are not explicitly defined. And like values and variables, functions are easier to read with explicit types.

Syntax: Defining a Function with a Return Type

```
def <identifier>: <type> = <expression>
```

This function definition is also input-less, but it demonstrates the "colon-and-type" format from value and variable definitions for function definitions. Here's the "hi" function again with an explicit type for better readability:

```
scala> def hi: String = "hi"
hi: String
```

Now we're ready to look at a full function definition.

Syntax: Defining a Function

```
def <identifier>(<identifier>: <type>[, ... ]): <type> = <expression>
```

Let's try creating a function that performs an essential mathematical operation:

```
scala> def multiplier(x: Int, y: Int): Int = { x * y }
multiplier: (x: Int, y: Int)Int

scala> multiplier(6, 7)
res0: Int = 42
```

The body of these functions consists essentially of expressions or expression blocks, where the final line becomes the return value of the expression and thus the function. While I do recommend continuing this practice for functions, there are times when you need to exit and return a value before the end of the function's expression block. You can use the return keyword to specify a function's return value explicitly and exit the function.

A common use of an early function exit is to stop further execution in the case of invalid or abnormal input values. For example, this "trim" function validates that the input value is nonnull before calling the JVM String's "trim" method:

```
scala> def safeTrim(s: String): String = {
     |   if (s == null) return null
     |   s.trim()
     | }
safeTrim: (s: String)String
```

You should now have a basic understanding of how to define and invoke functions in Scala.

 To become more familiar with Scala's functions, try rewriting some code examples from Chapter 2 and Chapter 3 as functions. When possible, move fixed values from the example expressions into input parameters of your new functions.

Procedures

A *procedure* is a function that doesn't have a return value. Any function that ends with a statement, such as a `println()` call, is also a procedure. If you have a simple function without an explicit return type that ends with a statement, the Scala compiler will infer the return type of the function to be `Unit`, the lack of a value. For procedures greater than a single line, an explicit unit type of `Unit` will clearly indicate to readers that there is no return value.

Here is a simple logging procedure, defined with an implicit return type and then with an explict return type:

```
scala> def log(d: Double) = println(f"Got value $d%.2f")
log: (d: Double)Unit

scala> def log(d: Double): Unit = println(f"Got value $d%.2f")
log: (d: Double)Unit

scala> log(2.23535)
Got value 2.24
```

An alternate but now unofficially deprecated syntax you will see for procedures is to define them without the `Unit` return type *and* without an equals sign before the procedure body. With this syntax the example `log()` method would be written like this:

```
scala> def log(d: Double) { println(f"Got value $d%.2f") }
log: (d: Double)Unit
```

As just noted, this syntax is unofficially deprecated by the maintainers of the Scala language. The problem with this syntax is that too many developers accidentally wrote procedures with return values, expecting the return value to be actually returned to the caller. With this procedure syntax, any return value (or final expression) will be discarded. To address this problem, it is recommended that developers stick to regular function definitions with an equals sign to reduce the possibility that valid return values will be ignored.

Functions with Empty Parentheses

An alternate way to define and invoke an input-less function (one which has no input parameters) is with empty parentheses. You might find this style preferable because it clearly distinguishes the function from a value.

Syntax: Defining a Function with Empty Parentheses

```
def <identifier>()[: <type>] = <expression>
```

You can invoke such a function using empty parentheses as well, or choose to leave them off:

```
scala> def hi(): String = "hi"
hi: ()String

scala> hi()
res1: String = hi

scala> hi
res2: String = hi
```

The reverse is not true, however. Scala does not allow a function that was defined without parentheses to be invoked with them. This rule prevents confusion from invoking a function without parentheses versus invoking the return value of that function as a function.

Functions with Side Effects Should Use Parentheses

A Scala convention for input-less functions is that they should be defined with empty parentheses if they have side effects (i.e., if the function modifies data outside its scope). For example, an input-less function that writes a message to the console should be defined with empty parentheses.

Function Invocation with Expression Blocks

When invoking functions using a single parameter, you can choose to use an expression block surrounded with curly braces to send the parameter instead of surrounding the value with parentheses. Using an expression block to invoke a function makes it possible to handle calculations or other actions and then call the function with the return value of the block.

Syntax: Invoking a Function with an Expression Block

```
<function identifier> <expression block>
```

One example where using an expression block to invoke a function may be preferable is when you have to send a calculated value to the function. Instead of calculating the amount and storing it in local values to be passed to the function, you can do the calculations inside the expression block. The expression block will be evaluated before the function is called and the block's return value will be used as the function argument.

Here is an example of calculating values inside a function block used for invoking a function:

```
scala> def formatEuro(amt: Double) = f"€$amt%.2f"
formatEuro: (amt: Double)String

scala> formatEuro(3.4645)
res4: String = €3.46
```

```
scala> formatEuro { val rate = 1.32; 0.235 + 0.7123 + rate * 5.32 }
res5: String = €7.97
```

If the value we want to pass to the function is already calculated, using parentheses to specify the function parameter is the natural way to go. But if you have calculations that will only be used for the function, and you can keep the code readable to others, a function invocation with an expression block may be a good choice.

Recursive Functions

A *recursive* function is one that may invoke itself, preferably with some type of parameter or external condition that will be checked to avoid an infinite loop of function invocation. Recursive functions are very popular in functional programming because they offer a way to iterate over data structures or calculations without using mutable data, because each function call has its own *stack* for storing function parameters.

Here's an example of a recursive function that raises an integer by a given positive exponent:

```
scala> def power(x: Int, n: Int): Long = {
     |    if (n >= 1) x * power(x, n-1)
     |    else 1
     | }
power: (x: Int, n: Int)Long

scala> power(2, 8)
res6: Long = 256

scala> power(2, 1)
res7: Long = 2

scala> power(2, 0)
res8: Long = 1
```

One problem with using recursive functions is running into the dreaded "Stack Overflow" error, where invoking a recursive function too many times eventually uses up all of the allocated stack space.

To prevent this scenario, the Scala compiler can optimize some recursive functions with *tail-recursion* so that recursive calls do not use additional stack space. With tail-recursion–optimized functions, recursive invocation doesn't create new stack space but instead uses the current function's stack space. Only functions whose last statement is the recursive invocation can be optimized for tail-recursion by the Scala compiler. If the result of invoking itself is used for anything but the direct return value, a function can't be optimized.

Fortunately there is a *function annotation* available to mark a function as being intended to be optimized for tail-recursion. A function annotation is special syntax carried over from the Java programming language where the "at" sign (@) and an annotation type is placed before a function definition to mark it for special use. A function marked with the tail-recursion function annotation will cause an error at compilation time if it cannot be optimized for tail-recursion.

To mark a function as intended for tail-recursion, add the text @annotation.tailrec before the function definition or on the previous line.

Here's the same example again only marked with the "tailrec" annotation, to let the Scala compiler know we expect it to be optimized for tail-recursion and that if it cannot be, the compiler should treat it as an error:

```
scala> @annotation.tailrec
     | def power(x: Int, n: Int): Long = {
     |   if (n >= 1) x * power(x, n-1)
     |   else 1
     | }
<console>:9: error: could not optimize @tailrec annotated method power:
it contains a recursive call not in tail position
       if (n >= 1) x * power(x, n-1)
```

Ah, the function couldn't be optimized because the recursive call is not the last statement in the function. This is understandable. I'll switch the "if" and "else" conditions and try again:

```
scala> @annotation.tailrec
     | def power(x: Int, n: Int): Long = {
     |   if (n < 1) 1
     |   else x * power(x, n-1)
     | }
<console>:11: error: could not optimize @tailrec annotated method power:
it contains a recursive call not in tail position
         else x * power(x, n-1)
                  ^
```

Hmm, the recursive call *is* the last item in the function. Oh I see, we're taking the result of the recursive call and multiplying it by a value, so that multiplication is actually the last statement in the function, not the recursive call.

A good way to fix this is to move the multiplication into the beginning of the invoked function instead of multiplying its result. Now the end of the function is a simple untouched result from the recursive call:

```
scala> @annotation.tailrec
     | def power(x: Int, n: Int, t: Int = 1): Int = {
     |   if (n < 1) t
     |   else power(x, n-1, x*t)
     | }
power: (x: Int, n: Int, t: Int)Int
```

```
scala> power(2,8)
res9: Int = 256
```

Success! The "tailrec" annotation and successful compile guarantees that the function will be optimized with tail-recursion, so that each successive call will not add more stack frames.

Although this example may seem challenging to get through, recursion and tail-recursion are still valuable methods for iterating without using mutable data. You'll find that many of the data structures we'll explore later in the book will be rich with functions that are implemented with tail-recursion.

Nested Functions

Functions are named, parameterized expression blocks and expression blocks are nestable, so it should be no great surprise that functions are themselves nestable.

There are times when you have logic that needs to be repeated inside a method, but would not benefit from being extrapolated to an external method. In these cases defining an internal function inside another function, to only be used in that function, may be worthwhile.

Let's have a look at a method that takes three integers and returns the one with the highest value:

```
scala> def max(a: Int, b: Int, c: Int) = {
     |    def max(x: Int, y: Int) = if (x > y) x else y
     |    max(a, max(b, c))
     | }
max: (a: Int, b: Int, c: Int)Int

scala> max(42, 181, 19)
res10: Int = 181
```

The logic inside the max(Int, Int) nested function was defined once but used twice inside the outer function, making it possible to reduce duplicated logic and simplify the overall function.

The nested function here has the same name as its outer function, but because their parameters are different (the nested one only takes two integers) there is no conflict between them. Scala functions are differentiated by their name and the list of their parameter types. However, even if the names and parameter types were the same there would be no confict because the local (nested) one takes precedence over the outer one.

Calling Functions with Named Parameters

The convention for calling functions is that the parameters are specified in the order in which they are originally defined. However, in Scala you can call parameters by name, making it possible to specify them out of order.

Syntax: Specifying a Parameter by Name

```
<function name>(<parameter> = <value>)
```

In this example, a simple two-parameter function is invoked twice, first using the convention of specifying parameters by their order and then by assigning values by parameter name:

```
scala> def greet(prefix: String, name: String) = s"$prefix $name"
greet: (prefix: String, name: String)String

scala> val greeting1 = greet("Ms", "Brown")
greeting1: String = Ms Brown

scala> val greeting2 = greet(name = "Brown", prefix = "Mr")
greeting2: String = Mr Brown
```

Read the next section on default values to see how calling parameters by name can be very useful.

Parameters with Default Values

A common problem when defining functions is deciding which input parameters they should take to maximize reuse. In Scala, Java, and other languages, a common solution is to provide multiple versions of the same function with the same name but different lists of input parameters. This practice is known as *function overloading* due to the function's name being reused for different inputs. The common practice is to copy a function with x number of parameters to a new function with x–1 parameters that invokes the original function using a default value for the missing parameter.

Scala provides a cleaner solution for this problem: specifying default values for any parameter, making the use of that parameter optional for callers.

Syntax: Specifying a Default Value for a Function Parameter

```
def <identifier>(<identifier>: <type> = <value>): <type>
```

Here is the greeting example from the previous section again with a default value for the "prefix" parameter. Because the "name" parameter is still required we will call the function with only this parameter, calling it by name because we can't call it in order (because the "prefix" parameter comes first!):

```
scala> def greet(prefix: String = "", name: String) = s"$prefix$name"
greet: (prefix: String, name: String)String
```

```
scala> val greeting1 = greet(name = "Paul")
greeting1: String = Paul
```

This is pretty useful, except it would be better to be able to call the function without having to specify the parameter name. By reorganizing the function so that the required parameter comes first, we can call it without using a parameter name:

```
scala> def greet(name: String, prefix: String = "") = s"$prefix$name"
greet: (name: String, prefix: String)String

scala> val greeting2 = greet("Ola")
greeting2: String = Ola
```

As a matter of style it's better to organize function parameters so that those with default values follow required parameters. This emphasizes the importance of the required parameters as well as making it possible to call the function without specifying the default parameters and not require the use of parameter names.

Vararg Parameters

Java and C developers will recognize the term *vararg*, a function parameter that can match zero or more arguments from the caller. Its most popular usage is in string interpolation functions such as C's `printf()` and Java's `String.format()`.

Scala also supports vararg parameters, so you can define a function with a variable number of input arguments. The vararg parameter cannot be followed by a nonvararg parameter because there would be no way to distinguish them. Inside the function, the vararg parameter, implemented as a collection (which we'll study in Chapter 6), can be used as an iterator in for loops.

To mark a function parameter as matching one or more input arguments, add an asterisk symbol (*) after the parameter's type in the function definition.

Here is an example of using a vararg parameter to create a summing function that returns a sum of all of its input integers:

```
scala> def sum(items: Int*): Int = {
     |    var total = 0
     |    for (i <- items) total += i
     |    total
     | }
sum: (items: Int*)Int

scala> sum(10, 20, 30)
res11: Int = 60

scala> sum()
res12: Int = 0
```

Parameter Groups

So far we have looked at parameterized function definitions as a list of parameters surrounded by parentheses. Scala provides the option to break these into groups of parameters, each separated with their own parentheses.

Here is an example of the "max" function where the two input parameters have been split into their own parameter groups:

```
scala> def max(x: Int)(y: Int) = if (x > y) x else y
max: (x: Int)(y: Int)Int

scala> val larger = max(20)(39)
larger: Int = 39
```

Given this example, parameter groups may appear to provide little benefit. After all, why not just keep all of the parameters together in one group? The real benefits come when you use them with function literals, which we will investigate in "Invoking Higher-Order Functions with Function Literal Blocks" on page 78.

Type Parameters

Until this point, the only parameters to functions we have discussed are "value" parameters, the input data passed to functions. In Scala, to complement the value parameters, you can also pass type parameters, which dictate the types used for the value parameters or for the return value. Using type parameters can increase the flexibility and reusability of functions as they transition these types from being fixed to being set by the caller of the function.

Here is the syntax for defining a function with a type parameter. I've removed everything after the return type to keep the syntax simple, and changed the typical "identifier" notation to denote its actual purpose (because otherwise every item after "def" would be an identifier).

Syntax: Defining a Function's Type Parameters

```
def <function-name>[type-name](parameter-name): <type-name>): <type-name>...
```

This is where I normally put an example of a new feature, but because type parameters can be a tricky subject to learn I'll change the formula here to show how this feature solves a given problem.

 Here is one of the times when I'm showing the wrong way to do something. It is a useful exercise for demonstrating the usefulness of type parameters, but be forewarned that some of the example code exercises will not be correct.

Let's say I want to have a simple function that only returns its input (known as an *identity* function), in this case one defined for a `String`:

```
def identity(s: String): String = s
```

Well, that could be useful, but I can only call it for a `String`. There is no way to call it for, say, an `Int` unless I define a separate function:

```
def identity(i: Int): Int = i
```

Now I have defined this for `Int`s, but it will be a pain to have to redefine this for every type I want to use. What if I just use the root type, `Any`, which will work for all types? I'll try that out and pass it a new `String`, then store the return value:

```
scala> def identity(a: Any): Any = a
identity: (a: Any)Any

scala> val s: String = identity("Hello")
<console>:8: error: type mismatch;
 found    : Any
 required: String
       val s: String = identity("Hello")
                               ^
```

This example didn't work out. I had hoped to assign the result to a `String` but because the function's return type is `Any` there was no way to do this, thus resulting in a Scala compilation error.

The solution? Instead of defining the function to use a specific type (e.g., `String` or `Int`) or a generic "root" type (e.g., `Any`), parameterize the type so it will suit whatever callers want to use.

Here is the identity function defined with a type parameter, making it usable with any type you give it:

```
scala> def identity[A](a: A): A = a
identity: [A](a: A)A

scala> val s: String = identity[String]("Hello")
s: String = Hello

scala> val d: Double = identity[Double](2.717)
d: Double = 2.717
```

The identity function's type parameter is `A`, which like the value parameter `a` is simply a unique identifier. It is used to define the type of the value parameter `a` and the return type of the function.

Now that the identity function has been defined with a type parameter, I can call it with `[String]` to convert the value parameter type and return type into a `String` for the scope of my function call. I can then call it with [Double] to convert it to work with Double values for the scope of the function call.

Of course, another excellent feature that we know Scala provides is type inference. In the preceding example it wasn't really necessary to pass the [String] type parameter to the "identity" method because the compiler could have inferred this from either the String literal we passed it or the String value to which we assigned the function's return value.

Let's take the two function calls from the previous example and remove their type parameters, demonstrating that type parameters can be inferred by the compiler:

```
scala> val s: String = identity("Hello")
s: String = Hello

scala> val d: Double = identity(2.717)
d: Double = 2.717
```

This looks great. There is just one remaining explicit type we can remove, the types of the values. With input values of a String and a Double, the Scala compiler can infer the types of the type parameters *and* of the values to which the return values are assigned:

```
scala> val s = identity("Hello")
s: String = Hello

scala> val d = identity(2.717)
d: Double = 2.717
```

Here you have witnessed a triumph of type parameters and type inference. The literals passed to a function are enough to change its value parameter type, return value type, and the type of the values to which its return value is assigned.

In regular practice this may not be the most readable way to define values, because a reader of the code would need to check the function definition carefully to figure out what the values assigned to its return value would become. It does, however, serve as a successful demonstration of the flexibility and functionality of Scala's type system and support for highly reusable functions.

Methods and Operators

Until this point we have been discussing the use of functions without reference to *where* they will actually be used. Functions on their own, as defined in the REPL, are helpful for learning the core concepts. However, in practice they will typically exist in objects and act on data from the object, so a more appropriate term for them will often be "methods."

A *method* is a function defined in a class and available from any instance of the class. The standard way to invoke methods in Scala (as in Java and Ruby) is with *infix dot notation*, where the method name is prefixed by the name of its instance and the dot (.) separator.

Syntax: Invoking a Method with Infix Dot Notation

```
<class instance>.<method>[(<parameters>)]
```

Let's try this out by calling one of the many useful methods on the String type:

```
scala> val s = "vacation.jpg"
s: String = vacation.jpg

scala> val isJPEG = s.endsWith(".jpg")
isJPEG: Boolean = true
```

If it isn't clear, the value s is an instance of type String, and the String class has a method called endsWith( ). In the future we'll refer to methods using the full class name, like String.endsWith( ), even though you typically invoke them with the instance name, not the type name.

You'll find that most of the types in Scala have a wide variety of methods available for use with them. Part of the process of becoming a proficient Scala developer is learning the Scala library well enough to be familiar with many of its types and their methods. The official Scala API Documention (*http://bit.ly/ls-scalaapi*) has a full list of the available types and their methods. I highly recommend taking the time to learn the types you are using and try out new methods on them.

Finding Documentation for the String Type

The documentation for the String type is split between the String Ops page in the Scala documentation and the java.lang.String Javadocs (*http://bit.ly/ls-string*), because Scala wraps Java's String, providing complementary functionality.

Let's continue exploring new methods by trying out some of the useful ones in the Double type:

```
scala> val d = 65.642
d: Double = 65.642

scala> d.round
res13: Long = 66

scala> d.floor
res14: Double = 65.0

scala> d.compare(18.0)
res15: Int = 1
```

```
scala> d.+(2.721)
res16: Double = 68.363
```

The round and floor methods are relatively simple. They have no parameters and only return a modified version of the value in the object (where the object in question is a Double with the value 65.642). The compare method takes a single parameter and returns either 1, 0, or –1 if the given parameter is less, equal to, or greater than the value of d.

The last method has a single character as its name, the addition operator (+), but is still a valid function that takes a single parameter and returns the sum of d and the parameter. It may seem odd to provide a method for handling addition when one could just use the addition operator, but this method is actually the implementation of the addition operator.

Let me explain that in plainer terms. There actually is no addition operator in Scala, nor are there any other arithmetic operators. All of the arithmetic operators we have used in Scala are actually methods, written as simple functions using their operator symbol as the function name and bound to a specific type.

This is possible because of an alternate form of invoking methods on objects known as *operator notation*, which forsakes the traditional dot notation and uses spaces to separate the object, its operator method, and the single parameter to the method. Every time we write 2 + 3, the Scala compiler recognizes this as operator notation and treats it as if you had written 2.+(3), where the addition method of an Int with the value 2 is called with the parameter 3 and the value 5 is returned.

To invoke an object's methods with operator notation, pick a method that takes a single parameter and separate the object, method, and single parameter with spaces. No other puncuation is necessary.

Syntax: Invoking a Method with Operator Notation

```
<object> <method> <parameter>
```

A more precise term for this notation would be *infix operator notation*, because the operator (the object's method) is located in between the two operands.

Let's repeat the last two method calls in the previous example, but rewrite them using operator notation. The first two methods in the previous example aren't eligible for infix operator notation because they lack a parameter:

```
scala> d compare 18.0
res17: Int = 1

scala> d + 2.721
res18: Double = 68.363
```

The results are equivalent to the results in the previous example, which we should expect because they are calling the same functions with the same input values.

What About Methods with More Than One Parameter?

Operator notation is meant for single-parameter methods, akin to simple mathematical operations, but can be used on methods with more than one parameter. To do so, wrap the list of parameters in parentheses and treat it as a single (but wrapped) parameter. For example, you can invoke String.substring(start,end) as "star ing" substring (1,4).

Here is an addition of three numbers. In terms of operators, there are two additions taking place. How would you expect this gets converted into method calls?

```scala
scala> 1 + 2 + 3
res19: Int = 6
```

The answer is that the first operation is one method call, 1 + 2. The second operation is a separate method call applied to the result from the first call, or 3 + 3. You can use the same technique to chain regular method calls as long as each method's result is an object on which you can call the next operator method.

Scala's support for infix operator notation for invoking object methods has multiple benefits for the language. Operators, instead of being a part of the syntax and implemented in hidden ways, are just methods implemented in their objects that can be viewed or called directly. The syntax is thus reduced and simplified. Developers are free to implement their own operators because every single-parameter method can be used as an operator, and are motivated to simplify methods to only take a single parameter to make them eligible for operator notation. Finally, the code readability may be improved, removing otherwise necessary punctuation to focus on the simple object, method, and parameter components.

About the only drawback to using operator notation is when it reduces code readability instead of improving it. For example, a chain of 10 method calls separated only by spaces may be a bit harder to read than with regular dot notation, because the operators and operands may be hard to discern. Or an overeager developer may define his own type with an addition operator that, unknowingly to callers, performs a completely different type of operation.

Make sure to use care to invoke operator notation only when it can be clearly read, and you may find yourself using it regularly.

Writing Readable Functions

We'll wrap up this chapter with a more general discussion of *how* to write functions.

The entire point of writing functions is to reuse them (because otherwise you would have left them as single-use expressions). And the best way to ensure your functions will get reused is to make them *readable* by other developers. Readable functions are clear, understandable, and simple.

There are two ways to make sure your functions are readable. First, keep them short, well-named, and obvious. Break your complex functions into simpler functions that are shorter than the height of a standard visible page of text (say, 40 lines), so a reader won't need to scroll up and down to see the entire function. Use a name that reasonably sums up what your function is trying to accomplish. If you have these two right, your function's intent and implementation should be fairly obvious to developers.

The other way to make your functions readable is to add comments where appropriate. Scala supports the same commenting syntax as Java and C++ do. A double-slash (//) starts a *line comment*, continuing until the end of the line it starts on. A slash-and-star (/*) starts a *range comment* that continues until a closing star-and-slash (*/). Use them within your function to point out details and context that may be missed by readers, as well as to indicate potential problems or future work to be done.

An additional type of commenting is adding Scaladoc headers to your function. The Scaladoc tool, included with your Scala package, can generate API documentation based on these function headers. Scaladoc headers follow the same format as Javadoc headers, with a starting range comment of two stars (e.g., /**), an indented start prefixing every following line, and a regular ending range comment (*/). Parameters can be called out with a @param keyword followed by the parameter name and its description.

Scaladoc (or Javadoc, if you prefer) headers are a standard format for function comments. Adding them to your functions is a good practice to follow even if you don't plan on generating API documentation. Developers reading your function will likely start with the Scaladoc header before reading the function's code, so make sure to keep it accurate and concise.

Here is an example Scaladoc header for a function:

```scala
scala> /**
     |  * Returns the input string without leading or trailing
     |  * whitespace, or null if the input string is null.
     |  * @param s the input string to trim, or null.
     |  */
     | def safeTrim(s: String): String = {
     |   if (s == null) return null
     |   s.trim()
     | }
safeTrim: (s: String)String
```

An additional benefit of using Scaladoc headers for your function is the support from IDEs such as Eclipse and IntelliJ IDEA. They allow developers to read the documentation for your function without even reading your source code. Developers who invoke your function (or method) can view the Scaladoc header's contents with a mouse-over of a function invocation, or by browsing a list of functions.

Summary

Because most of the language's logical structures were covered in Chapter 3, it made sense to focus this, the chapter following expressions, on how to organize and reuse them as functions. Indeed, while a function's name, input parameters, and return value type are important parts of a function's definition, the actual contents of a function are one big expression.

An entire chapter about functions should be no less than expected from a book itself devoted to a functional programming language. However, though you just finished an entire chapter *about* functions, you have not yet learned everything there is to know about functions. Namely, that in Scala you can treat your functions as data and pass them into other functions to invoke.

This concept of functions as data, with their own literals and types, brings functions up to par with other forms as data. You'll learn all about how functions can receive the same treatment as other data types, making them "first-class" citizens of the language, in the next chapter.

Exercises

1. Write a function that computes the area of a circle given its radius.

2. Provide an alternate form of the function in exercise 1 that takes the radius as a String. What happens if your function is invoked with an empty String?

3. Write a recursive function that prints the values from 5 to 50 by fives, without using for or while loops. Can you make it tail-recursive?

4. Write a function that takes a milliseconds value and returns a string describing the value in days, hours, minutes, and seconds. What's the optimal type for the input value?

5. Write a function that calculates the first value raised to the exponent of the second value. Try writing this first using math.pow, then with your own calculation. Did you implement it with variables? Is there a solution available that only uses immutable data? Did you choose a numeric type that is large enough for your uses?

6. Write a function that calculates the difference between a pair of 2D points (x and y) and returns the result as a point. Hint: this would be a good use for tuples (see "Tuples" on page 25).

7. Write a function that takes a 2-sized tuple and returns it with the Int value (if included) in the first position. Hint: this would be a good use for type parameters and the isInstanceOf type operation.

8. Write a function that takes a 3-sized tuple and returns a 6-sized tuple, with each original parameter followed by its String representation. For example, invoking

the function with (`true`, `22.25`, `"yes"`) should return (`true`, `"true"`, `22.5`, `"22.5"`, `"yes"`, `"yes"`). Can you ensure that tuples of all possible types are compatible with your function? When you invoke this function, can you do so with explicit types not only in the function result but in the value that you use to store the result?

CHAPTER 5

First-Class Functions

One of the core values of functional programming is that functions should be *first-class*. The term indicates that they are not only declared and invoked but can be used in every segment of the language as just another data type. A first-class function may, as with other data types, be created in literal form without ever having been assigned an identifier; be stored in a container such as a value, variable, or data structure; and be used as a parameter to another function or used as the return value from another function.

Functions that accept other functions as parameters and/or use functions as return values are known as *higher-order functions*. You may have heard of two of the most famous higher-order functions, `map()` and `reduce()`. The `map()` higher-order function takes a function parameter and uses it to convert one or more items to a new value and/or type. The `reduce()` higher-order function takes a function parameter and uses it to reduce a collection of multiple items down to a single item. The popular Map/Reduce computing paradigm uses this concept to tackle large computing challenges, by mapping the computation across a range of distributed nodes and reducing their results back to a meaningful size.

One of the benefits of using higher-order functions to work with data is that the actual *how* of processing the data is left as an implementation detail to the framework that has the higher-order function. A caller can specify *what* should be done and leave the higher-order functions to handle the actual logic flow. There's actually a name for this methodology, *declarative programming*, typically correlated with the use of functional programming and indicating that higher-order functions or some other mechanism is used to simply declare the work to be done without manually doing it. The opposite of this approach is the more mundane *imperative programming* style, wherein the logic flow of an operation is always explicitly stated.

So how does all of this apply to Scala?

Scala has full support for first-class functions, higher-order functions, and the use of declarative programming. As with other types of data such as String or Int, functions have types based on the types of their input arguments and their return value. A function can be stored in a value or variable, passed to a function, returned from a function, and used with data structures to support map(), reduce(), fold(), and filter(), among many other higher-order functions.

In this chapter, we will explore Scala's use of first-class functions, higher-order functions, and the use of function literals to easily create or pass logical expressions anywhere a regular function could be used.

Function Types and Values

The *type* of a function is a simple grouping of its input types and return value type, arranged with an arrow indicating the direction from input types to output type.

Syntax: A Function Type

```
([<type>, ...]) => <type>
```

Until now, all of the types we have used have been simple words like String and Int, so a type that includes punctuation and whitespace is likely to appear to be a bit odd. However, if you think about it, this is the only way to really describe a function without using a specific name. Because a function's signature is its name, inputs, and outputs, the type of a function should be the inputs and outputs.

For example, the function def double(x: Int): Int = x * 2 has the function type Int => Int, indicating that it has a single Int parameter and returns an Int. The function name, "double," is an identifier and isn't part of the type. The body of the function, a simple multiplication of the input by 2, does not affect the type of the function. The rest of the information is the input types and return type, and so these make up the function type itself.

Let's try using a function type in the REPL, by creating a function and then assigning it to a function value:

```
scala> def double(x: Int): Int = x * 2
double: (x: Int)Int

scala> double(5)
res0: Int = 10

scala> val myDouble: (Int) => Int = double                    ❶
myDouble: Int => Int = <function1>

scala> myDouble(5)                                            ❷
res1: Int = 10
```

```
scala> val myDoubleCopy = myDouble
myDoubleCopy: Int => Int = <function1>

scala> myDoubleCopy(5)
res2: Int = 10
```
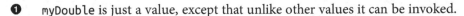

❸

❶ myDouble is just a value, except that unlike other values it can be invoked.

❷ Invoking myDouble as a function has the same result as invoking double.

❸ Assigning a function value to a new value works as with any other value.

The explicit type for the "myDouble" value was required to distinguish it as a function value and not a function invocation. An alternate way to define function values, assigned with a function, is with the wildcard operator, _.

Function types with a single parameter can leave off the parentheses. For example, a function that takes and returns a single integer can be written as the type Int => Int.

Syntax: Assigning a Function with the Wildcard Operator

```
val <identifier> = <function name> _
```

Let's try this out with the "myDouble" function value:

```
scala> def double(x: Int): Int = x * 2
double: (x: Int)Int

scala> val myDouble = double _
myDouble: Int => Int = <function1>

scala> val amount = myDouble(20)
amount: Int = 40
```

This time, the explicit function type for myDouble wasn't required to distinguish it from a function invocation. The underscore (_) served as a placeholder for a future invocation of the function, returning a function value that we could store in myDouble.

Let's revisit the explicit function type again to explore functions with multiple inputs. A function type with multiple inputs requires explicit parentheses around the input types, which ends up having the appearance of a function definition without parameter names.

Here's an example of a function value defined with an explicit function type using multiple parameters, enclosed with parentheses:

```
scala> def max(a: Int, b: Int) = if (a > b) a else b
max: (a: Int, b: Int)Int
```

```
scala> val maximize: (Int, Int) => Int = max
maximize: (Int, Int) => Int = <function2>

scala> maximize(50, 30)
res3: Int = 50
```

We could have also used a wildcard operator here, in place of the explicit type, but this example serves to demonstrate how to specify the multiple parameters in the type.

Finally, here's a function type that has no inputs. Do the empty parentheses remind you of a certain core Scala type? This is also the literal repesentation of the Unit type (as seen in Table 2-4), which indicates the lack of a value:

```
scala> def logStart() = "=" * 50 + "\nStarting NOW\n" + "=" * 50
logStart: ()String

scala> val start: () => String = logStart
start: () => String = <function0>

scala> println( start() )
==================================================
Starting NOW
==================================================
```

This was a gentle introduction to how functions may be treated as data, by storing them in values and assigning them static types. I hope you can try out these examples and gain some familiarity with specifying function types and storing functions in values, because the next few sections on higher-order functions and function literals are going to build on this knowledge and cover some challenging new syntax. Everything's about to get seriously fun now.

Higher-Order Functions

We have already defined values that have a function type. A *higher-order* function is a function that has a value with a function type as an input parameter or return value.

Here's a good use case for a higher-order function: calling other functions that act on a String, but only if the input String is not null. Adding this check can prevent a NullPointerException in the JVM by avoiding a method call on null:

```
scala> def safeStringOp(s: String, f: String => String) = {
     |     if (s != null) f(s) else s
     | }
safeStringOp: (s: String, f: String => String)String

scala> def reverser(s: String) = s.reverse
reverser: (s: String)String

scala> safeStringOp(null, reverser)
```

```
res4: String = null

scala> safeStringOp("Ready", reverser)
res5: String = ydaeR
```

The call with "null" safely returned the same value back, whereas the call with a valid String returned the reverse of the input value.

This example demonstrated how to pass an existing function as a parameter to a higher-order function. An alternative to using functions as parameters is to define them inline with function literals, as we will see in the next section.

Function Literals

Now we'll tackle a difficult concept covered by a variety of names by starting with an easy example. In this example we will create a *function literal*, a working function that lacks a name, and assign it to a new function value:

```
scala> val doubler = (x: Int) => x * 2
doubler: Int => Int = <function1>

scala> val doubled = doubler(22)
doubled: Int = 44
```

The function literal in this example is the syntax (x: Int) => x * 2, which defines a typed input argument (x) and the function body (x * 2). Function literals can be stored in function values and variables, or defined as part of a higher-order function invocation. You can express a function literal in any place that accepts a function type.

Although function literals are nameless functions, their concept and the use of the arrow syntax have many names. Here are a few that you may know:

Anonymous functions
> Literally true, because function literals do not include a function name. This is the Scala language's formal name for function literals.

Lambda expressions
> Both C# and Java 8 use this term, derived from the original *lambda calculus* syntax (e.g., x → x*2) in mathematics.

Lambdas
> A shortened version of *lambda expressions*.

function0, function1, function2, ..
> The Scala compiler's term for function literals, based on the number of input arguments. You can see how the single-argument function literal in the preceding example was given the name <function1>.

Why Not Just Call Them Anonymous Functions?

Although *The Scala Language Specification* (Odersky, 2011) uses the term *anonymous function*, this term focuses more attention on the lack of a name than on the interesting arrow-based syntax for defining its logic. Thus I prefer the clarifying term *function literal*, which indicates that the entire logic of a function body is being specified inline! You can think of a function literal as being to a function value what a string literal (e.g., "Hello, World") is to a string value: a literal expression of the assigned data.

Syntax: Writing a Function Literal

```
([<identifier>: <type>, ... ]) => <expression>
```

Let's define a function value and assign it a new function literal:

```
scala> val greeter = (name: String) => s"Hello, $name"
greeter: String => String = <function1>

scala> val hi = greeter("World")
hi: String = Hello, World
```

If you think about it, a function literal is essentially a parameterized expression. We know about expressions that return a value, but now have a way to parameterize their input.

Let's try a longer example to compare function assignment with function literals. We'll start with the max() function from the chapter introduction, assign it to a function value, and then reimplement the max() function as a function literal:

```
scala> def max(a: Int, b: Int) = if (a > b) a else b        ❶
max: (a: Int, b: Int)Int

scala> val maximize: (Int, Int) => Int = max                ❷
maximize: (Int, Int) => Int = <function2>

scala> val maximize = (a: Int, b: Int) => if (a > b) a else b   ❸
maximize: (Int, Int) => Int = <function2>

scala> maximize(84, 96)
res6: Int = 96
```

❶ The original max() function

❷ .. as assigned to a function value

❸ .. as redefined with a function literal

Function literals do not always need input arguments. Let's try defining one that doesn't take any arguments. We'll rewrite another function as a function literal, this time with the logStart() function from the chapter introduction:

```
scala> def logStart() = "=" * 50 + "\nStarting NOW\n" + "=" * 50
logStart: ()String

scala> val start = () => "=" * 50 + "\nStarting NOW\n" + "=" * 50
start: () => String = <function0>

scala> println( start() )
==================================================
Starting NOW
==================================================
```

Did you note that the REPL referred to the function literal as a "function0," its name for input-less functions? This is not the type of the value, however, which was inferred as () => String, an input-less function that returns a string.

As noted, function literals can be defined inside of higher-order function invocations. As an example, we will invoke the "safeStringOp" example (see "Higher-Order Functions" on page 68) with a function literal:

```
scala> def safeStringOp(s: String, f: String => String) = {
     |    if (s != null) f(s) else s
     | }
safeStringOp: (s: String, f: String => String)String

scala> safeStringOp(null, (s: String) => s.reverse)
res7: String = null

scala> safeStringOp("Ready", (s: String) => s.reverse)
res8: String = ydaeR
```

The function "safeStringOp" receives a function value parameter named "f" and invokes it conditionally. It makes no distinction between a regular function value being used to invoke it versus our function literal.

In the example, the type of the function parameter "f" is String => String. With this type already defined, we could have removed the explicit type from our function literal, because the compiler could easily infer its expected type. Removing the explicit type means that we could then remove the parentheses from the function literal, because they are unnecessary for single, untyped inputs.

Let's invoke the "safeStringOp" function again with a function literal that uses this simpler syntax:

```scala
scala> safeStringOp(null, s => s.reverse)
res9: String = null

scala> safeStringOp("Ready", s => s.reverse)
res10: String = ydaeR
```

The function literals here, stripped of their explicit types or parentheses, are reduced down to the basic essence of the function. They take an input parameter and return a value based on an operation on that parameter.

Although these function literals are very simple expressions of functions, Scala supports even simpler expressions with *placeholder syntax*.

Placeholder Syntax

Placeholder syntax is a shortened form of function literals, replacing named parameters with wildcard operators (_). It can be used when (a) the explicit type of the function is specified outside the literal and (b) the parameters are used no more than once.

Here is an example of a doubling function literal using wildcard operators in place of named parameters:

```scala
scala> val doubler: Int => Int = _ * 2
doubler: Int => Int = <function1>
```

Placeholder syntax is valid here because the input parameter is only used once and the literal's type has an external explicit definition (in the value).

As another example, let's invoke the "safeStringOp" example with placeholder syntax:

```scala
scala> def safeStringOp(s: String, f: String => String) = {
     |    if (s != null) f(s) else s
     | }
safeStringOp: (s: String, f: String => String)String

scala> safeStringOp(null, _.reverse)
res11: String = null

scala> safeStringOp("Ready", _.reverse)
res12: String = ydaeR
```

The body of the function literal is operationally the same as s => s.reverse, but simplified with placeholder syntax. The reference to the input parameter s has been replaced with a wildcard (_) representing the first input parameter to the function. Essentially the wildcard is the single String input parameter.

Let's demonstrate how this ordering of placeholders works by trying an example with two placeholders:

```
scala> def combination(x: Int, y: Int, f: (Int,Int) => Int) = f(x,y)
combination: (x: Int, y: Int, f: (Int, Int) => Int)Int

scala> combination(23, 12, _ * _)
res13: Int = 276
```

The use of two placeholders admittedly makes the syntax more abstract. Try to keep in mind that they are positionally replacing the input parameters (x and y, respectively).

Using an additional placeholder here would result in an error, because the number of placeholders must match the number of input arguments. If I call the reduce method with one or three placeholders, an error would ensue.

Let's kick the number of placeholders up for the last time, from two to three. Is this example still easily readable?

```
scala> def tripleOp(a: Int, b: Int, c: Int, f: (Int, Int, Int) => Int) = f(a,b,c)
tripleOp: (a: Int, b: Int, c: Int, f: (Int, Int, Int) => Int)Int

scala> tripleOp(23, 92, 14, _ * _ + _)
res14: Int = 2130
```

The tripleOp function takes four parameters: three Int values and a function that can reduce them down to a single Int. The actual function body is far shorter than the parameter list, and applies the function to the input values.

This example function, tripleOp, is limited to integer values. However, wouldn't it be more useful if it was generic and supported type parameters?

Let's redefine the tripleOp function using two type parameters, one for the common input type and one for the single return value type. This will give us some flexibility to call the tripleOp function with any type of inputs or anonymous functions that we choose (as long as the anonymous function takes three inputs):

```
scala> def tripleOp[A,B](a: A, b: A, c: A, f: (A, A, A) => B) = f(a,b,c)
tripleOp: [A, B](a: A, b: A, c: A, f: (A, A, A) => B)B

scala> tripleOp[Int,Int](23, 92, 14, _ * _ + _)
res15: Int = 2130

scala> tripleOp[Int,Double](23, 92, 14, 1.0 * _ / _ / _)
res16: Double = 0.017857142857142856

scala> tripleOp[Int,Boolean](93, 92, 14, _ > _ + _)
res17: Boolean = false
```

This syntax is admittedly a bit difficult to comprehend if you aren't experienced with Scala. Eventually, after reading the material and working on the exercises at the end of this chapter, the use of placeholders will feel like just another tool to you.

Placeholder syntax is especially helpful when working with data structures and collections. Many of the core sorting, filtering, and other data structure methods tend to use first-class functions, and placeholder syntax reduces the amount of extra code required to call these methods.

Partially Applied Functions and Currying

Invoking functions, both regular and higher-order, typically requires specifying all of the function's parameters in the invocation (the exception being those functions with default parameter values). What if you wanted to *reuse* a function invocation and retain some of the parameters to avoid typing them in again?

To demonstrate this answer, I'll use the example of a two-parameter function that checks if a given number is a factor of the other number:

```
scala> def factorOf(x: Int, y: Int) = y % x == 0
factorOf: (x: Int, y: Int)Boolean
```

If you want a shortcut to the function without retaining any parameters, you can use the wildcard operator (_) assignment we covered in this chapter's introduction:

```
scala> val f = factorOf _
f: (Int, Int) => Boolean = <function2>

scala> val x = f(7, 20)
x: Boolean = false
```

If you want to retain some of the parameters, you can *partially apply* the function by using the wildcard operator to take the place of one of the parameters. The wildcard operator here requires an explicit type, because it is used to generate a function value with a declared input type:

```
scala> val multipleOf3 = factorOf(3, _: Int)
multipleOf3: Int => Boolean = <function1>

scala> val y = multipleOf3(78)
y: Boolean = true
```

The new function value, multipleOf3, is a partially applied function, because it contains some but not all of the parameters for the factorOf() function.

A cleaner way to partially apply functions is to use functions with multiple parameter lists. Instead of breaking up a parameter list into applied and unapplied parameters, apply the parameters for one list while leaving another list unapplied. This is a technique known as *currying* the function:

```
scala> def factorOf(x: Int)(y: Int) = y % x == 0
factorOf: (x: Int)(y: Int)Boolean

scala> val isEven = factorOf(2) _
isEven: Int => Boolean = <function1>

scala> val z = isEven(32)
z: Boolean = true
```

In terms of a function type, a function with multiple parameter lists is considered to be a chain of multiple functions. Each separate parameter list is considered to be a separate function call.

Our example function def `factorOf(x: Int, y: Int)` has the function type `(Int, Int) => Boolean`. But the updated example function "def factorOf(x: Int)(y: Int)" has the function type `Int => Int => Boolean`. When curried, the function type becomes the second chained function, `Int => Boolean`. In the preceding example, the function value "isEven" curries the first part of the chained function with the integer value 2.

With some ingenuity you could write your own function literals that handle the job that partially applied functions and curried functions provide. Retaining a reusable parameter in a function literal and invoking a new function with it and new parameters isn't a complex trick. The benefit that partially applied functions and curried functions provide is an expressive syntax for doing so.

By-Name Parameters

We have studied higher-order functions that take a function value as a parameter. An alternate form of a function type parameter is a *by-name* parameter, which can take either a value or a function that eventually returns the value. By supporting invocations with both values and functions, a function that takes a by-name parameter leaves the choice of which to use up to its callers.

Syntax: Specifying a By-Name Parameter

```
<identifier>: => <type>
```

Each time a by-name parameter is used inside a function, it gets evaluated into a value. If a value is passed to the function then there is no effect, but if a function is passed then that function is invoked for every usage.

When you pass a function to a by-name parameter, make sure that you understand any cost of repeated accesses of your function. For example, an expression that searches a database and returns its value may have acceptable performance if used once to pass a fixed value to a function. But if that expression is used for a by-name parameter, it becomes a function value that is invoked every time the parameter is accessed in the method.

The main benefit of using by-name parameters, as opposed to value or function parameters, is the flexibility they provide. Functions that take by-name parameters can be used when values are available, and also when a function needs to be used instead. Although multiple parameter accesses implies multiple invocations of the function parameter, the inverse is also true. A function passed in a by-name parameter will not be invoked if the parameter is not accessed, so a costly function call can be avoided if necessary.

Let's try invoking a function that has a by-name parameter. We'll use it with a regular value and then with a function to verify that it invokes the function every time the parameter is accessed:

```scala
scala> def doubles(x: => Int) = {
     |     println("Now doubling " + x)          ❶
     |     x * 2
     | }
doubles: (x: => Int)Int

scala> doubles(5)                                ❷
Now doubling 5
res18: Int = 10

scala> def f(i: Int) = { println(s"Hello from f($i)"); i }
f: (i: Int)Int

scala> doubles( f(8) )                           ❸
Hello from f(8)
Now doubling 8
Hello from f(8)                                  ❹
res19: Int = 16
```

❶   The x by-name parameter is accessed here just like a normal by-value parameter.

❷   Invoke the `doubles` method with a regular value and it will operate normally.

❸   …but when you invoke it with a function value, that function value will get invoked inside the `doubles` method.

❹   Because the `double` method refers to the x param twice, the "Hello" message gets invoked twice.

Partial Functions

All of the functions we have studied so far are known as *total functions*, because they properly support every possible value that meets the type of the input parameters. A simple function like `def double(x: Int) = x*2` can be considered a total function; there is no input x that the `double()` function could not process.

However, there are some functions that do not support every possible value that meets the input types. For example, a function that returns the square root of the input number would certainly not work if the input number was negative. Likewise, a function that divides by a given number isn't applicable if that number is zero. Such functions are called *partial functions* because they can only partially apply to their input data.

Scala's partial functions are function literals that apply a series of case patterns to their input, requiring that the input match at least one of the given patterns. Invoking one of these partial functions with data that does not meet at least one case pattern results in a Scala error.

What Is the Difference Between Partial and Partially Applied Functions?
The two terms look and sound almost the same, causing many developers to mix them up. A partial function, as opposed to a total function, only accepts a partial amount of all possible input values. A partially applied function is a regular function that has been partially invoked, and remains to be fully invoked (if ever) in the future.

Let's take one of the examples of match expressions (from "Match Expressions" on page 31) and reuse it as a new partial function:

```
scala> val statusHandler: Int => String = {
     |     case 200 => "Okay"
     |     case 400 => "Your Error"
     |     case 500 => "Our error"
     | }
statusHandler: Int => String = <function1>
```

We now have a function literal that is only applicable to integers with the values 200, 400, and 500. We'll test it out with valid inputs first:

```
scala> statusHandler(200)
res20: String = Okay

scala> statusHandler(400)
res21: String = Your Error
```

What do you expect to happen if we call it with an integer that doesn't match one of its case patterns?

```
scala> statusHandler(401)
scala.MatchError: 401 (of class java.lang.Integer)
  at $anonfun$1.apply(<console>:7)
  at $anonfun$1.apply(<console>:7)
  ... 32 elided
```

A MatchError resulted because the input value, while having the correct Int type, did not match any of the partial function's case patterns.

Partial functions may seem like an odd feature, because when they are not applicable they can lead to errors like this. One method to prevent such errors is to use a wildcard pattern at the end to catch all other errors, but then the term "partial function" wouldn't really be applicable. You'll find partial functions more useful when working with collections and pattern matching. For example, you can "collect" every item in a collection that is accepted by a given partial function.

Invoking Higher-Order Functions with Function Literal Blocks

We covered how to invoke functions with expression blocks instead of parentheses or spaces (see "Function Invocation with Expression Blocks" on page 49). You can reuse this notation with higher-order functions, invoking them with function literal blocks in addition to or in place of parentheses. A function invoked by its name and a large expression block takes the block as a function literal, which can then be invoked zero or more times. A common use of this syntax is to invoke utility functions with an expression block. For example, a higher-order function can wrap a given expression block in a single database session or transaction.

I'll use the "safeStringOps" function to demonstrate when this syntax may be desirable and how to use it. To start, here is the "safeStringOps" function used with a regular function literal, before converting it to the desired syntax:

```scala
scala> def safeStringOp(s: String, f: String => String) = {
     |   if (s != null) f(s) else s
     | }
safeStringOp: (s: String, f: String => String)String

scala> val uuid = java.util.UUID.randomUUID.toString                    ❶
uuid: String = bfe1ddda-92f6-4c7a-8bfc-f946bdac7bc9

scala> val timedUUID = safeStringOp(uuid, { s =>
     |   val now = System.currentTimeMillis                             ❷
     |   val timed = s.take(24) + now                                   ❸
     |   timed.toUpperCase
     | })
timedUUID: String = BFE1DDDA-92F6-4C7A-8BFC-1394546043987
```

❶ A UUID utility in Java's `java.util` package, accessible (as are all JDK classes) from Scala.

❷ `System.currentTimeMillis` provides the epoch time (elapsed time since January 1, 1970 GMT) in milliseconds, useful for creating timestamps.

❸ The `take(x)` method returns the first x items from the `String`, in this case the first four sections of the UUID.

In this example, a multiline function literal is passed along with a value parameter to a function. This works, but including these together in the same parenthesis block is unwieldy.

We can improve this by splitting the parameters in "safeStringOp" into two separate groups (see "Parameter Groups" on page 55). The second parameter group, containing the function type, can then be invoked with expression block syntax:

```scala
scala> def safeStringOp(s: String)(f: String => String) = {
     |    if (s != null) f(s) else s
     | }
safeStringOp: (s: String)(f: String => String)String

scala> val timedUUID = safeStringOp(uuid) { s =>
     |    val now = System.currentTimeMillis
     |    val timed = s.take(24) + now
     |    timed.toUpperCase
     | }
timedUUID: String = BFE1DDDA-92F6-4C7A-8BFC-1394546915011
```

We now have a cleaner invocation of `safeStringOp`, passing it the value parameter in parentheses and the function parameter as a free-standing function literal block.

Here is an alternate example, one that takes a single by-name parameter. We'll make the function more generic with a type parameter used for the by-name parameter return type and the main function's return type:

```scala
scala> def timer[A](f: => A): A = {                          ❶
     |    def now = System.currentTimeMillis                 ❷
     |    val start = now; val a = f; val end = now
     |    println(s"Executed in ${end - start} ms")
     |    a
     | }
timer: [A](f: => A)A

scala> val veryRandomAmount = timer {                        ❸
     |    util.Random.setSeed(System.currentTimeMillis)
     |    for (i <- 1 to 100000) util.Random.nextDouble      ❹
     |    util.Random.nextDouble
     | }
Executed in 13 ms
veryRandomAmount: Double = 0.5070558765221892
```

❶ The type parameter "A" helps the return type of the "f" by-name parameter become the return type of the "timer" function, reducing the impact of wrapping code with the "timer" function.

❷ This inner, nested function is here for purely aesthetic reasons, enabling us to retrieve the current millisecond amount compactly.

❸   Finally, we have reduced the expression block syntax for higher-order functions to its simplest form: the function name and the block. You can view the code between the braces as being an expression block, or as a function literal block, or as regular code being *wrapped* by the "timer" function.

❹   This line generates and discards 100,000 random floating-point numbers. It's useful for running out the clock for a timing demonstration, but I wouldn't recommend using this in production code.

The "timer" function is used here to wrap a discrete unit of code, but it could also be integrated into an existing code base. You could use it to wrap the last part of any function, measuring its performance while ensuring the function's return value passes from the code block through "timer" and is returned by the function.

Functions that can wrap indiscriminate blocks of code with utilities in this way are a major benefit of using the "expression block" style of higher-order function invocations. Some of the other uses for this invocation style include:

- Managing database transactions, where the higher-order function opens the session, invokes the function parameter, and then closes the transaction with a commit or rollback.

- Handling expected errors with retries, by calling the function parameter a set number of times until it stops causing errors.

- Conditionally invoking the function parameter based on local, global, or external values (e.g., a database setting or environment variable).

As with many other features in Scala, you have more than one way to invoke higher-order functions. I find the use of this syntax to be a clean break from using the traditional parentheses, but the most important criteria for when and where to use it is if it seems right to you.

Summary

Scala treats functions as first-class data types, as demonstrated throughout this chapter and supported by the notions of higher-order functions, function literals, and function types. While simply stated, until you have some experience working with first-class functions you may find the concept a difficult one to understand. If you haven't already done so, I highly recommend trying out the code samples and experimenting with writing your own first-class function-based code. And then, after you have become familiar with storing functions as data and using them to invoke higher-order functions, you'll find the following exercises will help to increase your comfort level with this challenging topic.

The real beauty and utility of higher-order functions, however, cannot be demonstrated with the data types we have thus far learned. To really demonstrate them we will need to learn a critical component of writing any kind of useful and data-driven code. I'm talking about collections, data structures that scale from zero to many elements and make it possible to collect multiple values of a given type. From lists to maps, Scala not only supports the data structures that you're well familiar with, but provides ample use of higher-order functions to maximize your productivity. We'll cover not only creating and iterating through collections, but how you'll use `map()`, `reduce()`, and `filter()` to manage them with amazingly expressive code.

From this point forward you can expect to see first-class functions and higher-order functions play a prominent role in code examples and exercises. Whether demonstrated with the data types we have learned thus far or with the higher-order function-based collections library, these are the shining stars of the Scala language.

Exercises

1. Write a function literal that takes two integers and returns the higher number. Then write a higher-order function that takes a 3-sized tuple of integers plus this function literal, and uses it to return the maximum value in the tuple.

2. The library function `util.Random.nextInt` returns a random integer. Use it to invoke the "max" function with two random integers plus a function that returns the larger of two given integers. Do the same with a function that returns the smaller of two given integers, and then a function that returns the second integer every time.

3. Write a higher-order function that takes an integer and returns a function. The returned function should take a single integer argument (say, "x") and return the product of x and the integer passed to the higher-order function.

4. Let's say that you happened to run across this function while reviewing another developer's code:

    ```
    def fzero[A](x: A)(f: A => Unit): A = { f(x); x }
    ```

    What does this function accomplish? Can you give an example of how you might invoke it?

5. There's a function named "square" that you would like to store in a function value. Is this the right way to do it? How else can you store a function in a value?

    ```
    def square(m: Double) = m * m
    val sq = square
    ```

6. Write a function called "conditional" that takes a value x and two functions, p and f, and returns a value of the same type as x. The p function is a predicate, taking the value x and returning a `Boolean` b. The f function also takes the value x and returns

a new value of the same type. Your "conditional" function should only invoke the function f(x) if p(x) is true, and otherwise return x. How many type parameters will the "conditional" function require?

7. Do you recall the "typesafe" challenge from the exercises in Chapter 3? There is a popular coding interview question I'll call "typesafe," in which the numbers 1-100 must be printed one per line. The catch is that multiples of 3 must replace the number with the word "type," while multiples of 5 must replace the number with the word "safe." Of course, multiples of 15 must print "typesafe."

Use the "conditional" function from exercise 6 to implement this challenge.

Would your solution be shorter if the return type of "conditional" did not match the type of the parameter x? Experiment with an altered version of the "conditional" function that works better with this challenge.

CHAPTER 6

Common Collections

A *collections* framework provides data structures for collecting one or more values of a given type such as arrays, lists, maps, sets, and trees. Most of the popular programming languages have their own collections framework (or, at the least, lists and maps) because these data structures are the building blocks of modern software projects.

The term "collections" was popularized by the Java collections library, a high-performance, object-oriented, and type-parameterized framework. Because Scala is a JVM language, you can access and use the entire Java collections library from your Scala code. Of course, if you did, you would miss out on all the glory of the higher-order operations in Scala's own collections.

Scala has a high-performance, object-oriented, and type-parameterized collections framework just as Java does. However, Scala's collections also have higher-order operations like map, filter, and reduce that make it possible to manage and manipulate data with short and expressive expressions. It also has separate mutable versus immutable collection type hierarchies, which make switching between immutable data (for stability) and mutable data (when necessary) convenient.

The root of all iterable collections, Iterable, provides a common set of methods for (you guessed it) iterating through and manipulating collection data. We'll now explore some of its most popular and immutable collections.

Lists, Sets, and Maps

Let's start with the List type, an immutable singly linked list. You can create a list by invoking it as a function, passing in its contents in the form of comma-separated parameters:

```
scala> val numbers = List(32, 95, 24, 21, 17)
numbers: List[Int] = List(32, 95, 24, 21, 17)
```

```
scala> val colors = List("red", "green", "blue")
colors: List[String] = List(red, green, blue)

scala> println(s"I have ${colors.size} colors: $colors")
I have 3 colors: List(red, green, blue)
```

The size method, available on all collections and String instances, returns the number of items in the collection. Defined without parentheses (see "Functions with Empty Parentheses" on page 48), the size method is simply invoked by name.

In Chapter 4 you learned how functions can use type parameters to parameterize the type of their input values and return values. Collections are also type-parameterized, ensuring that they remember and adhere to the type they were initialized with. You can see this in the preceding example, where the REPL displays the type-parameterized collections as List[Int] and List[String].

Use the Lisp-style head() and tail() methods to access the first and remaining elements of a list, respectively. To access a single element directly, invoke the list as a function and pass it the zero-based index of that element:

```
scala> val colors = List("red", "green", "blue")
colors: List[String] = List(red, green, blue)

scala> colors.head
res0: String = red

scala> colors.tail
res1: List[String] = List(green, blue)

scala> colors(1)
res2: String = green

scala> colors(2)
res3: String = blue
```

In "Loops" on page 37 you learned about the Range collection, a consecutive range of numbers, and how to iterate over it with a for-loop. It turns out that for-loops are also excellent for iterating over lists (or any other collection, really).

Let's try out using for-loops to iterate over the "numbers" and "colors" lists:

```
scala> val numbers = List(32, 95, 24, 21, 17)
numbers: List[Int] = List(32, 95, 24, 21, 17)

scala> var total = 0; for (i <- numbers) { total += i }
total: Int = 189

scala> val colors = List("red", "green", "blue")
colors: List[String] = List(red, green, blue)

scala> for (c <- colors) { println(c) }
```

```
red
green
blue
```

In Chapter 5 you learned how to use functions as data and pass them to higher-order functions. Scala's collections use higher-order functions extensively to iterate, map (convert a list item-by-item to a different list), reduce (fold a list into a single element), and perform a wide range of other useful operations.

Here's an example of the `foreach()`, `map()`, and `reduce()` higher-order functions available in `List` and other collections. Respectively, these functions iterate over the list, convert the list, and reduce the list down to a single item. For each method, a function literal is passed in, including the input parameter in parentheses and its function body:

```
scala> val colors = List("red", "green", "blue")
colors: List[String] = List(red, green, blue)

scala> colors.foreach( (c: String) => println(c) ) ❶
red
green
blue

scala> val sizes = colors.map( (c: String) => c.size ) ❷
sizes: List[Int] = List(3, 5, 4)

scala> val numbers = List(32, 95, 24, 21, 17)
numbers: List[Int] = List(32, 95, 24, 21, 17)

scala> val total = numbers.reduce( (a: Int, b: Int) => a + b ) ❸
total: Int = 189
```

❶   `foreach()` takes a function (a procedure, to be accurate) and invokes it with every item in the list.

❷   `map()` takes a function that converts a single list element to another value and/or type.

❸   `reduce()` takes a function that combines two list elements into a single element.

A `Set` is an immutable and unordered collection of unique elements, but works similarly to `List`. Here is an example of creating a `Set` with duplicate items. As another subtype of `Iterable`, a `Set` instance supports the same operations as a `List` instance does:

```
scala> val unique = Set(10, 20, 30, 20, 20, 10)
unique: scala.collection.immutable.Set[Int] = Set(10, 20, 30)

scala> val sum = unique.reduce( (a: Int, b: Int) => a + b )
sum: Int = 60
```

A `Map` is an immutable key-value store, also known as a hashmap, dictionary, or associative array in other languages. Values stored in a `Map` with a given unique key may be retrieved using that key. The key and the value are type-parameterized; you can just as easily create a mapping from strings to integers as a mapping from integers to strings.

When creating a Map, specify the key-value pairs as tuples (see "Tuples" on page 25). You can use the relation operator (->) to specify the key and value tuple.

Here is an example of a color name to numeric color value Map built with pairs of relation operators. As with Set, the Map type is a subtype of Iterable and so supports the same operations as List does:

```
scala> val colorMap = Map("red" -> 0xFF0000, "green" -> 0xFF00,
  "blue" -> 0xFF)
colorMap: scala.collection.immutable.Map[String,Int] =
  Map(red -> 16711680, green -> 65280, blue -> 255)

scala> val redRGB = colorMap("red")
redRGB: Int = 16711680

scala> val cyanRGB = colorMap("green") | colorMap("blue")
cyanRGB: Int = 65535

scala> val hasWhite = colorMap.contains("white")
hasWhite: Boolean = false

scala> for (pairs <- colorMap) { println(pairs) }
(red,16711680)
(green,65280)
(blue,255)
```

In this section we were introduced to the common collections List, Map, and Set, all subtypes of the root Iterable type. We also learned about some of the methods available in Iterable and its subtypes, foreach(), map(), and reduce(). However, we have only scratched the surface of what is possible with these collections.

In the rest of this chapter we'll examine the structure and operations of these common collections, focusing on the List type for consistency.

What's in a List?

The standard way to create a List or other type of collection is by invoking it as a function with the desired contents:

```
scala> val colors = List("red", "green", "blue")
colors: List[String] = List(red, green, blue)
```

You can store values of any type in collections, instead of just the numbers and strings we have used so far. For example, you can create a collection of collections:

```
scala> val oddsAndEvents = List(List(1, 3, 5), List(2, 4, 6))
oddsAndEvents: List[List[Int]] = List(List(1, 3, 5), List(2, 4, 6))
```

Or you can have a collection of 2-sized tuples, and create a List that looks similar to a Map:

```scala
scala> val keyValues = List(('A', 65), ('B',66), ('C',67))
keyValues: List[(Char, Int)] = List((A,65), (B,66), (C,67))
```

You can access a single element from a list by invoking it as a function with a (zero-based) index number. Here is an example of accessing the first and fourth elements of a List by their index:

```scala
scala> val primes = List(2, 3, 5, 7, 11, 13)
primes: List[Int] = List(2, 3, 5, 7, 11, 13)

scala> val first = primes(0)
first: Int = 2

scala> val fourth = primes(3)
fourth: Int = 7
```

You can decompose a list into its *head*, the first item in the list, and its *tail*, the remaining items in the list:

```scala
scala> val first = primes.head
first: Int = 2

scala> val remaining = primes.tail
remaining: List[Int] = List(3, 5, 7, 11, 13)
```

A List is an immutable and recursive data structure, so each item in the list has its own head and incrementally shorter tail. You could use this to create your own List iterator, by starting with the head and making your way through successive tails.

The challenging part in creating such an iterator would be in figuring out when you arrived at the end of the list. We could try checking if `list.size > 0` but, because this is a linked list, the `size` method would have to traverse to the end of the list each time. Fortunately, there is an `isEmpty` method on lists we can use that does not need to traverse the list.

Here is an iterator built with a `while` loop that traverses the list until `isEmpty` returns true:

```scala
scala> val primes = List(2, 3, 5, 7, 11, 13)
primes: List[Int] = List(2, 3, 5, 7, 11, 13)

scala> var i = primes
i: List[Int] = List(2, 3, 5, 7, 11, 13)

scala> while(! i.isEmpty) { print(i.head + ", "); i = i.tail }
2, 3, 5, 7, 11, 13,
```

Or, in recursive form, here is a function that traverses the list without using a mutable variable:

```
scala> val primes = List(2, 3, 5, 7, 11, 13)
primes: List[Int] = List(2, 3, 5, 7, 11, 13)

scala> def visit(i: List[Int]) { if (i.size > 0) { print(i.head + ", ");
         visit(i.tail) } }
visit: (i: List[Int])Unit

scala> visit(primes)
2, 3, 5, 7, 11, 13,
```

This recursive function is representative of how many of the methods in List (and Iterable collections in general) are implemented. Except that, in most cases, they are written as functions whose return values can be collected into a single result or a new list.

Calling isEmpty to check for the end of a list is efficient, but there is yet another efficient way to do this. All lists end with an instance of Nil as their terminus, so an iterator can check for the list's end by comparing the current element to Nil:

```
scala> val primes = List(2, 3, 5, 7, 11, 13)
primes: List[Int] = List(2, 3, 5, 7, 11, 13)

scala> var i = primes
i: List[Int] = List(2, 3, 5, 7, 11, 13)

scala> while(i != Nil) { print(i.head + ", "); i = i.tail }
2, 3, 5, 7, 11, 13,
```

Nil is essentially a singleton instance of List[Nothing]. The Nothing type, as you'll recall from Table 2-4, is a noninstantiable subtype of all other Scala types. A list of Nothing types is thus compatible with lists of all other types and can be safely used as their terminus.

Creating a new, empty list will actually return Nil instead of a fresh instance. Because Nil is immutable, there is essentially no difference between it and a fresh, empty list instance. Likewise, creating a new list that has a single entry just creates a single list element that points to Nil as its tail.

Let's demonstrate these points with some examples:

```
scala> val l: List[Int] = List()
l: List[Int] = List()

scala> l == Nil
res0: Boolean = true

scala> val m: List[String] = List("a")
m: List[String] = List(a)
```

```
scala> m.head
res1: String = a

scala> m.tail == Nil
res2: Boolean = true
```

I have used lists of two explicit types, Int and String, to demonstrate that regardless of the type of their data, a List will always end with Nil.

The Cons Operator

There is an alternate way to construct lists that takes advantage of this relationship with Nil. As another nod to Lisp, Scala supports use of the *cons* (short for *construct*) operator to build lists. Using Nil as a foundation and the right-associative cons operator :: for binding elements, you can build a list without using the traditional List(…) format.

Right-Associative Notation

All of the operators we have used so far in space-delimited operator notation have been *left-associative* in that they are invoked on the entity to their immediate left (e.g., 10 / 2). In *right-associative* notation, triggered when operators end with a colon (:), operators are invoked on the entity to their immediate right.

Here is an example of building a list with the cons operator:

```
scala> val numbers = 1 :: 2 :: 3 :: Nil
numbers: List[Int] = List(1, 2, 3)
```

This may look a bit odd, but remember that :: is simply a method in List. It takes a single value that becomes the head of a new list, its tail pointing to the list on which :: was called. You could use traditional dot notation with the cons operator, but it would look a bit odd.

OK, let's try it out anyway:

```
scala> val first = Nil.::(1)
first: List[Int] = List(1)

scala> first.tail == Nil
res3: Boolean = true
```

As noted, this does look a bit odd, so let's stick to using the cons operator (::) as a right-associative operator. This time we will use it to prepend (insert at the front) a value to an existing list, thus creating a brand new list. We have actually tried this before, because it is the same as the operation of prepending a value to Nil, the empty list:

```
scala> val second = 2 :: first
second: List[Int] = List(2, 1)

scala> second.tail == first
res4: Boolean = true
```

Although the "second" list includes the "first" list, both are valid lists that can be used independently. This example of building one list by adding a value to another demonstrates the recursive and reusable nature of Scala's immutable lists, and provides a good summary of this section.

List Arithmetic

Now we have explored the essential internals of List types and written our own iterator. With this understanding, let's leave this manual labor behind and start exploring the rich array of List methods. In this section we will focus on basic arithmetic operations on lists. By "arithmetic," a term I use loosely, I mean operations that add, remove, split, combine, and otherwise modify the organization of lists without changing the list elements (i.e., their contents) themselves. And of course by "modify" I mean "return a new list with the requested changes" because List is an immutable collection.

Table 6-1 shows a selection of the arithmetic methods on List. For a full list of all the methods see the official Scaladoc page (*http://bit.ly/ls-scalalist*) for the List type.

Table 6-1. Arithmetic operations on lists

Name	Example	Description
::	1 :: 2 :: Nil	Appends individual elements to this list. A right-associative operator.
:::	List(1, 2) ::: List(2, 3)	Prepends another list to this one. A right-associative operator.
++	List(1, 2) ++ Set(3, 4, 3)	Appends another collection to this list.
==	List(1, 2) == List(1, 2)	Returns true if the collection types and contents are equal.
distinct	List(3, 5, 4, 3, 4).distinct	Returns a version of the list without duplicate elements.
drop	List('a', 'b', 'c', 'd') drop 2	Subtracts the first *n* elements from the list.
filter	List(23, 8, 14, 21) filter (_ > 18)	Returns elements from the list that pass a true/false function.
flatten	List(List(1, 2), List(3, 4)).flatten	Converts a list of lists into a single list of elements.
partition	List(1, 2, 3, 4, 5) partition (_ < 3)	Groups elements into a tuple of two lists based on the result of a true/false function.
reverse	List(1, 2, 3).reverse	Reverses the list.

Name	Example	Description
slice	List(2, 3, 5, 7) slice (1, 3)	Returns a segment of the list from the first index up to but not including the second index.
sortBy	List("apple", "to") sortBy (_.size)	Orders the list by the value returned from the given function.
sorted	List("apple", "to").sorted	Orders a list of core Scala types by their natural value.
splitAt	List(2, 3, 5, 7) splitAt 2	Groups elements into a tuple of two lists based on if they fall before or after the given index.
take	List(2, 3, 5, 7, 11, 13) take 3	Extracts the first *n* elements from the list.
zip	List(1, 2) zip List("a", "b")	Combines two lists into a list of tuples of elements at each index.

Using Operator Versus Dot Notation

In Table 6-1 some examples used operator notation (e.g., list drop 2) whereas others used dot notation (e.g., list.flatten). Selecting the right notation is a personal choice, except where dot notation is required due to lack of an operation parameter (as in list.flatten).

Did you spot the higher-order functions in the table? Here are the three examples of higher-order operations, filter, partition, and sortBy, executed in the Scala REPL:

```scala
scala> val f = List(23, 8, 14, 21) filter (_ > 18)
f: List[Int] = List(23, 21)

scala> val p = List(1, 2, 3, 4, 5) partition (_ < 3)
p: (List[Int], List[Int]) = (List(1, 2),List(3, 4, 5))

scala> val s = List("apple", "to") sortBy (_.size)
s: List[String] = List(to, apple)
```

The sortBy method takes a function that returns a value for use in ordering the elements of the list, while the filter and partition methods each take a predicate function. A *predicate function* takes an input value and returns either true or false. In the case of the partition function, the predicate uses placeholder syntax (see "Placeholder Syntax" on page 72) to return true if the input value is less than three and false otherwise.

Collection methods that are also higher-order functions, such as filter, map, and partition, are excellent candidates for using placeholder syntax. The function parameter they take as input acts on a single element in their list. Thus the underscore (_) in an anonymous function sent to one of these methods represents each item in the list.

For example, the anonymous function we passed to the partition method, _ < 3, indicates that each element in the list will be checked to see if it is less than 3. The values 1 and 2 were less than 3 and thus partitioned into a separate list.

An important point to make about these arithmetic methods is that ::, drop, and take act on the front of the list and thus do not have performance penalties. Recall that List is a linked list, so adding items to or removing items from its front does not require a full traversal. A list traversal is a trivial operation for short lists, but when you start getting into lists of thousands or millions of items, an operation that requires a list traversal can be a big deal.

That said, these operations have corollary operations that act on the end of the list and thus do require a full list traversal. Additionally, because adding items to the end of a list would mutate it, they require copying the entire list and returning the copy. Again, not an important memory consideration unless you are working with large lists, but in general it is best to operate on the front of a list, not its end.

The corollary operations to ::, drop, and take are +: (a left-associative operator), dropRight, and takeRight. The arguments to these operators are the same as to their corollary operations.

Here are examples of these list-appending operations:

```
scala> val appended = List(1, 2, 3, 4) :+ 5
appended: List[Int] = List(1, 2, 3, 4, 5)

scala> val suffix = appended takeRight 3
suffix: List[Int] = List(3, 4, 5)

scala> val middle = suffix dropRight 2
middle: List[Int] = List(3)
```

With the extremely small list sizes used in these examples, the additional time and memory space required to traverse the list and copy its contents to a new array is miniscule. However, it's still considered good form to prefer operations on the start of a list over those that work on the end.

Mapping Lists

Map methods are those that take a function and apply it to every member of a list, collecting the results into a new list. In set theory, and the field of mathematics in general, to *map* is to create an assocation between each element in one set to each element in another set. In a sense, both definitions describe what the map methods in List are doing: mapping each item from one list to another list, so that the other list has the same size as the first but with different data or element types. Table 6-2 shows a selection of these map methods available on Scala's lists.

Table 6-2. List mapping operations

Name	Example	Description
collect	`List(0, 1, 0) collect {case 1 =>` `"ok"}`	Transforms each element using a partial function, retaining applicable elements.
flatMap	`List("milk,tea")` `flatMap (_.split(','))`	Transforms each element using the given function and "flattens" the list of results into this list.
map	`List("milk","tea")` `map (_.toUpperCase)`	Transforms each element using the given function.

Let's see how these list-mapping operators work in the REPL:

```scala
scala> List(0, 1, 0) collect {case 1 => "ok"}
res0: List[String] = List(ok)

scala> List("milk,tea") flatMap (_.split(','))
res1: List[String] = List(milk, tea)

scala> List("milk","tea") map (_.toUpperCase)
res2: List[String] = List(MILK, TEA)
```

The `flatMap` example uses the `String.split()` method to convert pipe-delimited text into a list of strings. Specifically this is the `java.lang.String.split()` method, and it returns a Java array, not a list. Fortunately, Scala converts Java arrays to its own type, `Array`, which extends `Iterable`. Because `List` is also a subtype of `Iterable`, and the `flatMap` method is defined at the `Iterable` level, a list of string arrays can be safely flattened into a list of strings.

Reducing Lists

We have studied ways to change the size and structure of lists, and ways to convert lists into completely different values and types. Now let's look at ways to shrink down all that work to a single value, an action known as *reducing* a list.

List reduction is a common operation for working with collections. Need to sum up a list of grades, or calculate the average duration of several benchmarks? How about if you want to check if a collection contains a specific element, or to see if a predicate function will return "true" for every element in the list? These are all list reductions, because they use logic to reduce a list down to a single value.

Scala's collections support mathematical reduction operations (e.g., finding the sum of a list) and Boolean reduction operations (e.g., determining if a list contains a given element). They also support generic higher-order operations known as *folds* that you can use to create any other type of list reduction algorithm.

We'll start by looking at the built-in mathematical reduction operations. See Table 6-3 for a selection of these methods.

Table 6-3. Math reduction operations

Name	Example	Description
max	List(41, 59, 26).max	Finds the maximum value in the list.
min	List(10.9, 32.5, 4.23, 5.67).min	Finds the minimum value in the list.
product	List(5, 6, 7).product	Multiplies the numbers in the list.
sum	List(11.3, 23.5, 7.2).sum	Sums up the numbers in the list.

The next set of operations we'll look at reduces lists down to a single Boolean value. See Table 6-4 for a selection of these methods.

Table 6-4. Boolean reduction operations

Name	Example	Description
contains	List(34, 29, 18) contains 29	Checks if the list contains this element.
endsWith	List(0, 4, 3) endsWith List(4, 3)	Checks if the list ends with a given list.
exists	List(24, 17, 32) exists (_ < 18)	Checks if a predicate holds true for *at least one* element in the list.
forall	List(24, 17, 32) forall (_ < 18)	Checks if a predicate holds true for *every* element in the list.
startsWith	List(0, 4, 3) startsWith List(0)	Tests whether the list starts with a given list.

These Boolean list reduction operations work great with infix operator notation, not only because they take a single argument but also due to their names being verbs. The phrase "list contains x" reads more like a written description about an operation, even though it is actually a valid, statically typed function invocation.

In addition to being highly readable, they are also rather similar. Choosing the right operation for a task may be more of a question of readability than suitability. As an example of their similar nature, let's search through a list of validation results for a "false" entry using three different operations:

```scala
scala> val validations = List(true, true, false, true, true, true)
validations: List[Boolean] = List(true, true, false, true, true, true)

scala> val valid1 = !(validations contains false)
valid1: Boolean = false

scala> val valid2 = validations forall (_ == true)
valid2: Boolean = false

scala> val valid3 = validations.exists(_ == false) == false
valid3: Boolean = false
```

Logically, checking that a list of validations does not contain "false" is the same as ensuring that the list only contains "true."

These operations are useful enough to have been included with Scala collections, but are not so complex that we couldn't implement them ourselves. Let's create our own list reduction operation to demonstrate how it is done. Doing so simply requires iterating over a collection with an *accumulator* variable, which contains the current result so far, and logic that updates the accumulator based on the current element:

```scala
scala> def contains(x: Int, l: List[Int]): Boolean = {
     |   var a: Boolean = false
     |   for (i <- l) { if (!a) a = (i == x) }
     |   a
     | }
contains: (x: Int, l: List[Int])Boolean

scala> val included = contains(19, List(46, 19, 92))
included: Boolean = true
```

This works perfectly well, but could also stand to be improved. How about if we separate the "contains" logic from the work of maintaining an accumulator value and iterating through the list? By moving the "contains" logic to a function parameter, we could create a reusable function to support additional list reduction operations.

Here's the same logic as in the previous example except with the core "contains" logic moved to a function parameter. We'll name this common function boolReduce to indicate that it is a Boolean list reduction operation:

```scala
scala> def boolReduce(l: List[Int], start: Boolean)(f: (Boolean, Int) =>
     |     Boolean): Boolean = {
     |
     |   var a = start
     |   for (i <- l) a = f(a, i)
     |   a
     | }
boolReduce: (l: List[Int], start: Boolean)(f: (Boolean, Int) => Boolean)Boolean

scala> val included = boolReduce(List(46, 19, 92), false) { (a, i) =>
     |   if (a) a else (i == 19)
     | }
included: Boolean = true
```

Our generic-sounding boolReduce function is no longer tied to determining if a list contains an element, and could be reused for any of the other Boolean reduction operations. We could theoretically implement exists, forall, startsWith, and the rest of the Boolean operations.

Let's take this example one step further and make it even more generally applicable. The boolReduce function is fine for Boolean operations on integer lists, but we could "genericize" it to make it applicable to lists and reduction operations of any type. Once this function takes type parameters for its list elements and the accumulator value and result (which necessarily need to match), we could use it to implement max, sum, and other mathematical operations.

Here is the boolReduce operation rewritten as reduceOp, renamed because it is no longer Boolean-specific, with the Int and Boolean types replaced with the type parameters A and B, respectively. What's really nice is that our sample invocation doesn't require any changes from working with boolReduce thanks to Scala's inference of type parameters. To verify that this new operation isn't limited to an integer list and a Boolean result, I have added an implementation of the sum example:

```scala
scala> def reduceOp[A,B](l: List[A], start: B)(f: (B, A) => B): B = {  ❶
     |   var a = start
     |   for (i <- l) a = f(a, i)
     |   a
     | }
reduceOp: [A, B](l: List[A], start: B)(f: (B, A) => B)B

scala> val included = reduceOp(List(46, 19, 92), false) { (a, i) =>  ❷
     |   if (a) a else (i == 19)
     | }
included: Boolean = true

scala> val answer = reduceOp(List(11.3, 23.5, 7.2), 0.0)(_ + _)  ❸
answer: Double = 42.0
```

❶ Replacing real types with type parameters can make the code less readable. If it isn't clear what the A and B parameters are referring to, have a look at the bool Reduce function definition and compare the parameters in both functions.

❷ I've chosen "a" as the name of the accumulator value and "i" as the name of the current element in the list. Writing function literals gives you the option to define your own names for input parameters!

❸ In this case I chose placeholder syntax because the parameters are each accessed only once in the function body.

Our reduceOp method is now a generic, left-to-right (or, start-to-finish) list reduction operation. It could be used to implement a math reduction operation such as max or a Boolean reduction operation such as contains. In fact, it could be used to create any other list reduction operation, at least one that supports its use of scanning the list from left to right (i.e., from the first element to the last).

Fortunately, you won't need to write down or remember the reduceOp function in order to take advantage of its functionality. Scala's collections provide built-in operations similar to reduceOp that are flexible enough to provide left-to-right, right-to-left, and order-agnostic versions, as well as offering different ways to work with the accumulator and accumulated values. These higher-order functions to reduce a list based on the input function are popularly known as *list-folding* operations, because the function of reducing a list is better known as a *fold*.

Table 6-5 displays a selection of the list-folding operations in Scala's collections. To simplify the process of comparing the functions, each operation's example reuses the "sum" function implemented in the previous example.

Table 6-5. Generic list reduction operations

Name	Example	Description
fold	List(4, 5, 6).fold(0)(_ + _)	Reduces the list given a starting value and a reduction function.reduction function.
foldLeft	List(4, 5, 6).foldLeft(0)(_ + _)	Reduces the list from left to right given a starting value and a reduction function.
foldRight	List(4, 5, 6).foldRight(0)(_ + _)	Reduces the list from right to left given a starting value and a reduction function.
reduce	List(4, 5, 6).reduce(_ + _)	Reduces the list given a reduction function, starting with the first element in the list.
reduceLeft	List(4, 5, 6).reduceLeft(_ + _)	Reduces the list from left to right given a reduction function, starting with the first element in the list.
reduceRight	List(4, 5, 6).reduceRight(_ + _)	Reduces the list from right to left given a reduction function, starting with the first element in the list.
scan	List(4, 5, 6).scan(0)(_ + _)	Takes a starting value and a reduction function and returns a list of each accumulated value.
scanLeft	List(4, 5, 6).scanLeft(0)(_ + _)	Takes a starting value and a reduction function and returns a list of each accumulated value from left to right.
scanRight	List(4, 5, 6).scanRight(0)(_ + _)	Takes a starting value and a reduction function and returns a list of each accumulated value from right to left.

The three folding operations, fold, reduce, and scan, are really not very different from each other. Can you figure out how you might implement reduce as a specific case of fold, or implement fold if you were given the scan function?

Interestingly, the differences between the left/right directional varieties of each operation, e.g., foldLeft, and the nondirectional variety, e.g., fold, may be more significant than the differences between the three folding operations. For one thing, fold, reduce, and scan are all limited to returning a value of the same type as the list elements, while the left/right varities of each operation support unique return types. Thus you could implement the forall Boolean operation on a list of Integers with foldLeft but would not be able to do so with fold.

Another major difference is in the ordering. Whereas foldLeft and foldRight, as an example, specify the direction in which they will iterate through the list, the nondirectional operations specify no order to their iteration. This often puzzles developers, because it doesn't make clear which direction will be used.

For example, what if your collection is not sequential but is distributed among a dozen different computers? Or what if it is all on the same computer, but your fold operation is so expensive that you want it to run in parallel? In such cases, it makes sense to distinguish between a fold that iterates through the list sequentially versus a fold that may, based on the collection that implements it, run in any order it needs to.

Unless you are specifically using distributed or parallel collections, or you are developing a library that may be reused with such collections, it is safe to simply choose the left/right directional varieties. I will also recommend that, unless you require right-to-left iteration, it is better to select the "left" operations because they require fewer traversals through the list in their implementation.

So, before studying the three list-folding operations we implemented the contains and sum operations the hard way. Now let's reimplement them using the new folding operations we just covered:

```
scala> val included = List(46, 19, 92).foldLeft(false) { (a, i) =>  ❶
     |    if (a) a else (i == 19)
     | }
included: Boolean = true

scala> val answer = List(11.3, 23.5, 7.2).reduceLeft(_ + _)          ❷
answer: Double = 42.0
```

❶ Not much has changed here other than that we're calling foldLeft, a list operation. Would reduceLeft work here?

❷ This operation is now even shorter thanks to reduceLeft, which uses the first element in the list for a starting value instead of taking it as a parameter.

In this section we covered list reduction/folding operations, both specific and generic. The numeric and Boolean list reduction operations are widely useful, but in case you need additional operations, you now know how to create your own.

Converting Collections

Lists are ubiquitous, especially in the examples in this chapter, but the other collections are certainly also important for their own uses. I find myself reaching for lists by default when I need a collection, but sometimes you do need a map, set, or other type. Fortunately, it is easy to convert between these types, so you can create a collection with one type and end up with the other.

Table 6-6 contains a selection of these methods. Because a `List.toList()` operation would be silly (but possible), the examples demonstrate converting from one type to a completely different type.

Table 6-6. Operations to convert collections

Name	Example	Description
mkString	List(24, 99, 104).mkString(", ")	Renders a collection to a Set using the given delimiters.
toBuffer	List('f', 't').toBuffer	Converts an immutable collection to a mutable one.
toList	Map("a" -> 1, "b" -> 2).toList	Converts a collection to a List.
toMap	Set(1 -> true, 3 -> true).toMap	Converts a collection of 2-arity (length) tuples to a Map.
toSet	List(2, 5, 5, 3, 2).toSet	Converts a collection to a Set.
toString	List(2, 5, 5, 3, 2).toString	Renders a collection to a String, including the collection's type.

Consider these operations when you have a map but only want a list of its keys, or are given a list and want to generate a lookup map with it. As immutable collections, `List`, `Map`, and `Set` cannot be built from empty collections and so are better suited to being mapped from existing collections. With these operations you can map data in one type to another type, even if you're going from a sequence to a key-value store (or back).

Java and Scala Collection Compatibility

There is another important angle to converting collections that we need to cover. Because Scala compiles to and runs on the JVM, interacting with the JDK as well as any Java libraries you may add is a common requirement. Part of this task of interacting is to convert between Java and Scala collections, because the two collection types are incompatible by default.

You can add the following command to enable manual conversions between Java and Scala collections. Although this command is a bit esoteric now, it'll make more sense when we study it in the context of object-oriented Scala later in the book:

```
scala> import collection.JavaConverters._
import collection.JavaConverters._
```

This `import` command adds `JavaConverters` and its methods to the current namespace. In the REPL this means the current session, while in source files this means the rest of the file or local scope, wherever the `import` command is added. Table 6-7 displays the operations added to Java and Scala collections when `JavaConverters` has been imported.

Table 6-7. Java and Scala collection conversions

Name	Example	Description
asJava	`List(12, 29).asJava`	Converts this Scala collection to a corresponding Java collection.
asScala	`new java.util.ArrayList(5).asScala`	Converts this Java collection to a corresponding Scala collection.

By exercising this import of `JavaConverters`, a greater selection of Java libraries and JVM functions is made available without significantly changing how you use Scala collections.

Pattern Matching with Collections

The final operation that we'll review in this chapter isn't a named collection method, but the use of match expressions (see "Match Expressions" on page 31) with collections. If you recall, we have used match expressions to match single value patterns:

```scala
scala> val statuses = List(500, 404)
statuses: List[Int] = List(500, 404)

scala> val msg = statuses.head match {
     |    case x if x < 500 => "okay"
     |    case _ => "whoah, an error"
     | }
msg: String = whoah, an error
```

With a pattern guard (see "Matching with Pattern Guards" on page 36), you could also match a single value inside a collection:

```scala
scala> val msg = statuses match {
     |    case x if x contains(500) => "has error"
     |    case _ => "okay"
     | }
msg: String = has error
```

Because collections support the equals operator (==) it shouldn't be a surprise that they also support pattern matching. To match the entire collection, use a new collection as your pattern:

```scala
scala> val msg = statuses match {
     |    case List(404, 500) => "not found & error"
     |    case List(500, 404) => "error & not found"
     |    case List(200, 200) => "okay"
     |    case _ => "not sure what happened"
     | }
msg: String = error & not found
```

You can use value binding (see "Matching with Wildcard Patterns" on page 34) to bind values to some or all elements of a collection in your pattern guard:

```
scala> val msg = statuses match {
     |   case List(500, x) => s"Error followed by $x"
     |   case List(e, x) => s"$e was followed by $x"
     | }
msg: String = Error followed by 404
```

Lists are decomposable into their head element and their tail. In the same way, as patterns they can be matched on their head and tail elements:

```
scala> val head = List('r','g','b') match {
     |   case x :: xs => x
     |   case Nil => ' '
     | }
head: Char = r
```

Tuples, while not officially collections, also support pattern matching and value binding. Because a single tuple can support values of different types, their pattern-matching capability is at times even more useful than that of collections:

```
scala> val code = ('h', 204, true) match {
     |   case (_, _, false) => 501
     |   case ('c', _, true) => 302
     |   case ('h', x, true) => x
     |   case (c, x, true) => {
     |     println(s"Did not expect code $c")
     |     x
     |   }
     | }
code: Int = 204
```

Pattern matching is a core feature of the Scala language, not simply another operation in its standard collection library. It is broadly applicable to Scala's data structures, and when used wisely can shorten and simplify logic that would require expansive work in other languages.

Summary

Working with collections, whether creating, mapping, filtering, or performing other operations, is a major component of software development. And lists, maps, and sets, some of the main building blocks for scalable data structures, are included as part of the default libraries for Java, Ruby, Python, PHP, and C++. What sets Scala's collections library apart from the others is its core support for immutable data structures and higher-order operations.

The core data structures in Scala, List, Map, and Set, are immutable. They cannot be resized, nor can their contents be swapped out. As a way of giving precedence over mutable collections, their package (collection.immutable) is automatically imported into Scala namespaces by default. This precedence aims to steer developers toward the immutable collections and immutable data in general, a "best practice" in functional programming circles. This is not to say that mutable collections are less powerful or less capable than immutable ones. Scala's mutable collections have all the same features as the immutable ones and also support a range of modification operations. We'll learn about mutable collections and how to convert mutable to immutable ones (and vice versa) in the next chapter.

The ability to take a collection and iterate or map it with an anonymous function is common to many languages, including Ruby and Python. However, the ability to do so while ensuring the type requirements of both the collection and the input and return types of the anonymous functions *is* relatively uncommon. Collections with type-safe higher-order functions support a declarative programming style, the ability to create expressive code, and very few runtime type conversion errors. This powerful combination of features helps to set the Scala collections library apart from those available in other languages and frameworks and provides a fairly large productivity boost to its users. In addition, Scala collections are *monadic*, supporting the ability to chain operations together in a high-level, type-safe manner. We'll learn about monadic collections as well in the next chapter.

Exercises

Do you recall the suggestion I previously made (see "Exercises" on page 42) to switch your development environment from inside-the-REPL to an external Scala source file? If you haven't made the switch yet, you'll find working on these exercises in the REPL to be downright impractical given their size and complexity.

I also recommend working on these exercises using a professional IDE such as IntelliJ IDEA CE or the Eclipse-based Scala IDE. You'll gain instant feedback about whether code is compilable and get code completion and documentation for Scala library functions. There are also plug-ins for simpler editing environments like Sublime Text, VIM, and Emacs that enable this functionality, but if you're getting started with Scala a full-fledged IDE will probably be easier and quicker to use.

The exercises in this section will help you become familiar with the core collections and operations we have studied in this chapter. I recommend spending time to not only write the most basic solution, but to find alternate methods for each implementation. This will help you become familiar with the subtle differences between similar functions such as fold and reduce, or head and slice, in addition to giving you the tools to bypass these functions and develop your own solutions.

1. Create a list of the first 20 odd Long numbers. Can you create this with a for-loop, with the filter operation, and with the map operation? What's the most efficient and expressive way to write this?

2. Write a function titled "factors" that takes a number and returns a list of its factors, other than 1 and the number itself. For example, `factors(15)` should return `List(3, 5)`.

   Then write a new function that applies "factors" to a list of numbers. Try using the list of `Long` numbers you generated in exercise 1. For example, executing this function with `List(9, 11, 13, 15)` should return `List(3, 3, 5)`, because the factor of 9 is 3 while the factors of 15 are 3 again and 5. Is this a good place to use `map` and `flatten`? Or would a for-loop be a better fit?

3. Write a function, `first[A](items: List[A], count: Int): List[A]`, that returns the first x number of items in a given list. For example, `first(List('a','t','o'), 2)` should return `List('a','t')`. You could make this a one-liner by invoking one of the built-in list operations that already performs this task, or (preferably) implement your own solution. Can you do so with a for-loop? With `foldLeft`? With a recursive function that only accesses `head` and `tail`?

4. Write a function that takes a list of strings and returns the longest string in the list. Can you avoid using mutable variables here? This is an excellent candidate for the list-folding operations (Table 6-5) we studied. Can you implement this with both `fold` and `reduce`? Would your function be more useful if it took a function parameter that compared two strings and returned the preferred one? How about if this function was applicable to generic lists, i.e., lists of any type?

5. Write a function that reverses a list. Can you write this as a recursive function? This may be a good place for a match expression.

6. Write a function that takes a `List[String]` and returns a `(List[String],List[String])`, a tuple of string lists. The first list should be items in the original list that are palindromes (written the same forward and backward, like "racecar"). The second list in the tuple should be all of the remaining items from the original list. You can implement this easily with `partition`, but are there other operations you could use instead?

7. The last exercise in this chapter is a multipart problem. We'll be reading and processing a forecast from the excellent and free OpenWeatherMap API.

   To read content from the URL we'll use the Scala library operation `io.Source.+fromURL(url: String)`, which returns an `+io.Source` instance. Then we'll reduce the source to a collection of individual lines using the `getLines.toList` operation. Here is an example of using `io.Source` to read content from a URL, separate it into lines, and return the result as a list of strings:

   ```
   scala> val l: List[String] = io.Source.fromURL(url).getLines.toList
   ```

   Here is the URL we will use to retrieve the weather forecast, in XML format:

   ```
   scala> val url =
     "http://api.openweathermap.org/data/2.5/forecast?mode=xml&lat=55&lon=0"
   ```

Go ahead and read this URL into a list of strings. Once you have it, print out the first line to verify you've captured an XML file. The result should look pretty much like this:

```
scala> println( l(0) )
<?xml version="1.0" encoding="utf-8"?>
```

If you don't see an XML header, make sure that your URL is correct and your Internet connection is up.

Let's begin working with this `List[String]` containing the XML document.

a. To make doubly sure we have the right content, print out the top 10 lines of the file. This should be a one-liner.

b. The forecast's city's name is there in the first 10 lines. Grab it from the correct line and print out its XML element. Then extract the city name and country code from their XML elements and print them out together (e.g., "Paris, FR"). This is a good place to use regular expressions to extract the text from XML tags (see "Regular expressions" on page 19).

   If you don't want to use regular expression capturing groups, you could instead use the `replaceAll()` operation on strings to remove the text surrounding the city name and country name.

c. How many forecast segments are there? What is the shortest expression you can write to count the segments?

d. The "symbol" XML element in each forecast segment includes a description of the weather forecast. Extract this element in the same way you extracted the city name and country code. Try iterating through the forecasts, printing out the description.

   Then create an informal weather report by printing out the weather descriptions over the next 12 hours (not including the XML elements).

e. Let's find out what descriptions are used in this forecast. Print a sorted listing of all of these descriptions in the forecast, with duplicate entries removed.

f. These descriptions may be useful later. Included in the "symbol" XML element is an attribute containing the symbol number. Create a `Map` from the symbol number to the description. Verify this is accurate by manually accessing symbol values from the forecast and checking that the description matches the XML document.

g. What are the high and low temperatures over the next 24 hours?

h. What is the average temperature in this weather forecast? You can use the "value" attribute in the temperature element to calculate this value.

Now that you have solved the exercises, are there simpler or shorter solutions than the ones you chose? Did you prefer infix dot notation or infix operator notation? Was using `for..yield` easier than higher-order operations like `map` and `filter`?

This is a good place to rework some of your solutions to really find your favored coding style, which is often the intersection between ease of writing, ease of reading, and expressiveness.

CHAPTER 7

More Collections

In Chapter 6 we were introduced to the Iterable root type and three of its immutable subtypes: the ordered collection List and the unordered collections Set and Map. These collections were labeled *common* because they are ubiquitous in modern programming languages, not to imply that they are basic and unadorned. In this chapter we will uncover Scala collections that may not be ubiquitous but are just as important.

We'll start with mutable collections, which probably can be considered ubiquitous because more languages support them than they do immutable collections. Then we'll move on to arrays, streams, and other collections.

Mutable Collections

The List, Set, and Map immutable collections we are familiar with cannot be changed after they have been created (see the definition of "immutable"). They *can*, however, be transformed into new collections. For example, we can create an immutable map, and then transform it by removing one mapping and adding another:

```scala
scala> val m = Map("AAPL" -> 597, "MSFT" -> 40)  ❶
m: scala.collection.immutable.Map[String,Int] =
  Map(AAPL -> 597, MSFT -> 40)

scala> val n = m - "AAPL" + ("GOOG" -> 521)      ❷
n: scala.collection.immutable.Map[String,Int] =
  Map(MSFT -> 40, GOOG -> 521)

scala> println(m)                                ❸
Map(AAPL -> 597, MSFT -> 40)
```

❶   A new map with "AAPL" and "MSFT" keys.

❷   Removing "APPL" and adding "GOOG" gives us a different collection…

❸   … while the original collection in "m" remains the same.

What you end up with is a completely new collection stored in "n". The original collection, stored in the "m" value, remains untouched. And this is exactly the point of *immutable data*, namely that data and data structures should not be mutable or change their state in order to improve code stability and prevent bugs. As an example, data structures that are rigid and never change state are safer to use with concurrent code than data structures that may change at any point and are prone to corruption (e.g., reading a data structure while it is undergoing a state change).

However, there *are* times when you do want mutable data, and when it is arguably safe to use it. For example, creating a mutable data structure that is only used within a function, or one that is converted to immutability before being returned, are considered to be safe use cases. You may want to add elements to a list in the course of a series of "if" condition blocks, or add them in the course of iterating over a separate data structure, without having to store each transformation in a series of local values.

In this section we will explore three methods for building mutable collections.

Creating New Mutable Collections

The most straightforward way to modify collections is with a mutable collection type. See Table 7-1 for the mutable counterparts to the standard immutable `List`, `Map`, and `Set` types.

Table 7-1. Mutable collection types

Immutable type	Mutable counterpart
collection.immutable.List	collection.mutable.Buffer
collection.immutable.Set	collection.mutable.Set
collection.immutable.Map	collection.mutable.Map

Whereas the `collection.immutable` package is automatically added to the current namespace in Scala, the `collection.mutable` package is not. When creating mutable collections, make sure to include the full package name for the type.

The `collection.mutable.Buffer` type is a general-purpose mutable sequence, and supports adding elements to its beginning, middle, and end.

Here is an example of using it to build a list of integers starting from a single element:

```
scala> val nums = collection.mutable.Buffer(1)
nums: scala.collection.mutable.Buffer[Int] = ArrayBuffer(1)

scala> for (i <- 2 to 10) nums += i

scala> println(nums)
Buffer(1, 2, 3, 4, 5, 6, 7, 8, 9, 10)
```

Here is an example of using the same buffer but starting with an empty collection. Because there is no default value, we will have to specify the collection's type with a type parameter (Int, in this case):

```
scala> val nums = collection.mutable.Buffer[Int]()
nums: scala.collection.mutable.Buffer[Int] = ArrayBuffer()

scala> for (i <- 1 to 10) nums += i

scala> println(nums)
Buffer(1, 2, 3, 4, 5, 6, 7, 8, 9, 10)
```

Building maps and sets is a similar process. Specifying the type parameter for a new set, or the key and value type parameters for a new map, is only required when creating an empty collection.

You can convert your mutable buffer back to an immutable list at any time with the toList method:

```
scala> println(nums)
Buffer(1, 2, 3, 4, 5, 6, 7, 8, 9, 10)

scala> val l = nums.toList
l: List[Int] = List(1, 2, 3, 4, 5, 6, 7, 8, 9, 10)
```

Likewise for sets and maps, use the toSet and toMap methods to convert these mutable collections to their immutable counterparts.

Creating Mutable Collections from Immutable Ones

An alternative to creating mutable collections directly is to convert them from immutable collections. This is useful when you already have a starting immutable collection that you want to modify, or would just rather type "List()" instead of "collection.mutable.Buffer()."

The List, Map, and Set immutable collections can all be converted to the mutable collection.mutable.Buffer type with the toBuffer method. For lists this is obviously straightforward, because the buffer and list type are both sequences. Maps, as subtypes of Iterable, can be considered as sequences as well, and are converted to buffers as sequences of key-value tuples. Converting sets to buffers is trickier, however, because buffers do not honor the uniqueness constraint of sets. Fortunately, any duplicates in the buffer's data will be removed when converted back to a Set.

Here is an example of converting an immutable map to a mutable one and then changing it back:

```
scala> val m = Map("AAPL" -> 597, "MSFT" -> 40)
m: scala.collection.immutable.Map[String,Int] =
  Map(AAPL -> 597, MSFT -> 40)

scala> val b = m.toBuffer                                   ❶
b: scala.collection.mutable.Buffer[(String, Int)] =
  ArrayBuffer((AAPL,597), (MSFT,40))

scala> b trimStart 1                                        ❷

scala> b += ("GOOG" -> 521)                                 ❸
res1: b.type = ArrayBuffer((MSFT,40), (GOOG,521))

scala> val n = b.toMap                                      ❹
n: scala.collection.immutable.Map[String,Int] =
  Map(MSFT -> 40, GOOG -> 521)
```

❶   The map, containing key-value pairs, is now a sequence of tuples.

❷   trimStart removes one or more items from the start of the buffer.

❸   After removing the "AAPL" entry we'll add a "GOOG" entry.

❹   This buffer of tuples is now an immutable map again.

The buffer methods toList and toSet can be used in addition to toMap to convert a buffer to an immutable collection.

Let's try converting this buffer of 2-sized tuples to a List and to a Set. After all, there's no reason that a collection of 2-sized tuples created from a map *must* be converted back to its original form.

To verify that Set imposes a uniqueness constraint, we'll first add a duplicate entry to the buffer. Let's see how this works out:

```
scala> b += ("GOOG" -> 521)
res2: b.type = ArrayBuffer((MSFT,40), (GOOG,521), (GOOG,521))

scala> val l = b.toList
l: List[(String, Int)] = List((MSFT,40), (GOOG,521), (GOOG,521))

scala> val s = b.toSet
s: scala.collection.immutable.Set[(String, Int)] = Set((MSFT,40), (GOOG,521))
```

The list "l" and set "s" were created successfully, with the list containing the duplicated entries and the set restricted to contain only unique entries.

The Buffer type is a good, general-purpose mutable collection, similiar to a List but able to add, remove, and replace its contents. The conversion methods it supports, along with the toBuffer methods on its immutable counterparts, makes it a useful mechanism for working with mutable data.

About the only drawback of a buffer is that it may be too broadly applicable. If all you need is to put together a collection iteratively, e.g., inside a loop, a builder may be a good choice instead.

Using Collection Builders

A Builder is a simplified form of a Buffer, restricted to generating its assigned collection type and supporting only append operations.

To create a builder for a specific collection type, invoke the type's newBuilder method and include the type of the collection's element. Invoke the builder's result method to convert it back into the final Set. Here is an example of creating a Set with a builder:

```
scala> val b = Set.newBuilder[Char]
b: scala.collection.mutable.Builder[Char,scala.collection.immutable.
  Set[Char]] = scala.collection.mutable.SetBuilder@726dcf2c

scala> b += 'h'        ❶
res3: b.type = scala.collection.mutable.SetBuilder@d13d812

scala> b ++= List('e', 'l', 'l', 'o')   ❷
res4: b.type = scala.collection.mutable.SetBuilder@d13d812

scala> val helloSet = b.result      ❸
helloSet: scala.collection.immutable.Set[Char] = Set(h, e, l, o)
```

❶ Adding a single item, one of two append operations.

❷ Adding multiple items, the second of two append operations.

❸ Unlike with buffers, a builder knows its immutable counterpart.

So, why use Builder versus Buffer or one of the mutable collection types? The Build er type is a good choice if you are only building a mutable collection iteratively in order to convert it to an immutable collection. If you need Iterable operations while building your mutable collection, or don't plan on converting to an immutable collection, using one of the Buffer or other mutable collection types is a better match.

In this section we have investigated methods to convert between immutable and mutable collections, which are either unchangeable or fully modifiable. In the next section we'll cover a "collection" that breaks these rules, being immutable in size but mutable in content.

Arrays

An `Array` is a fixed-size, mutable, indexed collection. It's not officially a collection, because it isn't in the "scala.collections" package and doesn't extend from the root `Itera ble` type (although it has all of the `Iterable` operations like `map` and `filter`). The `Array` type is actually just a wrapper around Java's array type with an advanced feature called an *implicit class* allowing it to be used like a sequence. Scala provides the `Array` type for compatibility with JVM libraries and Java code and as a backing store for indexed collections, which really require an array to be useful.

Here are some examples of working with arrays, demonstrating their cell mutability and support for `Iterable` operations:

```
scala> val colors = Array("red", "green", "blue")
colors: Array[String] = Array(red, green, blue)

scala> colors(0) = "purple"   ❶

scala> colors ❷
res0: Array[String] = Array(purple, green, blue)

scala> println("very purple: " + colors) ❸
very purple: [Ljava.lang.String;@70cf32e3

scala> val files = new java.io.File(".").listFiles ❹
files: Array[java.io.File] = Array(./Build.scala, ./Dependencies.scala,
 ./build.properties, ./JunitXmlSupport.scala, ./Repositories.scala,
 ./plugins.sbt, ./project, ./SBTInitialization.scala, ./target)

scala> val scala = files map (_.getName) filter(_ endsWith "scala")
scala: Array[String] = Array(Build.scala, Dependencies.scala,
 JunitXmlSupport.scala, Repositories.scala, SBTInitialization.scala)
```

❶   Use a zero-based index to replace any item in an `Array`.

❷   The Scala REPL knows how to print an `Array` ...

❸   ... but not `println()`, which can only call a type's `toString()` method.

❹   The `listFiles` method in `java.io.File`, a JDK class, returns an array that we can easily map and filter.

Java arrays do not override the `toString()` method inherent in all Java and Scala objects, and thus use the default implementation of printing out the type parameter and reference. Thus, calling `toString()` on an `Array` results in the unreadable output seen in the last example. Fortunately you won't see this output with Scala collections, because they all override `toString()` to provide human-readable printouts of their contents and structure.

It's important to hear about and understand the Array type, but I don't recommend using it in regular practice unless you need it for JVM code. There are many other fine sequences that you can use instead, as you'll see in the next section.

Seq and Sequences

Seq is the root type of all sequences, including linked lists like List and indexed (direct-access) lists like Vector. The Array type, if it were a collection, could be considered an indexed sequence because its elements are directly accessible without traversal. As a root type, Seq itself cannot be instantiated, but you can invoke it as a shortcut for creating a List:

```scala
scala> val inks = Seq('C','M','Y','K')
inks: Seq[Char] = List(C, M, Y, K)
```

The Seq hierarchy of sequence collections appears in Figure 7-1, and Table 7-2 contains the descriptions for each of these types.

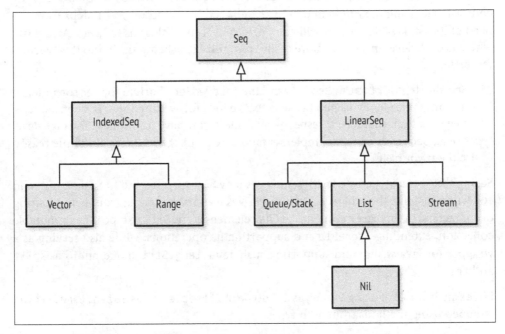

Figure 7-1. The sequence collections hierarchy

Table 7-2. Sequence types

Name	Description
Seq	The root of all sequences. Shortcut for `List()`.
IndexedSeq	The root of indexed sequences. Shortcut for `Vector()`.
Vector	A list backed by an `Array` instance for indexed access.
Range	A range of integers. Generates its data on-the-fly.
LinearSeq	The root of linear (linked-list) sequences.
List	A singly linked list of elements.
Queue	A first-in-last-out (FIFO) list.
Stack	A last-in-first-out (LIFO) list.
Stream	A lazy list. Elements are added as they are accessed.
String	A collection of characters.

The `Vector` type is implemented with an `Array` for storage. As an indexed sequence (since arrays are indexed), you can access items in a `Vector` directly by their index. By contrast, accessing the *nth* item of a `List` (a linked list) requires $n - 1$ steps from the head of its list. Java developers will recognize `Vector` as analogous to Java's "ArrayList," whereas C++ developers will (more easily) recognize it as being similar to the "Vector" template.

The `Seq` shortcut for `List` linked lists and the `IndexedSeq` shortcut for `Vector` indexed lists are only marginally useful, because the savings for writing them is one character and negative four characters, respectively. Unless you have a fondness for high-level types (e.g., `Seq`) over concrete implementations (e.g., `List`), you may find little reason to use them yourself.

Seeing the `String` type listed with sequences may be a surprise, but in Scala it is a valid collection just like the others. A "string" derives its name, after all, from being a string of characters, in this case a sequence of `Char` elements. The `String` type is an immutable collection, extending `Iterable` and supporting its operations, while also serving as a wrapper for Java strings and supporting such `java.lang.String` operations as `split` and `trim`.

Here's an example of using `String` as a subtype of `Iterable` *and* as a `java.lang.String` wrapper, using methods from both types:

```
scala> val hi = "Hello, " ++ "worldly" take 12 replaceAll ("w","W")
hi: String = Hello, World
```

The `++` and `take` operations derive from `Iterable` and act on the sequence of characters, while `replaceAll` is a `java.lang.String` operation invoked as a Scala operator.

The last sequence we'll discuss in this chapter is the `Stream` type, which builds itself as its elements are accessed. It's a popular collection in functional programming languages, but it takes some extra time to learn so it has its own section. Take the time to try out the examples and get familiar with `Stream` because it can be a very helpful collection to know about.

Streams

The `Stream` type is a *lazy* collection, generated from one or more starting elements and a recursive function. Elements are added to the collection only when they are accessed for the first time, in constrast to other immutable collections that receive 100% of their contents at instantiation time. The elements that a stream generates are cached for later retrieval, ensuring that each element is only generated once. Streams can be unbounded, theoretically infinite collections where elements are only realized upon access. They can also be terminated with `Stream.Empty`, a counterpart to `List.Nil`.

Streams, like lists, are recursive data structures consisting of a head (the current element) and a tail (the rest of the collection). They can be built with a function that returns a new stream containing the head element and a recursive invocation of that function to build the tail. You can use `Stream.cons` to construct a new stream with the head and tail.

Here is an example function that builds and recursively generates a new stream. By incrementing the starting integer value, it will end up creating a collection of consecutively increasing integers:

```scala
scala> def inc(i: Int): Stream[Int] = Stream.cons(i, inc(i+1))
inc: (i: Int)Stream[Int]

scala> val s = inc(1)
s: Stream[Int] = Stream(1, ?)
```

We have our stream but it only contains our starting value (1) and a promise of future values (?). Let's force it to build out the next four elements by "taking" them and retrieving the contents as a list:

```scala
scala> val l = s.take(5).toList
l: List[Int] = List(1, 2, 3, 4, 5)

scala> s
res1: Stream[Int] = Stream(1, 2, 3, 4, 5, ?)
```

We took the first five elements and retrieved them as a plain old list. Printing out the original stream instance shows that it now contains five elements and is ready to generate more. We could follow this up by taking 20, or 200, or 2,000 elements. The stream contains a recursive function call (specifically, a function value) that it can use to generate new elements without end.

An alternate syntax for the `Stream.cons` operator is the slightly cryptic `#::` operator, which we'll just call the *cons* operator for streams. This performs the same function as `Stream.cons` except with right-associative notation, complementing the cons operator for lists, `::` (see "The Cons Operator" on page 89).

Here's the "inc" function again, using the cons operator `#::`. I've also renamed the parameter to "head" to better demonstrate its use as the head element of the new `Stream` instance:

```scala
scala> def inc(head: Int): Stream[Int] = head #:: inc(head+1)
inc: (head: Int)Stream[Int]

scala> inc(10).take(10).toList
res0: List[Int] = List(10, 11, 12, 13, 14, 15, 16, 17, 18, 19)
```

Where Is the Stream Being Constructed?

Many developers find the stream cons operator syntax, `#::`, confusing because it lacks an explicit creation of the underlying collection. The confusion is indeed warranted, because an advanced feature called *implicit conversion* is used to generate the new `Stream` instance from the recursive function's type, `=> Stream[A]`. If you can accept that the recursive function invocation (`inc(i+1)` in the preceding example) magically generates a `Stream` that acts as the tail, then prefixing this magic tail with your head element to create a new `Stream` should be acceptable.

Let's try creating a bounded stream. We'll use two arguments to our recursive function, one specifying the new head element and another specifying the last element to add:

```scala
scala> def to(head: Char, end: Char): Stream[Char] = (head > end) match {
     |   case true => Stream.empty
     |   case false => head #:: to((head+1).toChar, end)
     | }
to: (head: Char, end: Char)Stream[Char]

scala> val hexChars = to('A', 'F').take(20).toList
hexChars: List[Char] = List(A, B, C, D, E, F)
```

Using the new "to" function, we were able to create a bounded stream consisting of the letters used in writing hexadecimal numbers. The stream's `take` operation only returned the available elements, ending after we placed `Stream.empty` to terminate the collection.

The recursive function is used to generate a new `Stream` and (in our examples thus far) derive the new head element each time. We have used one or two parameter functions in the examples thus far, but you could easily have a function that had zero or a dozen parameters. The important part is defining the head value for your new stream.

All of the collections we have covered can hold zero, one, two, or more items, with the expectation that they can scale as far as your machine's memory or the JVM environment will allow. Next, we'll learn about a set of collections that can scale no longer than a single element, but are surprisingly applicable to situations where you never considered a collection would fit.

Monadic Collections

The last set of collections we'll discuss in this chapter are the *monadic* ones, which support transformative operations like the ones in `Iterable` but can contain no more than one element. The term "monadic" applies in its Greek origins to mean a single unit, and in the category theory sense of a single link in a chain of operations.

We'll start with the `Option` type, the one monadic collection that extends `Iterable`.

Option Collections

As a collection whose size will never be larger than one, the `Option` type represents the presence or absence of a single value. This potentially missing value (e.g., it was never initialized, or could not be calculated) can thus be wrapped in an `Option` collection and have its potential absence clearly advertised.

Some developers see `Option` as a safe replacement for `null` values, notifying users that the value may be missing and reducing the likelihood that its use will trigger a `Null PointerException`. Others see it as a safer way to build chains of operations, ensuring that only valid values will persist for the duration of the chain.

The `Option` type is itself unimplemented but relies on two subtypes for the implementation: `Some`, a type-parameterized collection of one element; and `None`, an empty collection. The `None` type has no type parameters because it never contains contents. You can work with these types directly, or invoke `Option()` to detect null values and let it choose the appropriate subtype.

Let's try creating an `Option` with nonnull and null values:

```scala
scala> var x: String = "Indeed"
x: String = Indeed

scala> var a = Option(x)
a: Option[String] = Some(Indeed)

scala> x = null
x: String = null

scala> var b = Option(x)
b: Option[String] = None
```

You can use isDefined and isEmpty to check if a given Option is Some or None, respectively:

```
scala> println(s"a is defined? ${a.isDefined}")
a is defined? true

scala> println(s"b is not defined? ${b.isEmpty}")
b is not defined? true
```

Let's use a more realistic example by defining a function that returns an Option value. In this case we will wrap the divide operator (/) with a check to prevent division by zero. Valid inputs will return a Some wrapper and invalid inputs will return None:

```
scala> def divide(amt: Double, divisor: Double): Option[Double] = { ❶
     |   if (divisor == 0) None
     |   else Option(amt / divisor) ❷
     | }
divide: (amt: Double, divisor: Double)Option[Double]

scala> val legit = divide(5, 2)
legit: Option[Double] = Some(2.5) ❸

scala> val illegit = divide(3, 0)
illegit: Option[Double] = None ❹
```

❶   The return type is the Option with a Double type parameter, ensuring that valid results will retain the correct type.

❷   This will return a Some wrapper because the dividend will be a nonnull value.

❸   With a valid divisor, our dividend comes wrapped in a Some.

❹   With an invalid divisor we get None, the absence of a value.

A function that returns a value wrapped in the Option collection is signifying that it may not have been applicable to the input data, and as such may not have been able to return a valid result. It offers a clear warning to callers that its value is only potential, and ensures that its results will need to be carefully handled. In this way, Option provides a type-safe option for handling function results, far safer than the Java standard of returning null values to indicate missing data.

Scala's collections use the Option type in this way to provide safe operations for handling the event of empty collections. For example, although the head operation works for non-empty lists, it will throw an error for empty lists. A safer alternative is headOption, which (as you may have guessed) returns the head element wrapped in an Option, ensuring that it will work even on empty lists.

Here is an example of calling headOption to safely handle empty collections:

```
scala> val odds = List(1, 3, 5)
odds: List[Int] = List(1, 3, 5)
```

```
scala> val firstOdd = odds.headOption
firstOdd: Option[Int] = Some(1)

scala> val evens = odds filter (_ % 2 == 0)
evens: List[Int] = List()

scala> val firstEven = evens.headOption
firstEven: Option[Int] = None
```

Another use of options in collections is in the find operation, a combination of fil
ter and headOption that returns the first element that matches a predicate function.
Here is an example of successful and unsuccessful collection searches with find:

```
scala> val words = List("risible", "scavenger", "gist")
words: List[String] = List(risible, scavenger, gist)

scala> val uppercase = words find (w => w == w.toUpperCase)
uppercase: Option[String] = None

scala> val lowercase = words find (w => w == w.toLowerCase)
lowercase: Option[String] = Some(risible)
```

In a way, we have used list reduction operations to reduce a collection down to a single
Option. Because Option is itself a collection, however, we can continue to transform it.

For example, we could use filter and map to transform the "lowercase" result in a way
that retains the value, or in a way that loses the value. Each of these operations is type-
safe and will not cause null pointer exceptions:

```
scala> val filtered = lowercase filter (_ endsWith "ible") map (_.toUpperCase)
filtered: Option[String] = Some(RISIBLE)

scala> val exactSize = filtered filter (_.size > 15) map (_.size)
exactSize: Option[Int] = None
```

In the second example, the filter is inapplicable to the "RISIBLE" value and so it
returns None. The ensuing map operation against None has no effect and simply returns
None again.

This is a great example of the Option as a *monadic* collection, providing a single unit
that can be executed safely (and type-safely) in a chain of operations. The operations
will apply to present values (Some) and not apply to missing values (None), but the
resulting type will still match the type of the final operation (an Option[Int] in the
preceding example).

We have covered creating and transforming the Option collection. You may be wondering, however, what you *do* with an Option after you transform it into the desired
value, type, or existence.

Extracting values from Options

The Option collection provides a safe mechanism and operations for storing and transforming values that may or may not be present. You shouldn't be surprised that it also provides safe operations to extract its potential value.

For the curious, there *is* also an unsafe extraction operation, the get() method. If you call this for an Option that is actually a Some instance, you will successfully receive the value it contains. However, if you call get() on an instance of None, a "no such element" error will be triggered.

Avoid Option.get()

Option.get() is unsafe and should be avoided, because it disrupts the entire goal of type-safe operations and can lead to runtime errors. If possible, use an operation like fold or getOrElse that allows you to define a safe default value.

We will focus on the safe operations for extracting Option values. The core strategy of these operations is to provide a framework for handling missing values, such as a replacement (aka "default") value to use instead of the missing one, or a function that can either generate a replacement or raise an error condition.

Table 7-3 has a selection of these operations. The examples in the table could have been written with literal Option values like Some(10) or None, but these would not have helped to illustrate the challenges of working with potential data. Instead, the following examples call the function nextOption, which randomly returns either a valid or missing Option value each time. Try out this function and the examples in the REPL to see how Some and None change the result of these operations:

```
scala> def nextOption = if (util.Random.nextInt > 0) Some(1) else None
nextOption: Option[Int]

scala> val a = nextOption
a: Option[Int] = Some(1)

scala> val b = nextOption
b: Option[Int] = None
```

Table 7-3. Safe Option extractions

Name	Example	Description
fold	nextOption.fold(-1)(x => x)	Returns the value from the given function for Some (in this case, based on the embedded value) or else the starting value. The foldLeft, foldRight, and reduceXXX methods are also available for reducing an Option down to its embedded value or else a computed value.

Name	Example	Description
getOrElse	nextOption getOrElse 5 or nextOption getOrElse { println("error!"); -1 }	Returns the value for Some or else the result of a by-name parameter (see "By-Name Parameters" on page 75) for None.
orElse	nextOption orElse nextOption	Doesn't actually extract the value, but attempts to fill in a value for None. Returns this Option if it is nonempty, otherwise returns an Option from the given by-name parameter.
Match expressions	nextOption match { case Some(x) => x; case None => -1 }	Use a match expression to handle the value if present. The Some(x) expression extracts its data into the named value "x", which can be used as the return value of the match expression or reused for further transformation.

The Option type is a great example of a monadic collection, being a singular and chainable unit. It is used throughout Scala's collections library, for example in the find and headOption operations for sequences. It is also helpful in your own functions for input parameters and return values when you need to represent potential values. Many consider it a safer alternative than using null (i.e., the absence of an initialized value), as its potential nature is made clear, because its use cannot prevent all null pointer errors.

Option is a general-purpose monadic collection for potential values, able to contain any type of value as specified in its type parameters. We will now look at two monadic collections for specific purposes: Try for successful values and Future for eventual values.

Try Collections

The util.Try collection turns error handling into collection management. It provides a mechanism to catch errors that occur in a given function parameter, returning either the error or the result of the function if successful.

Scala provides the ability to raise errors by throwing *exceptions*, error types that may include a message or other information. Throwing an exception in your Scala code will disrupt your program's flow and return control to the closest handler for that particular exception. Unhandled exceptions will terminate applications, although most Scala application frameworks and web containers take care to prevent this.

Exceptions may be thrown by your own code, by library methods that you invoke, or by the Java Virtual Machine (JVM). The JVM will throw a java.util.NoSuchElementException if you call None.get or Nil.head (the head of an empty list) or a java.lang.NullPointerException if you access a field or method of a null value.

To throw an exception, use the `throw` keyword with a new `Exception` instance. The text message provided to `Exception` is optional:

```
scala> throw new Exception("No DB connection, exiting...")
java.lang.Exception: No DB connection, exiting...
   ... 32 elided
```

To really test out exceptions, let's create a function that will throw an exception based on the input criteria. We can then use it to trigger exceptions for testing:

```
scala> def loopAndFail(end: Int, failAt: Int): Int = {
     |    for (i <- 1 to end) {
     |       println(s"$i) ")
     |       if (i == failAt) throw new Exception("Too many iterations")
     |    }
     |    end
     | }
loopAndFail: (end: Int, failAt: Int)Int
```

Let's try `loopAndFail` with a larger iteration number than the check, ensuring we get an exception. This will demonstrate how the for-loop and the function overall get disrupted by an exception:

```
scala> loopAndFail(10, 3)
1)
2)
3)
java.lang.Exception: Too many iterations
   at $anonfun$loopAndFail$1.apply$mcVI$sp(<console>:10)
   at $anonfun$loopAndFail$1.apply(<console>:8)
   at $anonfun$loopAndFail$1.apply(<console>:8)
   at scala.collection.immutable.Range.foreach(Range.scala:160)
   at .loopAndFail(<console>:8)
   ... 32 elided
```

The corollary to throwing exceptions is catching and handling them. To "catch" an exception, wrap the potentially offending code in the `util.Try` monadic collection.

No try/catch Blocks?

Scala *does* support `try {} .. catch {}` blocks, where the `catch` block contains a series of `case` statements that attempt to match the thrown error. I recommend using `util.Try()` exclusively because it offers a safer, more expressive, and fully monadic approach to handling errors.

The `util.Try` type, like `Option`, is unimplemented but has two implemented subtypes, `Success` and `Failure`. The `Success` type contains the return value of the attempted expression if no exception was thrown, and the `Failure` type contains the thrown `Exception`.

Let's wrap some invocations of the loopAndFail function with util.Try and see what we get:

```
scala> val t1 = util.Try( loopAndFail(2, 3) ) ❶
1)
2)
t1: scala.util.Try[Int] = Success(2) ❷

scala> val t2 = util.Try{ loopAndFail(4, 2) } ❸
1)
2)
t2: scala.util.Try[Int] = Failure(
    java.lang.Exception: Too many iterations) ❹
```

❶ util.Try() takes a function parameter, so our invocation of loopAndFail is automatically converted to a function literal.

❷ The function literal (our safe invocation of loopAndFail) exited safely, so we have a Success containing the return value.

❸ Invoking util.Try with expression blocks (see "Function Invocation with Expression Blocks" on page 49) is also acceptable.

❹ An exception was thrown in this function literal, so we have a Failure containing said exception.

Now we'll look at how to handle potential errors. Because util.Try and its subtypes are also monadic collections, you can expect to find a number of thrilling and yet familiar methods for handling these situations. You may find that selecting the right error-handling approach (including whether to handle them at all) for your application will depend on its requirements and context, however. Few error-handling methods are generally applicable, in my experience.

Table 7-4 has a selection of strategies for handling errors. To better portray the inherent dichotomy of the success and failure states, let's define a randomized error function for use in the examples:

```
scala> def nextError = util.Try{ 1 / util.Random.nextInt(2) }
nextError: scala.util.Try[Int]

scala> val x = nextError
x: scala.util.Try[Int] = Failure(java.lang.ArithmeticException:
/ by zero)

scala> val y = nextError
y: scala.util.Try[Int] = Success(1)
```

Now when you try out the following examples you'll be able to test them with successes and failures.

Table 7-4. Error-handling methods with Try

Name	Example	Description
flatMap	nextError flatMap { _ => nextError }	In case of Success, invokes a function that also returns util.Try, thus mapping the current return value to a new, embedded return value (or an exception). Because our "nextError" demo function does not take an input, we'll use an underscore to represent the unused input value from the current Success.
foreach	nextError foreach(x => println("success!" + x))	Executes the given function once in case of Success, or not at all in case of a Failure.
getOrElse	nextError getOrElse 0	Returns the embedded value in the Success or the result of a by-name parameter in case of a Failure.
orElse	nextError orElse nextError	The opposite of flatMap. In case of Failure, invokes a function that also returns a util.Try. With orElse you can potentially turn a Failure into a Success.
toOption	nextError.toOption	Convert your util.Try to Option, where a Success becomes Some and a Failure becomes None. Useful if you are more comfortable working with options, but the downside is you may lose the embedded Exception.
map	nextError map (_ * 2)	In case of Success, invokes a function that maps the embedded value to a new value.
Match expressions	nextError match { case util.Success(x) => x; case util.Failure(error) => -1 }	Use a match expression to handle a Success with a return value (stored in "x") or a Failure with an exception (stored in "error"). Not shown: logging the error with a good logging framework, ensuring it gets noticed and tracked.
Do nothing	nextError	This is the easiest error-handling method of all and a personal favorite of mine. To use this method, simply allow the exception to propagate up the call stack until it gets caught or causes the current application to exit. This method may be too disruptive for certain sensitive cases, but ensures that thrown exceptions will never be ignored.

A common exception that many developers have to work with is validating numbers stored in strings. Here's an example using the orElse operation to try to parse a number out of a string, and the foreach operation to print the result if successful:

```
scala> val input = " 123 "
input: String = " 123 "

scala> val result = util.Try(input.toInt) orElse util.Try(input.trim.toInt)
result: scala.util.Try[Int] = Success(123)

scala> result foreach { r => println(s"Parsed '$input' to $r!") }
Parsed ' 123 ' to 123!

scala> val x = result match {
     |    case util.Success(x) => Some(x)
     |    case util.Failure(ex) => {
     |      println(s"Couldn't parse input '$input'")
     |      None
     |    }
     | }
x: Option[Int] = Some(123)
```

I'll repeat the assertion that the best error-handling strategy will depend on your current requirements and context. The one error-handling method to avoid is to encounter an exception and ignore it, e.g., by replacing it with a default value. If an exception was thrown, it at least deserves to be reported and handled.

Future Collections

The final monadic collection we'll review is concurrent.Future, which initiates a background task. Like Option and Try, a future represents a potential value and provides safe operations to either chain additional operations or to extract the value. Unlike with Option and Try, a future's value may not be immediately available, because the background task launched when creating the future could still be working.

By now you know that Scala code executes on the Java Virtual Machine, aka the JVM. What you may not know is that it also operates inside Java's "threads," lightweight concurrent processes in the JVM. By default Scala code runs in the JVM's "main" thread, but can support running background tasks in concurrent threads. Invoking a future with a function will execute that function in a separate thread while the current thread continues to operate. A future is thus a monitor of a background Java thread in addition to being a monadic container of the thread's eventual return value.

Fortunately, creating a future is a trivial task—just invoke it with a function you want to run in the background.

Let's try creating a future with a function that prints a message. Before creating the future, it is necessary to specify the "context" in the current session or application for running functions concurrently. We'll use the default "global" context, which makes use of Java's thread library for this purpose:

```scala
scala> import concurrent.ExecutionContext.Implicits.global
import concurrent.ExecutionContext.Implicits.global

scala> val f = concurrent.Future { println("hi") }
hi
f: scala.concurrent.Future[Unit] =
  scala.concurrent.impl.Promise$DefaultPromise@29852487
```

Our background task printed "hi" before the future could even be returned to the value. Let's try another example that "sleeps" the background thread with Java's Thread.sleep to make sure we get the future back while the background task is still running!

```scala
scala> val f = concurrent.Future { Thread.sleep(5000); println("hi") }
f: scala.concurrent.Future[Unit] =
  scala.concurrent.impl.Promise$DefaultPromise@4aa3d36

scala> println("waiting")
waiting

scala> hi
```

The background task, after sleeping for 5 seconds (i.e., 5,000 milliseconds), printed the "hi" message. In the meantime, our code in the "main" thread had time to print a "waiting" message before the background task completed.

You can set callback functions or additional futures to execute when a future's task completes. As an example, an API call could start an important but prolonged operation in the background while it returns control to the caller. You can also choose to wait, blocking the "main" thread until the background task completes. An already-asynchronous event such as a network file transfer could be started in a future while the "main" thread sleeps until the task completes or a "timeout" duration is reached.

Futures can be managed asynchronously (while the "main" thread continues to operate) or synchronously (with the "main" thread waiting for the task to complete). Because asynchronous operations are more efficient, allowing both the background and current threads to continue executing, we will review them first.

Handling futures asynchronously

Futures, in addition to spawning background tasks, can be treated as monadic collections. You can chain a function or another future to be executed following the completion of a future, passing the first future's successful result to the new function or feature.

A future handled this way will eventually return a util.Try containing either its function's return value or an exception. In case of success (with a return value), the chained function or future will be passed to the return value and converted into a future to return its own success or failure. In case of a failure (i.e., an exception was thrown), no additional functions or futures will be executed. In this way, the future-as-monadic-collection is just a chain in a sequence of operations that carry an embedded value. This is similar to Try, which breaks the chain when a failure is reached, and Option, which breaks the chain when the value is no longer present.

To receive the eventual result of a future, or of a chain of futures, you can specify a callback function. Your callback function receives the eventual successful value or the exception, freeing the original code that created the future to move on to other tasks.

Table 7-5 has a selection of operations for chaining futures and setting callback functions. As with the previous tables of operations, we'll start with a randomized function that can provide us with a realistic test case. This function, nextFtr, will sleep and then either return a value or throw an exception. Its inner function "rand" makes it easier to set a sleep time (up to 5 seconds / 5,000 milliseconds) and determine whether to succeed or fail:

```scala
scala> import concurrent.ExecutionContext.Implicits.global
import concurrent.ExecutionContext.Implicits.global

scala> import concurrent.Future
import concurrent.Future

scala> def nextFtr(i: Int = 0) = Future {
     |    def rand(x: Int) = util.Random.nextInt(x)
     |
     |    Thread.sleep(rand(5000))
     |    if (rand(3) > 0) (i + 1) else throw new Exception
     | }
nextFtr: (i: Int)scala.concurrent.Future[Int]
```

Is Thread.sleep() Safe to Use?
Some of the examples in this section on futures use the Java library method Thread.sleep to help demonstrate the concurrent and potentially delayed nature of running background tasks. However, actually using Thread.sleep in your own futures is a practice best avoided due to its inefficiencies. If you really need to put a future to sleep, you should consider using callback functions instead.

Table 7-5. Asynchronous future operations

Name	Example	Description
fallbackTo	nextFtr(1) fallbackTo nextFtr(2)	Chains the second future to the first and returns a new overall future. If the first is unsuccessful, the second is invoked.
flatMap	nextFtr(1) flatMap nextFtr()	Chains the second future to the first and returns a new overall future. If the first is successful, its return value will be used to invoke the second.

Name	Example	Description
map	nextFtr(1) map (_ * 2)	Chains the given function to the future and returns a new overall future. If the future is successful, its return value will be used to invoke the function.
onComplete	nextFtr() onComplete { _ getOrElse 0 }	After the future's task completes, the given function will be invoked with a util.Try containing a value (if success) or an exception (if failure).
onFailure	nextFtr() onFailure { case _ => "Error!" }	If the future's task throws an exception, the given function will be invoked with that exception.
onSuccess	nextFtr() onSuccess { case x => s"Got $x" }	If the future's task completes successfully, the given function will be invoked with the return value.
Future.sequence	concurrent.Future sequence List(nextFtr(1), nextFtr(5))	Runs the futures in the given sequence concurrently, returning a new future. If all futures in the sequence are successful, a list of their return values will be returned. Otherwise the first exception that occurs across the futures will be returned.

The code examples we have used with futures should help to illustrate how to create and manage them. However, futures require creation, management, *and* extraction to be useful. Let's try a more realistic example of futures that shows how to work with them from start to finish.

In this example we will use the OpenWeatherMap API (remember this from "Exercises" on page 102?) to check the current temperature (in Kelvin!) for two cities and report which one is warmer. Because calling a remote API can be time-intensive we will make the API calls in concurrent futures, running concurrently with our main thread:

```scala
scala> import concurrent.Future                                    ❶
import concurrent.Future

scala> def cityTemp(name: String): Double = {
     |   val url = "http://api.openweathermap.org/data/2.5/weather"
     |   val cityUrl = s"$url?q=$name"
     |   val json = io.Source.fromURL(cityUrl).mkString.trim        ❷
     |   val pattern = """.*"temp":([\d.]+).*""".r                   ❸
     |   val pattern(temp) = json                                   ❹
     |   temp.toDouble
     | }
cityTemp: (name: String)Double

scala> val cityTemps = Future sequence Seq(                        ❺
     |   Future(cityTemp("Fresno")), Future(cityTemp("Tempe"))
     | )
cityTemps: scala.concurrent.Future[Seq[Double]] =
 scala.concurrent.impl.Promise$DefaultPromise@51e0301d

scala> cityTemps onSuccess {
     |   case Seq(x,y) if x > y => println(s"Fresno is warmer: $x K")  ❻
     |   case Seq(x,y) if y > x => println(s"Tempe is warmer: $y K")
```

```
  | }
Tempe is warmer: 306.1 K
```

❶ Okay, sometimes typing "concurrent.Future" too many times is a pain. The `import` command brings a package's type into the current session's namespace.

❷ `io.Source` has many useful I/O operations for Scala applications.

❸ Capturing the "temp" field in a JSON response.

❹ Using `Regex` to produce a value from a capture group (see "Regular expressions" on page 19 for a refresh on this topic).

❺ By invoking `Future.sequence`, the sequence of futures are invoked concurrently and a list of their results are returned.

❻ Pattern matching on sequences using a pattern guard (see "Pattern Matching with Collections" on page 100 for an overview of using pattern matching with collections).

In this example we were able to make multiple concurrent calls to a remote API without blocking the main thread, i.e. the Scala REPL session. Calling a remote API and parsing its JSON result using regular expressions only took a few lines to implement ("few" = "less then a dozen" here), and executing this concurrently took up about the same amount of code.

You should now have a good understanding of how to create futures and work with them asynchronously. In the next section we will cover what to do if you absolutely must wait for a future to complete.

Handling futures synchronously

Blocking a thread while waiting for a background thread to complete is a potentially resource-heavy operation. It should be avoided for high-traffic or high-performance applications in favor of using callback functions like `onComplete` or `onSuccess`. However, there are some times when you just need to block the current thread and wait for a background thread to complete, successfully or otherwise.

To block the current thread and wait for another thread to complete, use `concurrent.Await.result()`, which takes the background thread and a maximum amount of time to wait. If the future completes in less time than the given duration, its result is returned, but a future that doesn't complete in time will result in a `java.util.concurrent.TimeoutException`. This thrown unwieldy exception may require using `util.Try` to manage timeout conditions safely, so be sure to choose acceptable durations that can minimize the chance of this occurring.

To demonstrate the use of `concurrent.Await.result`, let's use the "nextFtr" demonstration function we created for testing asynchronous operations (see "Handling futures asynchronously" on page 126). We'll start by importing the contents of the "duration" package to get access to the Duration type for specifying time spans as well as the types for their units:

```
scala> import concurrent.duration._                    ❶
import concurrent.duration._

scala> val maxTime = Duration(10, SECONDS)             ❷
maxTime: scala.concurrent.duration.FiniteDuration = 10 seconds

scala> val amount = concurrent.Await.result(nextFtr(5), maxTime)
amount: Int = 6                                        ❸

scala> val amount = concurrent.Await.result(nextFtr(5), maxTime)
java.lang.Exception                                    ❹
  at $anonfun$nextFtr$1.apply$mcI$sp(<console>:18)
  at $anonfun$nextFtr$1.apply(<console>:15)
  at $anonfun$nextFtr$1.apply(<console>:15)
  ...
```

❶ The underscore (_) at the end imports every member of the given package into the current namespace.

❷ SECONDS is a member of the concurrent.duration package and signifies that the given duration (10, in this case) is in seconds.

❸ When "nextFtr()" returns a successful value, concurrent.Await will return it...

❹ ... but when "nextFtr()" throws an exception, the current thread will be disrupted.

While our first call to concurrent.Await.result gave us a successful call, the second one caused an exception that disrupted the Scala REPL. When working with synchronous operations, you may want to add your own util.Try wrapper to ensure that exceptions thrown in a future will not disrupt the current flow. Doing so is not a requirement, because allowing exceptions to propagate may be a valid design choice.

Summary

Mutable collections, well known and available in most programming languages, have the best of both worlds in Scala. They can be used as incremental buffers to expand collections one item at a time using buffers, builders, or other approaches, but also support the wide variety of operations available to immutable collections.

And collections are, especially as Scala broadly defines them, more than simple containers for application data. Monadic collections provide type-safe chainable operations and management for sensitive and complex situations such as missing data, error conditions, and concurrent processing.

In Scala, immutable, mutable, and monadic collections are indispensable building blocks and foundations for safe *and* expressive software development. They are ubiquitous in Scala code, and are generally applicable to a wide range of uses.

By learning and becoming familiar with the core operations of Iterable, and with the safe operation chaining of monadic collections, you can better leverage them as a core foundation for your applications in Scala.

This chapter concludes the Scala instructions for Part 1. In Part 2 we will cover object-oriented Scala, a core feature of this programming language, while continuing to use what we have learned thus far.

Exercises

1. The Fibonacci series starts with the numbers "1, 1" and then computes each successive element as the sum of the previous two elements. We'll use this series to get familiarized with the collections in this chapter.

   a. Write a function that returns a list of the first x elements in the Fibonacci series Can you write this with a Buffer? Would a Builder be appropriate here?

   b. Write a new Fibonacci function that adds new Fibonacci numbers to an existing list of numbers. It should take a list of numbers (List[Int]) and the count of new elements to add and return a new list (List[Int]). Although the input list and returned lists are immutable, you should be able to use a mutable list inside your function. Can you also write this function using only immutable lists? Which version, using mutable versus immutable collections, is more appropriate and readable?

   c. The Stream collection is a great solution for creating a Fibonacci series. Create a stream that will generate a Fibonacci series. Use it to print out the first 100 elements in the series, in a formatted report of 10 comma-delimited elements per line.

   d. Write a function that takes an element in the Fibonacci series and returns the following element in the series. For example, fibNext(8) should return 13. How will you handle invalid input such as fixNext(9)? What are your options for conveying the lack of a return value to callers?

2. In the example for Array collections (see "Arrays" on page 112) we used the java.io.File(<path>).listFiles operation to return an array of files in the current directory. Write a function that does the same thing for a directory, and converts each entry into its String representation using the toString method. Filter out any dot-files (files that begin with the . character) and print the rest of the files separated by a semicolon (;). Test this out in a directory on your computer that has a significant number of files.

3. Take the file listing from exercise 2 and print a report showing each letter in the alphabet followed by the number of files that start with that letter.

4. Write a function to return the product of two numbers that are each specified as a String, not a numeric type. Will you support both integers and floating-point numbers? How will you convey if either or both of the inputs are invalid? Can you handle the converted numbers using a match expression? How about with a for-loop?

5. Write a function to safely wrap calls to the JVM library method `System.getProperty(<String>)`, avoiding raised exceptions or null results. `System.getProperty(<String>)` returns a JVM environment property value given the property's name. For example, `System.getProperty("java.home")` will return the path to the currently running Java instance, while `System.getProperty("user.timezone")` returns the time zone property from the operating system. This method can be dangerous to use, however, because it may throw exceptions or return `null` for invalid inputs. Try invoking `System.getProperty("")` or `System.getProperty("blah")` from the Scala REPL to see how it responds.

   Experienced Scala developers build their own libraries of functions that wrap unsafe code with Scala's monadic collections. Your function should simply pass its input to the method and ensure that exceptions and null values are safely handled and filtered. Call your function with the example property names used here, including the valid and invalid ones, to verify that it never raises exceptions or returns null results.

6. Write a function that reports recent GitHub commits for a project. GitHub provides an RSS feed of recent commits for a given user, repository, and branch, containing XML that you can parse out with regular expressions. Your function should take the user, repository, and branch, read and parse the RSS feed, and then print out the commit information. This should include the date, title, and author of each commit.

   You can use the following RSS URL to retrieve recent commits for a given repository and branch:

   ```
   https://github.com/<user name>/<repo name>/commits/<branch name>.atom
   ```

   Here is one way to grab the RSS feed as a single string:

   ```
   scala> val u = "https://github.com/scala/scala/commits/2.11.x.atom"
   u: String = https://github.com/scala/scala/commits/2.11.x.atom

   scala> val s = io.Source.fromURL(u)
   s: scala.io.BufferedSource = non-empty iterator

   scala> val text = s.getLines.map(_.trim).mkString("")
   text: String = <?xml version="1.0" encoding="UTF-8"?><feed xmlns=...
   ```

Working with the XML will be a bit tricky. You may want to use `text.split(<to` `ken>)` to split the text into the separate <entry> components, and then use regular expression capture groups (see "Regular expressions" on page 19) to parse out the <title> and other elements. You could also just try iterating through all the lines of the XML file, adding elements to a buffer as you find them, and then converting that to a new list.

Once you have completed this exercise (and there is a lot to do here), here are some additional features worth investigating:

a. Move the user, repo, and branch parameters into a tuple parameter.

b. Following exercise (a), have the function take a list of GitHub projects and print a report of each one's commits, in order of specified project.

c. Following exercise (b), retrieve all of the projects, commit data concurrently using futures, await the result (no more than 5 seconds), and then print a commit report for each project, in order of project specified.

d. Following exercise (c), mix the commits together and sort by commit date, then print your report with an additional "repo" column.

These additional features will take some time to implement, but are definitely worthwhile for learning and improving your Scala development skills.

Once you have finished these features, test out your commit report using entries from the following projects:

```
https://github.com/akka/akka/tree/master
https://github.com/scala/scala/tree/2.11.x
https://github.com/sbt/sbt/tree/0.13
https://github.com/scalaz/scalaz/tree/series/7.2.x
```

These features are all active (as of 2014), so you should see an interesting mix of commit activity data in your report. It's worthwhile to browse the repositories for these core open source Scala projects, or at least their documentation, to understand some of the excellent work being done.

7. Write a command-line script to call your GitHub commit report function from exercise 6 and print out the results. This will require a Unix shell; if you are on a Windows system you will need a compatible Unix environment such as Cygwin or Virtualbox (running a Unix virtual machine). You'll also need to install SBT (Simple Build Tool), a build tool that supports dependency management and plug-ins and is commonly used by Scala projects. You can download SBT from *http://www.scala-sbt.org/* for any environment, including an MSI Windows Installer version. SBT is also available from popular package managers. If you are using Homebrew on OS X you can install it with `brew install sbt`.

Isn't SBT Hard to Learn?

Maybe. In this exercise we'll only use it as a shell script launcher, so you can get comfortable with writing and executing shell scripts in Scala. We'll cover how to write SBT-built scripts to manage your own projects in later chapters.

Here is an example SBT-based Scala script that reads the command-line arguments as a `List` and prints a greeting. The comment block starting with triple asterisks is reserved for SBT settings. In this script we are specifying that we want version 2.11.1 of the Scala language to be used:

```
#!/usr/bin/env sbt -Dsbt.main.class=sbt.ScriptMain

/***
scalaVersion := "2.11.1"
*/

def greet(name: String): String = s"Hello, $name!"


// Entry point for our script
args.toList match {
  case List(name) => {
    val greeting = greet(name)
    println(greeting)
  }
  case _ =>
    println("usage: HelloScript.scala <name>")
}
```

Copy this into a file titled *HelloScript.scala*, and change the permissions to be executable (`chmod a+x HelloScript.scala` in a Unix environment). Then you can run the script directly:

```
$ ./HelloScript.scala Jason
[info] Set current project to root-4926629s8acd7bce0b (in
  build file:/Users/jason/.sbt/boot/4926629s8acd7bce0b/)
Hello, Jason!
```

Your commit report script will need to take multiple GitHub projects as arguments. To keep the arguments concise, you may want to combine each project's input into a single string to be parsed, such as `scala/scala/2.11.x`.

The printout should be clean, well-formatted, and easily readable. Using fixed column widths could help, using the `printf`-style formatting codes in string interpolation (see "String interpolation" on page 18).

PART II

Object-Oriented Scala

CHAPTER 8

Classes

In Part 1 of this book you learned about Scala's core types and how to group them into collections. Now it is time to build your own types with classes.

Classes are the core building block of object-oriented languages, a combination of data structures with functions ("methods"). A class defined with values and variables can be instantiated as many times as needed, each one initialized with its own input data. With *inheritance* classes can extend other classes, creating a hierarchy of subclasses and superclasses. *Polymorphism* makes it possible for these subclasses to stand in for their parent classes, while *encapsulation* provides privacy controls to manage the outward appearance of a class. If these terms are unfamiliar to you, I recommend reading up on general object-oriented programming methodology. Although we will cover the Scala object-oriented features that make use of these concepts, we won't be spending time on learning the concepts themselves. Understanding them can help you to make the most of Scala's object-oriented features and design expressive and reusable types.

We'll start by defining the simplest possible class and instantiating it:

```
scala> class User
defined class User

scala> val u = new User
u: User = User@7a8c8dcf

scala> val isAnyRef = u.isInstanceOf[AnyRef]
isAnyRef: Boolean = true
```

We now have our first class. When the REPL prints it out, you see the class name and a hexadecimal string. This is the JVM's internal reference for that instance. If you create a new instance, you should see a different value printed out, because the second instance would have a different memory location and thus a different reference from the first instance.

The hexadecimal number printed after the name of our "User" clas may look a bit odd. The actual method printing this is the JVM's `java.lang.Object.toString`. The `java.lang.Object` class is the root of all instances in the JVM, including Scala, and is essentially equivalent to the Scala root type Any. By printing an instance, the REPL is invoking the instance's `toString` method, which it inherits from the root type. The actual parent type of our User class is AnyRef (see Table 2-4), the root of all instantiable types. Thus, invoking `toString` on our User class resulted in a call to its parent, Any Ref, then to its parent, Any, which is the same as `java.lang.Object` and where the `toString` method is located.

Let's redesign our User class and make it more useful. We'll add a value and some methods that operate on the value. We'll also override the default `toString` method and provide a more informative version:

```scala
scala> class User {
     |    val name: String = "Yubaba"
     |    def greet: String = s"Hello from $name"
     |    override def toString = s"User($name)"
     | }
defined class User

scala> val u = new User
u: User = User(Yubaba)

scala> println( u.greet )
Hello from Yubaba
```

We have values and methods, and a rockin' `toString` method that actually reveals the contents of this instance.

Let's make this a bit more useful by converting the "name" field from a fixed value to a parameterized value. After all, no one really needs multiple instances of a User class that all have the same name. In Scala, class parameters (if any) are specified after the name of the class, much like a function's parameters follow the name of the function in its definition:

```scala
scala> class User(n: String) {
     |    val name: String = n
     |    def greet: String = s"Hello from $name"
     |    override def toString = s"User($name)"
     | }
defined class User

scala> val u = new User("Zeniba")
u: User = User(Zeniba)

scala> println(u.greet)
Hello from Zeniba
```

The class parameter "n" is used here to initialize the "name" value. However, it could not be used inside either of the methods. Class parameters are available for initializing fields (values and variables in a class) or for passing to functions, but once the class has been created the parameters aren't available.

Instead of using a class parameter for intitialization purposes, we can instead declare one of the fields as a class parameter. By adding the keywords val or var before a class parameter, the class parameter then becomes a field in the class. Let's try this by moving the "name" field to the class parameters:

```
scala> class User(val name: String) {
     |   def greet: String = s"Hello from $name"
     |   override def toString = s"User($name)"
     | }
defined class User
```

Now that we have a short and useful class, let's put it to use. Here's an example of using this new class with lists:

```
scala> val users = List(new User("Shoto"), new User("Art3mis"),
  new User("Aesch"))
users: List[User] = List(User(Shoto), User(Art3mis), User(Aesch))   ❶

scala> val sizes = users map (_.name.size)                          ❷
sizes: List[Int] = List(8, 7, 5)

scala> val sorted = users sortBy (_.name)
sorted: List[User] = List(User(Aesch), User(Art3mis), User(Shoto))

scala> val third = users find (_.name contains "3")                 ❸
third: Option[User] = Some(User(Art3mis))

scala> val greet = third map (_.greet) getOrElse "hi"               ❹
greet: String = Hello from Art3mis
```

❶ Did you notice that our new class is the type parameter to List? The to String method that we've overridden ensures that the List contents are cleanly displayed.

❷ Do you recall how operator notation ("Methods and Operators" on page 57) and placeholder syntax ("Placeholder Syntax" on page 72) work? Used together, they serve to make this line short and expressive.

❸ On this line we have a Scala operation (find, which returns the first match by a predicate function, if available) and a Java operation (contains, in java.lang.String) being used with operation notation.

❹ Can you see why String is the correct result of a combination of map and getOrElse against our Option[String]?

Lists and list operations aren't really the focus of this chapter, because we covered them rather extensively in Chapter 6 and Chapter 7. However, when Scala developers develop their own classes, they are more likely than not to use their own classes in collections. This example should demonstrate how well Scala collections work for not only the core Scala types, but any other classes you define yourself.

Let's round up our introduction to classes by working through examples of inheritance and polymorphism. A class can extend up to one other class in Scala with the ex tends keyword, and override (i.e., supplant) the behavior of an inherited method with the override keyword. The fields and methods in a class can be accessed (if strictly necessary) with the this keyword, while the fields and methods in the parent class(es) can be accessed with the super keyword. The super keyword is especially useful when a method needs to still access the similar method in its parent class that it is overriding.

I'll demonstrate this with a parent class, "A," and subclass, "C," and a class situtated between these two, "B":

```scala
scala> class A {
     |    def hi = "Hello from A"
     |    override def toString = getClass.getName
     | }
defined class A

scala> class B extends A
defined class B

scala> class C extends B { override def hi = "hi C -> " + super.hi }
defined class C

scala> val hiA = new A().hi
hiA: String = Hello from A

scala> val hiB = new B().hi
hiB: String = Hello from A

scala> val hiC = new C().hi
hiC: String = hi C -> Hello from A
```

A and B share the same "hi" method, because B *inherits* its parent's method. C defines its own version of "hi," both overriding the version in A and invoking it to include it in the message.

Are the results of these "hi" methods what you expected to see? Seeing an instance of B print out "Hello from A" may be misleading, but this hardcoded message (including the A class name) is what B picked up by extending A. A more informative "hi" method could have included the current class's name, as our "toString" method did, instead of hardcoding the class name "A." If we had done that, what do you think the "hi" method would have printed for B and C?

Let's try out Scala's polymorphism next, the ability for classes to take on the shape of other, compatible classes. By compatible I mean an instance of a subclass can be used in place of an instance of its parent class, but not the inverse. A subclass extends its parent class, and so supports 100% of the parent's fields and methods, but the reverse may not be true.

We'll reuse the A, B, and C classes we defined to test this out:

```scala
scala> val a: A = new A
a: A = A

scala> val a: A = new B
a: A = B

scala> val b: B = new A
<console>:9: error: type mismatch;
 found   : A
 required: B
       val b: B = new A
                  ^

scala> val b: B = new B
b: B = B
```

Storing an instance with the same type as its value works every time, as does storing an instance of a subclass into a value with its parent class's type. However, storing an instance of a parent class into a value of the type of its subclass won't work. The Scala compiler will correctly point out that an instance of A isn't compatible with the expected type of B. Another term for this situation is that the instance of A does not *conform* to the expected type of B. The B class is an *extension* of A, such that A's fields and methods are a subset of B's, not the other way around. The fact that B doesn't actually add any unique fields or methods doesn't change this situation.

Let's put this knowledge to use to create a list of instances of A, B, and C. What should we declare as the type of such a list, A, B, or C?

To ensure that the list can include instances of each of these classes, we should define the list as List[A], which is compatible with all of these classes:

```scala
scala> val misc = List(new C, new A, new B)
misc: List[A] = List(C, A, B)

scala> val messages = misc.map(_.hi).distinct.sorted
messages: List[String] = List(Hello from A, hi C -> Hello from A)
```

Whoops! Despite my warning to define the list as List[A], I forgot to add an explicit type. Fortunately, the Scala compiler was able to infer the common type of the three instances as being A, the parent class, and set the list's type parameter correctly. Come to think of it, that's a great use for the compiler's type inference feature—finding the lowest (most specific) common denominator of one or more instances.

This wraps up our introduction to classes in Scala. In the rest of the chapter we'll explore the full syntax for defining classes with fields and methods, the alternate types of classes, and the intricate details of specifying type parameters.

Defining Classes

A class is the definition of a type, containing fields (values and variables) of core types and/or other classes. They also contain methods, functions that may act on the contained fields, and nested class definitions. We'll start this section with a basic class definition and move on to more parameterized classes.

Syntax: Defining a Simple Class

```
class <identifier> [extends <identifier>] [{ fields, methods, and classes }]
```

The classes A, B, and C we defined in the introduction to this chapter demonstrate this class definition (other than the nested classes). The identifier is the class/type name, followed by the class being extended (if any), and then an optional set of curly braces in which are defined the fields and methods for the class. Fields are values or variables, and methods are functions defined as part of the class.

Like expressions and functions, classes can be nested inside each other. A nested class may access the fields and methods of its parent class(es) in addition to its own. In fact, expressions, functions, and classes can be nested inside each other, although it may look odd to have an "if..else" expression block defining and using its own private class.

You can invoke a class's methods, or access its fields, on an *instance* of the class, a memory allocation that provides storage for the class's fields. This action, of reversing memory to allocate a class's contents, is known as *instantiation*. Use the new keyword to instantiate a class by its name, with or without parentheses.

To be more useful, a class should take *class parameters*, input values used to initialize other fields and methods in the class or even to act as the class's fields. Class parameters are a comma-delimited list of names and types in the same format as a function's (and now, also a method's) input parameters.

Syntax: Defining a Class with Input Parameters

```
class <identifier> ([val|var] <identifier>: <type>[, ... ])
                    [extends <identifier>(<input parameters>)]
                    [{ fields and methods }]
```

A class with input parameters gives a programmer a reason to create multiple instances, because each instance can have its own unique contents. Let's try creating a class with both value and variable fields as parameters:

```
scala> class Car(val make: String, var reserved: Boolean) {
     |   def reserve(r: Boolean): Unit = { reserved = r }
     | }
```

```
defined class Car

scala> val t = new Car("Toyota", false)
t: Car = Car@4eb48298

scala> t.reserve(true)

scala> println(s"My ${t.make} is now reserved? ${t.reserved}")
My Toyota is now reserved? true
```

The fields and methods of a class can be accessed with standard infix dot notation, where the instance and its field or method are delimited by a period (.). When invoking an instance's single-parameter method, infix operator notation may be used as well.

Like functions, class parameters can be invoked with named parameters (see "Calling Functions with Named Parameters" on page 53). Any parameters invoked by position (starting with the first one) must appear before the first named parameter, but following this, named parameters may be used in any order.

As an example, we'll create a new instance of "Car" using named parameters in the opposite order of their position:

```
scala> val t2 = new Car(reserved = false, make = "Tesla")
t2: Car = Car@2ff4f00f

scala> println(t2.make)
Tesla
```

When you have classes that extend classes which take parameters, you'll need to make sure the parameters are included in the classes' definition. The class identified following the extends keyword should have its own set of input parameters as necessary.

In this example we have a new subclass of Car titled Lotus that specifies its parent's input parameters in the definition. I'll include the Car class definition for reference:

```
scala> class Car(val make: String, var reserved: Boolean) {
     |    def reserve(r: Boolean): Unit = { reserved = r }
     | }
defined class Car

scala> class Lotus(val color: String, reserved: Boolean) extends
  Car("Lotus", reserved)
defined class Lotus

scala> val l = new Lotus("Silver", false)
l: Lotus = Lotus@52c46334

scala> println(s"Requested a ${l.color} ${l.make}")
Requested a Silver Lotus
```

Our new subclass, Lotus, has its own new field, color, and takes a nonfield input parameter to initialize its parent class, Car.

In addition to input parameters, another feature that class parameters borrow from functions is the ability to define default values for parameters (see "Parameters with Default Values" on page 53). This allows callers to instantiate the class without specifying all of the class's parameters.

Syntax: Defining a Class with Input Parameters and Default Values

```
class <identifier> ([val|var] <identifier>: <type> = <expression>[, ... ])
                    [extends <identifier>(<input parameters>)]
                    [{ fields and methods }]
```

Let's redefine the Car class to use a default value for the "reserved" field, making it possible to instantiate the class with only the "make" field specified. We'll add a third field, also with a default value, so we can really experiment with mixing default and required parameters:

```
scala> class Car(val make: String, var reserved: Boolean = true,
     |           val year: Int = 2015) {
     |   override def toString = s"$year $make, reserved = $reserved"
     | }
defined class Car

scala> val a = new Car("Acura")                            ❶
a: Car = 2015 Acura, reserved = true

scala> val l = new Car("Lexus", year = 2010)              ❷
l: Car = 2010 Lexus, reserved = true

scala> val p = new Car(reserved = false, make = "Porsche") ❸
p: Car = 2015 Porsche, reserved = false
```

❶ Only the first parameter is required, and we can invoke it by position.

❷ Here, the first and third parameters are specified. Because the third parameter is out of order we'll have to specify it by name.

❸ This time none of the parameters are invoked by position, with the final one skipped.

The borrowing of features from functions for class definitions doesn't end with named parameters and default values, however. Type parameters (see "Type Parameters" on page 55), those nondata specifiers of input or return types in functions, are also available in class definitions.

Come to think of it, you have already used classes that have type parameters, so this shouldn't be a surprise. The most common one we've used is List[A], which uses a type parameter to determine the type of its elements and thus operations. For example, a

List[String] may contain String instances and support operations that take and return a String.

Let's revise our ever-growing class definition syntax to include support for one or more type parameters in a class.

Syntax: Defining a Class with Type Parameters

```
class <identifier> [type-parameters]
                ([val|var] <identifier>: <type> = <expression>[, ... ])
                [extends <identifier>[type-parameters](<input parameters>)]
                [{ fields and methods }]
```

You have seen collections as an example of classes using type parameters. A new list of integers will have the Int type parameter, List[Int](1, 2, 3).

Let's create our own collection and use a type parameter to ensure type safety. The new collection will extend Traversable[A], the parent class of Iterable (see Chapter 6).

Of course, there's not a lot of traversing going on due to only having one element. However, by extending this base collection we can pick up all of the useful collection operations we have become accustomed to using:

```
scala> class Singular[A](element: A) extends Traversable[A] {    ❶
     |    def foreach[B](f: A => B) = f(element)                   ❷
     | }
defined class Singular

scala> val p = new Singular("Planes")
p: Singular[String] = (Planes)                                    ❸

scala> p foreach println                                          ❹
Planes

scala> val name: String = p.head                                 ❺
name: String = Planes
```

❶ A good example of passing a type parameter to the parent class in the class definition.

❷ By defining a foreach() operation, Traversable will ensure our class is a real collection and can use this to enable every other collection operation.

❸ Here is a validation of our type-parameterized class, with the REPL printing the class name and the name of the parameterized type used to instantiate it (a String).

❹ An example usage of the foreach method we defined, reduced to its most unadorned invocation.

❺ Another example usage of `foreach`, indirectly this time, as we access `Traversa ble.head`, which invokes `foreach` for us. By extending `Traversable` we can access `head` and a range of other standard collection operations.

At this point we have covered named classes, inheritance, instantiation, input parameters, and type parameters. Believe it or not, there are still many other ways to customize your class definitions in Scala that you'll need to know. For example, controlling the levels of encapsulation (i.e., privacy) and building layers of abstraction, or defining methods in such a way that they can be accessed without their name! Read on for some of the really interesting features of object-oriented Scala.

More Class Types

Scala offers more than the basic class definitions we have tried out until now. In this section we will look at alternative ways to define and create classes.

Abstract Classes

An *abstract* class is a class designed to be extended by other classes but not instantiated itself. Abstract classes are designated so by the `abstract` keyword, placed before the `class` keyword when defining the class.

An abstract class can be used to define the core fields and methods required by its subclasses without providing an actual implementation. Thanks to polymorphism, a value with the type of the abstract class can actually point to an instance of one of its nonabstract subclasses, and invoke methods that actually end up being invoked on the subclass.

Abstract classes provide unimplemented fields and methods by *declaring* them without defining them. A declared field or method will include the name and parameters but not a starting value or implementation, respectively. A class that extends an abstract class with declared fields and methods, and is not itself marked as abstract, must provide their implementations. An abstract class can also have its own implemented fields and methods, which would not require implementations in subclasses.

Let's create our own abstract class with a declared value and method, and experiment with implementations:

```
scala> abstract class Car {
     |    val year: Int
     |    val automatic: Boolean = true
     |    def color: String
     | }
defined class Car

scala> new Car()
```

```
<console>:9: error: class Car is abstract; cannot be instantiated
              new Car()

scala> class RedMini(val year: Int) extends Car {
     |    def color = "Red"
     | }
defined class RedMini

scala> val m: Car = new RedMini(2005)
m: Car = RedMini@5f5a33ed
```

An experiment with instantiating our abstract class Car by itself didn't work, for the obvious reason that it is abstract and uninstantiatable. Still, it's nice to see that Scala's compiler pointed this out with a helpful message.

Creating a subclass that extends Car but adds a value parameter and a concrete implementation of the color method solved the problem. The RedMini class is a successful implementation of its parent abstract class and can be instantiated with only its year as a parameter.

On the other hand, what good is an automobile that only comes in a single color? A better version of a subclass should take the color as an input parameter. Let's make that change with a new subclass:

```
scala> class Mini(val year: Int, val color: String) extends Car
defined class Mini

scala> val redMini: Car = new Mini(2005, "Red")
redMini: Car = Mini@1f4dd016

scala> println(s"Got a ${redMini.color} Mini")
Got a Red Mini
```

Our new class, "Mini," now takes the color as an input parameter.

 Wait, Did You Just Implement an Abstract Method with a Value?
Invoking a parentheses- and parameter-free method on an instance has the same appearance as accessing one of its values, so it should be unsurprising that you can implement a required method using a value. The syntax is the same to callers, and because parenthesis-free methods are not expected to have side effects (see "Functions with Empty Parentheses" on page 48), the behavior should be the same.

Abstract classes are a useful tool in object-oriented design, making it possible to create a usable base type while delegating the implementation.

Anonymous Classes

In the previous section we saw a class definition, Mini, that implemented its parent class's declared methods. A less formal way to provide the implementation for a parent class's methods is with an *anonymous* class, a nonreusable and nameless class definition.

To define a one-time anonymous class, instantiate the parent (and potentially abstract) class and follow the class name and parameters with curly braces containing your implementation. The result is an instance that does extend the given parent class with a one-time implementation, but can be used like an instance from a traditional class definition.

Let's try it out with a "listener" class, a design pattern for sending notifications that is popularly used in Java applications:

```scala
scala> abstract class Listener { def trigger }
defined class Listener

scala> val myListener = new Listener {
     |   def trigger { println(s"Trigger at ${new java.util.Date}") }
     | }
myListener: Listener = $anon$1@59831016

scala> myListener.trigger
Trigger at Fri Jan 24 13:08:51 PDT 2014
```

The myListener value is a class instance, but its class definition is part of the same expression that instantiated itself. To create a new myListener it would be necessary to redefine the anonymous class again.

Here's a more illustrative example of when you may find it useful to create an anonymous class. We have a class, Listening, that can register a Listener and trigger it later as necessary. Instead of instantiating the anonymous class on one line and passing it to the registration function on another, we can combine these into a single step of defining the anonymous class as part of the method invocation. This should look familiar to those with JavaScript experience, especially if you have worked on jQuery-style event handlers:

```scala
scala> abstract class Listener { def trigger }
defined class Listener

scala> class Listening {
     |   var listener: Listener = null
     |   def register(l: Listener) { listener = l }
     |   def sendNotification() { listener.trigger }
     | }
defined class Listening

scala> val notification = new Listening()
notification: Listening = Listening@66596c4c
```

```
scala> notification.register(new Listener {
     |    def trigger { println(s"Trigger at ${new java.util.Date}") }
     | })

scala> notification.sendNotification
Trigger at Fri Jan 24 13:15:32 PDT 2014
```

With anonymous classes, class definitions don't need to be stable or reusable. When a subclass will only be needed once, the anonymous class syntax can help to simplify your code base.

More Field and Method Types

We just covered alternative class types, but there's also alternative fields and methods you can use. Let's have a look at some of the additional choices of fields (values and variables) and methods available in classes.

Overloaded Methods

An *overloaded* method is a strategy for providing choices to callers. A class may have two or more methods with the same name and return value but with different arrangements of input parameters. By overloading a method name with multiple implementations, multiple choices for invoking a method with a specific name are made available.

Here is an example of overloaded methods, where the methods share the same name but take different parameters. In the example the second overloaded method calls the first after modifying its input parameters appropriately:

```
scala> class Printer(msg: String) {
     |    def print(s: String): Unit = println(s"$msg: $s")
     |    def print(l: Seq[String]): Unit = print(l.mkString(", "))
     | }
defined class Printer

scala> new Printer("Today's Report").print("Foggy" :: "Rainy" :: "Hot" :: Nil)
Today's Report: Foggy, Rainy, Hot
```

It is not possible to have two methods with the same name *and* input parameters, but different return values. Doing so will cause a Scala compiler error, because there is no way for only one of the methods to be specifically selected during compilation.

Overloading may be a useful feature, but many Scala developers prefer to use default-value parameters versus overloading. A method that provides default values for its parameters instead of two methods (where one method without a parameter could call the other method, giving the default value) results in less unnecessary code being written.

Apply Methods

Methods named "apply," sometimes referred to as a default method or an injector method, can be invoked without the method name. The apply method is essentially a shortcut, providing functionality that can be triggered using parentheses but without a method name.

Let's try it with a class that multiplies numbers by a predefined amount:

```
scala> class Multiplier(factor: Int) {
     |    def apply(input: Int) = input * factor
     | }
defined class Multiplier

scala> val tripleMe = new Multiplier(3)
tripleMe: Multiplier = Multiplier@339cde4b

scala> val tripled = tripleMe.apply(10)
tripled: Int = 30

scala> val tripled2 = tripleMe(10)
tripled2: Int = 30
```

Our "tripleMe" instance can be used with or without the "apply" name to triple a given number. You might remember this syntax from retrieving an element from a list by its index, which happens to use the List.apply method:

```
scala> val l = List('a', 'b', 'c')
l: List[Char] = List(a, b, c)

scala> val character = l(1)
character: Char = b
```

Here, the List.apply(index) method provides access to an element by index, an operation so common that it makes a good candidate for being the default method of lists.

One potential disadvantage to making a method be the default one is if it makes the code look odd. Accessing the default method should be natural, like the accessor method for lists. Try to only use the apply method where it makes sense, like an accessor method for a list.

Lazy Values

We've looked at some really interesting things you can do with methods in Scala, but now let's see what you can do with fields. The fields (values and variables) we have used so far in classes are all created when the class is first instantiated. *Lazy* values, however, are only created the first time they are instantiated. You can create a lazy value by adding the keyword lazy before the val keyword when defining a value.

In a way, lazy values are a mechanism situated between regular class values and methods. The expression used to initialize a regular class value is only executed once and at instantiation time, whereas the expression that makes up a method is executed every time the method is invoked. However, the expression that initializes a lazy value is executed when the value is invoked, but only the very first time. In this way, a lazy value is a sort of cached function result.

This concept is perhaps better explained with an example. Here's one that shows when a regular value is calculated versus a lazy value:

```
scala> class RandomPoint {
     |   val x = { println("creating x"); util.Random.nextInt }
     |   lazy val y = { println("now y"); util.Random.nextInt }
     | }
defined class RandomPoint

scala> val p = new RandomPoint()
creating x
p: RandomPoint = RandomPoint@6c225adb

scala> println(s"Location is ${p.x}, ${p.y}")
now y
Location is 2019268581, -806862774

scala> println(s"Location is ${p.x}, ${p.y}")
Location is 2019268581, -806862774
```

Our class, RandomPoint, initializes its two fields with expressions that print a message before returning their randomly generated number. The "x" field, a regular value, is initialized when our instance "p" is created. The "y" field, a lazy value, is initialized the first time we access it, but only the first time. In the second printout, both values have been initialized and are stable.

Lazy values are a great way to ensure that time- or performance-sensitive operations can be executed only once in a class's lifetime. They are popularly used to store information such as file-based properties, open database connections, and other immutable data that should only be initialized if it is really necessary. By initializing this data in a lazy val's expression, you can ensure that it will only operate if the lazy val is accessed at least once in the class instance's lifetime.

Packaging

We have covered myriad ways to define classes, methods, and fields. After creating your own classes, at some point you'll want to start organizing them to prevent namespace cluttering.

Packages are Scala's (and Java's) system for code organization. They make it possible to organize Scala code by directory using period-separated paths. Use the package keyword at the top of a Scala source file to declare all classes in that file to be included in the package.

Syntax: Defining the Package for a Scala File

```
package <identifier>
```

Scala follows the Java standard for package naming, where packages start with the reverse domain of your organization or business and then are further classified with additional names on the path. For example, a Scala class that provides utility methods and is developed at Netflix might be packaged in "com.netflix.utilities."

Scala source files should be stored in directories that match their packages. For example, a "DateUtilities" class in the "com.netflix.utilities" package should be stored under *com/netflix/utilities/DateUtilities.scala*. The Scala compiler will store the generated *.class* files (the standard binary format for JVM-executable code) in a directory structure that matches the package.

Let's try this out by creating a source file with a package and compiling it. We'll use the `scalac` command to compile the source file and generate a class file local to the current directory:

```
$ mkdir -p src/com/oreilly

$ cat > src/com/oreilly/Config.scala
package com.oreilly

class Config(val baseUrl: String = "http://localhost")

$ scalac src/com/oreilly/Config.scala

$ ls com/oreilly/Config.class
com/oreilly/Config.class
```

The *src* directory is a nice way to separate the source code from whatever else is in the current directory, but it wasn't actually used by the compiler. It took the relative path to the source file, compiled it, and generated a class file relative to the directory you launched the compiler from.

Accessing Packaged Classes

A packaged class can be accessed by its full period-delimited package path and class name. In the preceding "Config" example, the class named "Config" can be accessed as "com.oreilly.Config."

Let's try this out by accessing the JDK's `Date` class, located in the `java.util` package:

```
scala> val d = new java.util.Date
d: java.util.Date = Wed Jan 22 16:42:04 PDT 2014
```

A more convenient way to access classes in other packages is to *import* them into the current namespace. That way, the class can be accessed without its package prefix. To import a class, use the `import` keyword followed by the full package and name of the class.

Syntax: Importing a Packaged Class

```
import <package>.<class>
```

Let's create a new `Date`, but only after importing the class into the namespace so we can refer to it by name:

```
scala> import java.util.Date
import java.util.Date

scala> val d = new Date
d: java.util.Date = Wed Jan 22 16:49:17 PDT 2014
```

The `Date` class we are instantiating still lives in its `java.util` package, but is now also part of the current namespace.

The `import` command is a statement, because it doesn't return a value. Unlike in Java (which has a similar `import` keyword), an `import` can be placed anywhere in your code where you might use a statement.

Let's exercise the ability to place imports wherever we might use any other statement. In this example I'll add an import for Java's UUID class in the middle of a `println` call:

```
scala> println("Your new UUID is " + {import java.util.UUID; UUID.randomUUID})
Your new UUID is 47ba6844-3df5-403e-92cc-e429e614c9e5
```

You may not always want to add imports in the restricted scope of a function call. However, adding your imports near the code where you are using the imported classes helps to make the intent of the import more clear. It may also prevent name conflicts caused by importing multiple classes of the same name from different packages. By adding the conflicting imports in separate scopes, as opposed to adding them at the top of the file, the classes can be used without conflict.

An alternative to importing the full package and class is to import part of the package, reducing the need to refer to the full package but not quite importing a class. Scala's imports are *accumulative*, so importing a package allows us to remove that package from the full path of a class in the package.

Here's the `Date` class again, accessed by its partial package path:

```
scala> import java.util
import java.util

scala> val d = new util.Date
d: java.util.Date = Wed Jan 2229 06:18:52 PDT 2014
```

Our accumulative import worked; we can now access classes in the java.util package using the util package alone.

Scala also supports importing the entire contents of a package at once with the underscore (_) operator. After doing so, every class in that package will be added to the namespace. You might remember when we used this to import multiple Future helper classes (see "Handling futures synchronously" on page 129) without importing them one at a time.

Let's use the import-all feature to import all of the mutable collections into our current namespace, and then experiment with the ArrayBuffer and Queue collections in that package:

```
scala> import collection.mutable._
import collection.mutable._

scala> val b = new ArrayBuffer[String]
b: scala.collection.mutable.ArrayBuffer[String] = ArrayBuffer()

scala> b += "Hello"
res0: b.type = ArrayBuffer(Hello)

scala> val q = new Queue[Int]
q: scala.collection.mutable.Queue[Int] = Queue()

scala> q.enqueue(3, 4, 5)

scala> val pop = q.dequeue
pop: Int = 3

scala> println(q)
Queue(4, 5)
```

The ArrayBuffer and Queue collections, fully packaged classes, are now accessible by name without explicitly importing both classes from their package. Of course, they aren't the only ones we could have used. Because we imported the entire contents of the collection.mutable package, the full range of mutable collections became available in our namespace.

Speaking of ArrayBuffer, did you notice that we imported everything in the collection.mutable package but the REPL printed its full class name as scala.collection.mutable.ArrayBuffer? Scala does its own automatic imports in every Scala class, importing the entire scala._ and java.lang._ packages. This makes it possible to access the classes and packages in scala and java.lang directly without using the full path. Thus, Scala's class for random-based utilities is at scala.util.Random but can be accessed as util.Random. Likewise, the class we use for sleeping the current thread is officially defined as java.lang.Thread but we can access it directly by its class name.

There is a potential downside to importing every class and subpackage from a package. If the package you're importing has a class name that duplicates one already in your namespace, the class that was already in your namespace will no longer be accessible. As an example, the collection.mutable package has a mutable version of Map with the same name, Map. After importing the entire mutable package, any Map I create would then be mutable. This may be the desired behavior, but in case it isn't, make sure to check the contents of packages that you mass-import.

An alternative to importing a full package is to use an *import group*. With this feature, you can list a group of class names to import intead of a complete package.

Syntax: Using an Import Group

```
import <package>.{<class 1>[, <class 2>...]}
```

With an import group I could have imported the Queue and ArrayBuffer collections directly without importing the mutable Map:

```
scala> import collection.mutable.{Queue,ArrayBuffer}
import collection.mutable.{Queue, ArrayBuffer}

scala> val q = new Queue[Int]
q: scala.collection.mutable.Queue[Int] = Queue()

scala> val b = new ArrayBuffer[String]
b: scala.collection.mutable.ArrayBuffer[String] = ArrayBuffer()

scala> val m = Map(1 -> 2)
m: scala.collection.immutable.Map[Int,Int] = Map(1 -> 2)
```

After importing only the mutable collections that we wanted, we can use the Queue and ArrayBuffer mutable collections while still accessing the Map immutable collection. In this example the import group is just a shortcut that saves us one line of code, but with several classes from the same package they can visibly reduce the size of an "import" section.

There's actually a way to add both the immutable and the mutable Map collections to the current namespace without having a conflict. To do this, use an *import alias* that renames one of the types inside the local namespace. What's renamed is the local namespace reference to the class, not the class itself, so there is no actual change to classes outside your namespace (typically the file you are editing).

Syntax: Using an Import Alias

```
import <package>.{<original name>=><alias>}
```

Let's use an import alias to bring the collection.mutable.Map collection into our namespace, but in a way that won't conflict with our standard immutable Map:

```
scala> import collection.mutable.{Map=>MutMap}
import collection.mutable.{Map=>MutMap}

scala> val m1 = Map(1 -> 2)
m1: scala.collection.immutable.Map[Int,Int] = Map(1 -> 2)

scala> val m2 = MutMap(2 -> 3)
m2: scala.collection.mutable.Map[Int,Int] = Map(2 -> 3)

scala> m2.remove(2); println(m2)
Map()
```

With our aliased collection "MutMap" (short for "mutable," not "mutt"!) we can create both mutable and immutable maps by name, without specifying their packages.

Knowing how to access classes in other packages (whether your own or a library's) is a required skill for Scala developers. Organizing your own classes in packages is more of an acquired art, because there is no real guide on how to best do this. I can only offer a recommendation that your code should be organized for findability and abstraction, so developers can find your code and will know which code they *should* be finding.

Packaging Syntax

We have covered the most popular form of stating the package for one or more classes, the package <identifier> command at the top of the file. Everything that follows in the file will then be considered as a member of that identified package.

A less common form of specifying a package is with the *packaging* syntax, where the package is a block that wraps its classes with curly braces. In this format, only the classes within the package block are designated to be members of that package. This makes it possible for the same file to contain classes that are members of different packages. It also makes it possible to clearly demarcate packages within a nonfile environment such as a REPL.

Syntax: Packaging Classes

```
package <identifier> { <class definitions> }
```

Let's rewrite our "Config" example (from "Packaging" on page 151) using packaging syntax. Because we aren't relying on a file to delimit the end of the package, we can write the entire package in the REPL:

The Scala REPL Requires "Raw" Paste Mode for Packages
Packages are traditionally used to mark files, and thus are unsupported in the standard editing mode in the REPL. The workaround is to enter the "raw" paste mode with :paste -raw and then paste the contents of a Scala file, which will be fully compiled but available from the REPL.

```
scala> :paste -raw
// Entering paste mode (ctrl-D to finish)

package com {
  package oreilly {
    class Config(val baseUrl: String = "http://localhost")
  }
}

// Exiting paste mode, now interpreting.

scala> val url = new com.oreilly.Config().baseUrl
url: String = http://localhost
```

Our new class is now available at `com.oreilly.Config` and clearly packaged.

Would you expect that packaging syntax can be nested? Given that expressions, functions, and class definitions can be nested this shouldn't come as a surprise, but you can indeed nest your packages. A benefit to nesting packages is that the package path is derived from the sum of the nested package names. Thus a multipart package like "com.oreilly" can be built from an outer package of "com" and inner package of "oreilly."

Okay, let's try that out. We'll enter the "raw" paste mode again to enable package support in the REPL:

```
scala> :paste -raw
// Entering paste mode (ctrl-D to finish)

package com {
  package oreilly {
    class Config(val baseUrl: String = "http://localhost")
  }
```

```
    }

// Exiting paste mode, now interpreting.


scala> val url = new com.oreilly.Config().baseUrl
url: String = http://localhost
```

We now have two ways to define packages for our classes: by file and by packaging syntax. Although the former tends to be the most popular among Scala developers (in my opinion), both versions are acceptable and end up with the exact same result after compilation.

Privacy Controls

A corollary to packaging code is using privacy controls to manage its access. While you are organizing your code into separate packages (or subpackages), you'll probably find certain functionality in one package that ought to be hidden from other packages. For example, low-level persistence code could be hidden from your user interface-level code to force your layers to use a middle layer for communication. Or you may want to limit who can extend a subclass so that your parent class can keep track of its implementers.

By default, Scala does not add privacy controls. Any class you write will be instantiable and its fields and methods accessible by any other code. If you have a class with stateless methods, such as utility functions, this may be perfectly acceptable to you.

If you do have some reason to add privacy controls, such as mutable state that should only be handled inside the class, you can add them on a field and method basis in your class.

One privacy control is marking fields and methods as *protected*, which will limit their access to code from the same class or its subclasses. No other code except that class or subclasses will have access. Use the `protected` keyword before a `val`, `var`, or `def` keyword to mark that entity as being protected.

Here's an example of protecting a field from access by outside classes. The field is still accessible by a subclass, however:

```
scala> class User { protected val passwd = util.Random.nextString(10) }
defined class User

scala> class ValidUser extends User { def isValid = ! passwd.isEmpty }
defined class ValidUser

scala> val isValid = new ValidUser().isValid
isValid: Boolean = true
```

To verify that the "passwd" field is only accessible to "User" and its subclasses, try creating a new instance of "User" and access its protected field directly. You should see an error from the compiler alerting you that the "passwd" field is not accessible from outside the class (or subclasses).

When you need a more stringent level of protection, mark fields and methods as *private* to limit their access to only the class in which they are defined. No other code outside the class, and not even subclasses, will have access to that field.

Let's take another stab at this "User" class. If we're really storing a password in plain text in a class, making it accessible to any subclass means that any code anywhere can subclass our class and get access to it. Of course you would need an instance of that subclass to access the field, but this could still be a problem for some applications. In our new version, we'll fix this by making the password private so only our "User" class can get to it. We'll also make it mutable, adding a public setter method with an alerting system so we'll be able to check the logs for password changes. Finally, we'll add a validation system, again without exposing our private (literally!) password to external reads or writes:

```scala
scala> class User(private var password: String) {
     |   def update(p: String) {
     |     println("Modifying the password!")
     |     password = p
     |   }
     |   def validate(p: String) = p == password
     | }
defined class User

scala> val u = new User("1234")
u: User = User@94f6bfb

scala> val isValid = u.validate("4567")
isValid: Boolean = false

scala> u.update("4567")
Modifying the password!

scala> val isValid = u.validate("4567")
isValid: Boolean = true
```

By removing access to the password field, the User class is made (slightly) more secure and more flexible. With the backing data decoupled from the methods, you have the ability to change where you're storing the data, such as a secure identification system, without changing how callers access the class. Protecting mutable state from unplanned changes and providing the ability to decouple it from its current usage are only some of the benefits of encapsulation and privacy control.

Privacy Access Modifiers

The `private` and `protected` keywords provide class-hierarchy restrictions, but there are times when you want more fine-grained access control for your class's members. For example, a class in a persistence package may only want to reveal some of its database-level methods to other classes in the same package to reduce bugs and ensure a single point of access.

You can add this level of control by specifying *access modifiers* in addition to your `private` or `protected` designation. An access modifier specifies that such a designation is only active up to a given point, such as a package, class, or instance, and then is inactive within that point. For example, a method may be private but only so for callers outside its package (i.e., "up to" its package), and then freely accessible within the package. A field may be marked as private not just within the package but from other instances of the same class, and thus can only be accessed from code within the same instance.

An additional benefit of access modifiers is that they enable access controls for classes. There's not much benefit to marking a class as private for everyone (how would you go about instantiating it?), but a class marked as private *for everything outside its package* could be very useful.

To specify an access modifier, write the name of the package or class, or else use `this` inside brackets after the `private` or `protected` keyword. The package or class name will specify that the keyword is only active up to that package or class (and freely available within), but `this` limits access to only the same instance.

Let's try this out with an example of specifying both package-level and instance-level protections. We'll use the packaging syntax to denote the class's package, and thus the "raw" paste mode in the REPL to support the packaging:

```
scala> :paste -raw
// Entering paste mode (ctrl-D to finish)


package com.oreilly {

  private[oreilly] class Config {                              ❶
    val url = "http://localhost"
  }

  class Authentication {
    private[this] val password = "jason" // TODO change me     ❷
    def validate = password.size > 0
  }

  class Test {
    println(s"url = ${new Config().url}")
  }
```

```
    }

    // Exiting paste mode, now interpreting.

    scala> val valid = new com.oreilly.Authentication().validate        ❸
    valid: Boolean = true

    scala> new com.oreilly.Test
    url = http://localhost                                              ❹
    res0: com.oreilly.Test = com.oreilly.Test@4c309d4d

    scala> new com.oreilly.Config
    <console>:8: error: class Config in package oreilly cannot be        ❺
      accessed in package com.oreilly
              new com.oreilly.Config
                  ^
```

❶ Access to the "Config" class is now restricted to the "com.oreilly" package. Only the last part of the package path is required here.

❷ Our secretive "password" field is now off-limits to everyone except code within the same instance of the same class.

❸ Here we are verifying "password" access from the same instance.

❹ The "Test" class was able to successfully instantiate a "Config" class…

❺ … but we were not able to do the same from outside the package.

Scala's access modifiers provide a useful complement to the notion of the strict access policy for private members and inheritance access policy for protected members. In the case of package-level protection, these policies can be overridden based on the proximity of another class. Instance-level protection, on the other hand, adds an additional restriction to these policies based on the actual instances of the classes. Using access modifiers to either loosen or restrict access can be helpful, if used correctly, in improving the encapsulation and security of your applications.

Final and Sealed Classes

The protected and private access controls and their modifiers can limit access to a class or its members overall or based on location. However, they lack the abililty to restrict creating subclasses. Well, unless you mark a class as being private outside of its package, but then it can neither be subclassed nor used in that circumstance.

Final class members can never be overridden in subclasses. Marking a value, variable, or method with the final keyword ensures that the implementation is the one that all subclasses will use. Entire classes can be marked as final as well, preventing any possible subclasses of that class.

If final classes are too restrictive for your needs, consider *sealed* classes instead. Sealed classes restrict the subclasses of a class to being located in the same file as the parent class. By sealing a class, you can write code that makes safe assumptions about its hierarchy. Classes are sealed by prefixing the class definition and `class` keyword with the `sealed` keyword.

One popular sealed class is `Option`, one of the monadic collections we covered in "Monadic Collections" on page 117. The `Option` class is both abstract and sealed, and implemented with the (proper!) assumption that it will only ever have two subclasses, `Some` and `None`. By ensuring that no other subclasses will ever exist, `Option` can refer to these implementations explicitly in its code. An unsealed version of this collection would be more difficult to implement, because anyone could add an extra subclass that may not follow the assumed behavior of `Some` and `None`.

As with the `Option` implementation, sealed classes are a useful way to implement an abstract parent class that "knows" and refers to specific subclasses. By restricting subclasses outside the same file, assumptions can be made about a class hierarchy that would otherwise have severe repercussions (read: bugs).

Summary

Classes are often a starting point for learning a programming language. Because they are built on a foundation of values and functions, however, it seemed more appropriate to cover those features first. Now that you have a solid understanding of classes, it is safe to point out that values and functions (now "methods") don't really exist outside of classes. Classes are the core building blocks of Scala applications, and values and methods make up their bodies.

They are not, however, the exclusive containers of values and methods. In the next chapter we'll explore how objects, the singletons of the Scala world, can be used alone or alongside classes. We'll also see how traits can contain their own values and functions before being combined and mixed into classes.

Exercises

1. We're working on a gaming site, and need to track popular consoles like the Xbox Two and Playstation 5 (I'm planning for the future here).

    a. Create a console class that can track the make, model, debut date, WiFi type, physical media formats supported, and maximum video resolution. Override the default `toString` method to print a reasonably sized description of the instance (< 120 chars).

- The debut date (or launch date) should be an instance of `java.util.Date`.
- Keep the WiFi type (b/g, b/g/n, etc.) field optional, in case some consoles don't have WiFi.
- The physical media formats should be a list. Is a `String` the best bet here, or an `Int` that matches a constant value?
- The maximum video resolution should be in a format that would make it possible to sort consoles in order of greatest number of pixels.

b. Test your new console class by writing a new class that creates four instances of this console class. All of the instances should have reasonably accurate values.

c. Now it's time for games. Create a game class that includes the name, maker, and a list of consoles it supports, plus an "isSupported" method that returns true if a given console is supported.

d. Test out this game class by generating a list of games, each containing one or more instances of consoles. Can you convert this list to a lookup table for consoles with a list of supported games? How about a function that prints a list of the games, sorted first by maker and then by game name?

2. Create a linked list, object-oriented-style.

a. Create a container class that has an instance of itself plus an instance of a parameterized type. The constructor should take a variable number of the instances (e.g., strings or ints or any other parameterized type), which can be implemented with *vararg parameters* (see "Vararg Parameters" on page 54). Implement a "foreach" method that users can call to iterate over the list, invoking their function for every element.

- How will you determine the end of the list?
- C-style lists often use a `null` value to denote the end of the list. Is that the best approach here?
- Do you have a good use for the `apply()` method here?

b. I'm sure your linked list works great, but let's try refactoring it with a more interesting approach. Make your container class abstract with two subclasses: one representing a node with a valid item and one representing a node without a valid item, signifying the last item in the list.

- Will you ever need more than one instance of the second subclass?
- Are there any helper methods that should be private?

- How about abstract methods that the subclasses will need to implement?

- If you implemented the `apply()` method, should each subclass have its own implementation?

c. Add the standard `head`, `tail`, `filter`, `size`, and `map` collection methods for your linked list. Can you implement any of these using lazy values? Which of these should be implemented in the parent class versus being implemented in its subclasses?

d. Implement the `head`, `tail`, `filter`, `size`, and `map` collection methods using recursion instead of iteration. Can you ensure these all use tail recursion (see "Recursive Functions" on page 50) to prevent stack overflow errors for massive collections?

3. For a change of pace, let's create a directory listing class. The constructor fields should be the full path to the directory and a predicate function that takes a `String` (the filename) and returns true if the file should be included. The method "list" should then list the files in the directory.

To implement this, create an instance of `java.io.File` and use its `listFiles(filter: FilenameFilter)` to list files that match the given filter. You'll find Javadocs for this method and for the `java.io.FilenameFilter` class, but you will need to figure out how this would be called from Scala. You should pass in the `FilenameFilter` argument as an anonymous class.

- Is there any part of this class that would work well as a lazy value?

- Would it make sense to store the anonymous subclass of `java.io.FilenameFilter` as a lazy val?

- How about the filtered directory listing?

4. The JVM library includes a working MIDI sound synthesizer. Here's an example of playing a short set of notes:

```scala
scala> val synth = javax.sound.midi.MidiSystem.getSynthesizer
synth: javax.sound.midi.Synthesizer = com.sun.media.sound
  .SoftSynthesizer@283a8ad6

scala> synth.open()

scala> val channel = synth.getChannels.head
channel: javax.sound.midi.MidiChannel = com.sun.media.sound
  .SoftChannelProxy@606d6d2c

scala> channel.noteOn(50, 80); Thread.sleep(250); channel.noteOff(30)

scala> synth.close()
```

Create a simpler interface to this by writing a class that plays a series of notes. The class's constructor should take the volume (set to 80 in the example) but always use the same duration (250 milliseconds in the example). Its "play" method should take a list of the notes, for example Seq(30, 35, 40, 45, 50, 55, 60, 65, 70), and play them in the synthesizer.

- Assume the getSynthesizer method call is expensive. How can you prevent unnecessarily calling it in case the "play" method is never called?

- Make sure to hide fields that callers don't need to know about.

- Can you support a Range as input, e.g., play(30 to 70 by 5)?

- Can you support multiple ranges, for example a series of notes that rise, fall, and then rise again?

- Assume we only ever need one instance, ever, with the volume set to 95. Can you use access controls to ensure that there will never be more than one instance of this class?

CHAPTER 9

Objects, Case Classes, and Traits

In the previous chapter we covered classes, a core component of object-oriented Scala. As you'll recall, classes are defined once but can be instantiated an unlimited number of times. In this chapter we will discover new components that may be used to complement and embellish classes, or replace some classes entirely, depending on your object-oriented design preferences. Many developers choose the latter, using them in place of "regular" classes when they can. Therefore I highly recommend taking the time to learn about each component, not only because you also may end up preferring them over classes but also because they all have something new to offer most developers.

The three new components—objects, case classes, and traits—are sufficiently discrete that there is little point in writing a common introduction for them. Therefore, in this chapter we will have separate introductions for each component, starting with the section on objects.

Objects

An *object* is a type of class that can have no more than one instance, known in object-oriented design as a *singleton*. Instead of creating an instance with a new keyword, just access the object directly by name. An object gets automatically instantiated the first time it is accessed in a running JVM, which also means that until it is accessed the first time it won't get instantiated.

Java and other languages have the ability to designate certain fields and methods of a class as being "static" or "global," meaning that they are not tied to an instance's data and so can be accessed without instantiating a class. Objects provide similar functionality but decouple them from instantiable classes. This separation helps to clarify the difference between global and instance-based fields and methods and provides a safer and more understandable design. With this model there is less chance of accidentally invoking a global method on a class, or of mistakenly storing mutable data in a globally accessible field.

Objects and classes are not completely decoupled. An object can extend another class, making its fields and methods available in a global instance. The reverse is not true, however, because an object cannot itself be extended. This should make sense, because there is no reason to subclass one. If only one of the objects or its subclasses could ever be instantiated, why wouldn't you just add the features you would have wanted into the object itself?

Use the object keyword, in place of class, to define an object. Objects do not take any parameters (they are automatically instantiated), but you can define the same fields, methods, and internal classes as you can with regular classes.

Syntax: Defining an Object

```
object <identifier> [extends <identifier>] [{ fields, methods, and classes }]
```

Let's design an object that will demonstrate how objects are automatically instantiated:

```
scala> object Hello { println("in Hello"); def hi = "hi" }
defined object Hello

scala> println(Hello.hi)
in Hello
hi

scala> println(Hello.hi)
hi
```

The println at the top level of the object is invoked at instantiation/initialization, which only occurs when it is accessed for the first time. Repeating the call to the object's "hi" method reused the same global instance so there was no additional initialization.

The standard class method is one that reads from or writes to the fields of its instance, providing complementary access points and business logic for the data. Likewise, the kinds of methods best suited for objects are pure functions and the functions that work with external I/O (Input/Output). *Pure* functions are ones that return results calculated exclusively from their inputs, have no side effects, and are referentially transparent (indistinguishable if replaced by the result of the function). I/O functions are those that work with external data, such as with files, databases, and external services. Neither of these function types are well suited to being class methods because they have little to do with a class's fields.

As an example, we'll create an object that provides pure functions as utilities, one of my favorite uses for objects:

```
scala> object HtmlUtils {
     |   def removeMarkup(input: String) = {
     |     input
```

```
|        .replaceAll("""</?\w[^>]*>""","")
|        .replaceAll("<.*>","")
|   }
| }
defined object HtmlUtils

scala> val html = "<html><body><h1>Introduction</h1></body></html>"
html: String = <html><body><h1>Introduction</h1></body></html>

scala> val text = HtmlUtils.removeMarkup(html)
text: String = Introduction
```

Our example utility method, removeMarkup, is a pure function that returns a result based only on the input data. As a member of the object HtmlUtils it is now globally accessible by any other code, available without explicitly initializing a class.

A Referential Transparency Test

As a test of referential transparency, we could replace the function with one that just returns the result, "Introduction," and there would have been no other effect on our system. A class method that reads from one of its fields or an object method that writes to the console could not make the same claim, because they are either dependent on their environment or make a change to the environment. The point is that, when possible, consider using pure functions to reduce dependency problems and make your code self-sufficient.

We have covered the basic use of objects as global (or static, if you prefer) classes, but you can do much more with them than just storing your functions. You can use them as companions to classes of the same name, granting them special permissions, or have them act as entry points for command-line applications. We'll look at more uses of objects in the next several sections.

Apply Methods and Companion Objects

We have covered the *apply* method for classes (see "Apply Methods" on page 150), which makes it possible to invoke an instance. The same feature works for objects, making it possible to invoke an object by name. By defining one or more of these methods, your object can be invoked by name, much like List(1, 2, 3).

In fact, this is how lists are instantiated in Scala. The List object has an apply() method that takes arguments and returns a new collection from them. You have also experienced this feature when creating monadic collections (see "Monadic Collections" on page 117). The apply() method on the Option object takes a single value and returns Some[A] containing the value if it is nonnull or else None. The Future object uses apply() to take your function parameter and invoke it in a background thread. This is known as the *factory* pattern in object-oriented programming, and is a popular use of the `apply()` method in objects.

Specifically, the factory pattern is a popular way to generate new instances of a class from its companion object. A *companion object* is an object that shares the same name as a class and is defined together in the same file as the class. Having a companion object for a class is a common pattern in Scala, but there is also a feature from which they can benefit. Companion objects and classes are considered a single unit in terms of access controls, so they can access each other's private and protected fields and methods.

Let's try out the `apply()` factory pattern and the companion object pattern in the same example. We will use the REPL's `:paste` mode to simulate a class and object defined together in the same file, because otherwise the REPL would assume they are separate:

```
scala> :paste
// Entering paste mode (ctrl-D to finish)

class Multiplier(val x: Int) { def product(y: Int) = x * y }

object Multiplier { def apply(x: Int) = new Multiplier(x) }

// Exiting paste mode, now interpreting.

defined class Multiplier
defined object Multiplier

scala> val tripler = Multiplier(3)
tripler: Multiplier = Multiplier@5af28b27

scala> val result = tripler.product(13)
result: Int = 39
```

The example class, `Multiplier`, takes an amount and provides a method, `product`, that multiplies it by another amount. Our companion object of the same name has an "apply" method with the exact same parameters as the instance, which makes it clear to users that it serves as a factory method for the class.

However, we haven't yet seen the benefit of a companion object, namely the special access controls that it shares with a companion class. Let's try this out in a new example where the class accesses private members of its companion object:

```
scala> :paste
// Entering paste mode (ctrl-D to finish)

object DBConnection {
  private val db_url = "jdbc://localhost"
  private val db_user = "franken"
  private val db_pass = "berry"

  def apply() = new DBConnection
```

```
}
class DBConnection {
  private val props = Map(
    "url" -> DBConnection.db_url,
    "user" -> DBConnection.db_user,
    "pass" -> DBConnection.db_pass
  )
  println(s"Created new connection for " + props("url"))
}

// Exiting paste mode, now interpreting.

defined object DBConnection
defined class DBConnection

scala> val conn = DBConnection()
Created new connection for jdbc://localhost
conn: DBConnection = DBConnection@4d27d9d
```

Our new DBConnection object stores the database connection data in private constants, while the class of the same name can read them when creating a connection. The constants are global, because the settings are constant across the application, and safe from being read by any other part of the system.

Another benefit to using the REPL's paste mode is that both the object and the class are compiled together at the same time. Besides the special companion access to private fields, we could not have entered them in the REPL without paste mode because the class and object refer to each other. A class referring to an undefined object, being compiled without the object, would have led to a compilation error.

In the exercises for previous chapters you may have been writing *.scala* files executed directly by the scala command. Defining classes and objects together in a *.scala* file will work, because they are part of the same namespace. And you can add commands to access the classes and objects right inside the *.scala* file, executed when you run it with scala.

This approach is suitable for testing, but doesn't make it possible to reuse your code. The scala command will execute the contents of your file as if they were entered in a REPL, but you don't end up with compiled classes. In order to write reusable, compiled code, you'll need to compile your classes and objects with the scalac command and then execute them from your own application. In the next section we'll learn how to write command-line applications with Scala so you can start reusing your classes and objects.

Command-Line Applications with Objects

Most languages have the ability to create command-line applications, ones that can be executed from a shell. At the most basic level they read input arguments, perhaps read from the input stream, and then write to the output stream. More complex applications may work with persistent data such as files and databases, access other computers over a network, or launch new applications.

Scala also supports this feature, using a "main" method in objects as the entry point for the application. To create a command-line application in Scala, add a "main" method that takes an array of strings as input arguments. When you have compiled your code, execute it by running the `scala` command with the name of the object.

Here's an example of a short command-line application that prints out the current date. Included are steps to create the file, compile it, and execute it as an application, all inside a shell. The entry point is a "main" method defined in an object:

```
$ cat > Date.scala
object Date {
  def main(args: Array[String]) {
    println(new java.util.Date)
  }
}

$ scalac Date.scala

$ scala Date
Mon Sep 01 22:03:09 PDT 2014
```

After compiling our "Date" object into *.class* files (the binary format for JVM classes), we are able to execute it as an application. This example demonstrated the basics of creating, compiling, and executing a command-line application, although it didn't really demonstrate the use of the input arguments.

Here is a new example that emulates the Unix command *cat*, which prints the contents of a file to the console. It takes one or more filenames (or paths) and prints each one to the console:

```
$ cat > Cat.scala
object Cat {
  def main(args: Array[String]) {
    for (arg <- args) {
      println( io.Source.fromFile(arg).mkString )
    }
  }
}

$ scalac Cat.scala

$ scala Cat Date.scala
```

```
object Date {
  def main(args: Array[String]) {
    println(new java.util.Date)
  }
}
```

This time we're making use of the input arguments. The `fromFile` method in the Scala library's `io.Source` object (we can call it by its correct name now) is used to read each file, and the collection method `mkString` is used to convert the lines back into a single `String` for printing.

In a way, the best command-line applications are like pure functions: they read input, process it, and write output. Like the operations in Scala's collections they are only good for a single task, but when chained together they create a bounty of new opportunities and possibilities. Command-line applications written in Scala may not replace native tools and shell scripts, because their slower startup time (a known problem in the JVM) and greater memory requirements may make them less desirable for all environments. They do make writing command-line tools more fun, however, and are a great way to learn the language. I recommend taking the time to rewrite some of your favorite (and shorter) shell scripts in Scala. It's a great way to continue learning and practicing with the language, and you may find your Scala applications to be shorter and more stable than those written in other languages.

To summarize this section, objects are not only a global alternative to instance-based classes and a way to create command-line applications. When paired with classes as companion objects they create a new synergy for creating cleaner, decoupled, and more readable applications.

Now that you have some experience using objects with classes, it's time to learn how to automate their interaction using case classes.

Case Classes

A *case class* is an instantiable class that includes several automatically generated methods. It also includes an automatically generated companion object with its own automatically generated methods. All of these methods in the class and in the companion object are based on the class's parameter list, with the parameters being used to formulate methods like an `equals` implementation that iteratively compares every field and a `to String` method that cleanly prints out the class name and all of its field values.

Case classes work great for data transfer objects, the kind of classes that are mainly used for storing data, given the data-based methods that are generated. They don't work well in hierarchical class structures, however, because inherited fields aren't used to build its utility methods. And extending a case class with a regular class could lead to invalid results from the generated methods, which can't take into account fields added by subclasses. However, if you want a class with a definitive set of fields, and these automatically generated methods are useful, then a case class may be right for you.

To create a case class, just add the keyword `case` before your class definition.

Syntax: Defining a Case Class

```
case class <identifier> ([var] <identifier>: <type>[, ... ])
                        [extends <identifier>(<input parameters>)]
                        [{ fields and methods }]
```

The val Keyword Is Assumed for Case Class Parameters
By default, case classes convert parameters to value fields so it isn't necessary to prefix them with the `val` keyword. You can still use the `var` keyword if you need a variable field.

Table 9-1 displays the class and object methods that get automatically generated for case classes.

Table 9-1. Generated case class methods

Name	Location	Description
apply	Object	A factory method for instantiating the case class.
copy	Class	Returns a copy of the instance with any requested changes. The parameters are the class's fields with the default values set to the current field values.
equals	Class	Returns true if every field in another instance match every field in this instance. Also invocable by the operator ==.
hashCode	Class	Returns a hash code of the instance's fields, useful for hash-based collections.
toString	Class	Renders the class's name and fields to a `String`.
unapply	Object	Extracts the instance into a tuple of its fields, making it possible to use case class instances for pattern matching.

The methods generated by the Scala compiler for case classes aren't *special* in any way, other than that they are automatically generated for you. You could skip using case classes and add the methods and companion object yourself. The benefit that case classes bring is convenience, because writing all of these methods correctly for every data-based class would require a lot of work and maintenance. They also add a certain level of consistency, because all case classes carry the same features.

Now that we have exhaustively reviewed what case classes can do let's see them in action. In this example we'll create a case class and see how many of its automatically generated methods we can hit:

```
scala> case class Character(name: String, isThief: Boolean)
defined class Character
```

```
scala> val h = Character("Hadrian", true)                    ❶
h: Character = Character(Hadrian,true)                        ❷

scala> val r = h.copy(name = "Royce")                        ❸
r: Character = Character(Royce,true)

scala> h == r                                                ❹
res0: Boolean = false

scala> h match {
     |   case Character(x, true) => s"$x is a thief"         ❺
     |   case Character(x, false) => s"$x is not a thief"
     | }
res1: String = Hadrian is a thief
```

❶ Here's our companion object's factory method, `Character.apply()`.

❷ The generated `toString` method, printed here by the REPL, is a clean and simple representation of the fields in our instance.

❸ Our second instance shares the same value for the second field, so we only need to specify a new value for the first field in the `copy` method.

❹ If both instances are nonnull, the `==` operator triggers an instance's `equals` method, acting as a useful shortcut to the field comparison–based method generated for us.

❺ The companion object's `unapply` method allows us to decompose the instance into its parts, binding the first field (see "Matching with Wildcard Patterns" on page 34) and using a literal value to match the second field.

All of the generated methods we used in the example depended on the case class having two fields, `name` and `isThief`, based on the case class parameters. If our case class had extended another class with its own fields, but we hadn't added the fields as case class parameters, the generated methods wouldn't have been able to make use of them. This is an important caveat to know about before using case classes.

If your case class doesn't need to take into account the fields of a parent class, you'll find case classes to be wildly useful throughout your code. They can reduce the need to write your own boilerplate code, make debugging and logging easier with their helpful to String methods, and overall make object-oriented programming more enjoyable.

I find myself using case classes over classes for data storage, and objects over classes for writing most functions. Well, objects *and* traits for writing functions, because traits provide convenience for reusing functions in the same way that case classes provide convenience for managing your data. We'll cover traits, the final type of class to introduce in this chapter, in the next section.

Traits

A *trait* is a kind of class that enables multiple inheritance. Classes, case classes, objects, and (yes) traits can all extend no more than one class but can extend multiple traits at the same time. Unlike the other types, however, traits cannot be instantiated.

Traits look about the same as any other type of class. However, like objects, they cannot take class parameters. Unlike objects, however, traits can take type parameters, which can help to make them extremely reusable.

To define a trait, use the `trait` keyword in place of where you would normally use the `class` keyword.

Syntax: Defining a Trait

```
trait <identifier> [extends <identifier>] [{ fields, methods, and classes }]
```

Remember the `HtmlUtils` object (from "Objects" on page 167) we created as an example? Let's implement that as a trait instead:

```
scala> trait HtmlUtils {
     |    def removeMarkup(input: String) = {
     |      input
     |        .replaceAll("""</?\w[^>]*>""","")
     |        .replaceAll("<.*>","")
     |    }
     | }
defined trait HtmlUtils

scala> class Page(val s: String) extends HtmlUtils {
     |    def asPlainText = removeMarkup(s)
     | }
defined class Page

scala> new Page("<html><body><h1>Introduction</h1></body></html>").asPlainText
res2: String = Introduction
```

Our `Page` class can now use the `removeMarkup` method directly without specifying an object name.

This works pretty well, but a class version of `HtmlUtils` could have done the same job. Let's make it more interesting by adding a second trait. This time we'll use a new keyword, `with`, which is required for extending the second and later traits:

Traits Come After the Parent Class
If you are extending a class and one or more traits, you will need to extend the class *before* you can add the traits using the `with` keyword. A parent class, if specified, must always come before any parent traits.

```
scala> trait SafeStringUtils {
     |
     |    // Returns a trimmed version of the string wrapped in an Option,
     |    // or None if the trimmed string is empty.
     |    def trimToNone(s: String): Option[String] = {
     |      Option(s) map(_.trim) filterNot(_.isEmpty)
     |    }
     | }
defined trait SafeStringUtils

scala> class Page(val s: String) extends SafeStringUtils with HtmlUtils {
     |    def asPlainText: String = {
     |      trimToNone(s) map removeMarkup getOrElse "n/a"
     |    }
     | }
defined class Page

scala> new Page("<html><body><h1>Introduction</h1></body></html>").asPlainText
res3: String = Introduction

scala> new Page("  ").asPlainText
res4: String = n/a

scala> new Page(null).asPlainText
res5: String = n/a
```

Our new, more robust Page class now extends two traits and can handle null or empty strings by returning the message n/a.

If you're familiar with the JVM you may be wondering how Scala can support multiple inheritance with traits. After all, JVM classes can only extend one parent class. The answer is that although the language supports multiple inheritance in theory, the compiler actually creates copies of each trait to form a tall, single-column hierarchy of the class and traits. So, a class extending class A and traits B and C is actually extending one class, which extends another class, which extends another class, when compiled to the .class binary file.

This process of taking a horizontal list of a class and traits being extended, and reforming them into a vertical chain of one class extending another, is known as *linearization*. It is a kind of coping mechanism for supporting multiple inheritance in an execution environment that only supports single inheritance. The fact that the JVM only supports single inheritance ensures that all class hierarchies are nondeterministic and prevents the possibility of confusing two traits that have competing members.

What Happens If You Have Traits with Competing Members?
A class importing two traits that have the same field or method, but lack an override keyword, will fail to compile. The compilation error is the same as if you were extending a class and providing your own version of a method but failed to add an override keyword. In the case of the traits, adding a common base class and then overriding the field or method with the override keyword will ensure the traits can be extended by the same class.

The most important point to understand about linearization is in what *order* the Scala compiler arranges the traits and optional class to extend one another. The multiple inheritance ordering, from the lowest subclass up to the highest base class, is *right to left*.

Thus, a class defined as class D extends A with B with C, where A is a class and B and C are traits, would be reimplemented by the compiler as class D extends C extends B extends A. The rightmost trait is the immediate parent of the class being defined, and either the class or the first trait becomes the last parent class.

This is a lot to remember, so let's write a quick test to verify this ordering:

```
scala> trait Base { override def toString = "Base" }
defined trait Base

scala> class A extends Base { override def toString = "A->" + super.toString }
defined class A

scala> trait B extends Base { override def toString = "B->" + super.toString }
defined trait B

scala> trait C extends Base { override def toString = "C->" + super.toString }
defined trait C

scala> class D extends A with B with C { override def toString = "D->" +
     super.toString }
defined class D

scala> new D()
res50: D = D->C->B->A->Base
```

The toString method overridden in D prints the class name and then appends the output of its parent class's implementation. Fortunately all of its parent classes also override this method, so we can see the exact ordering of methods called. First the toString in D was invoked, followed by the one in trait C, trait B, class A, and finally the common base class Base.

The process of linearization may seem odd, but it's a useful compromise between the theory of a language supporting multiple inheritance versus the practice of an environment that doesn't. It also provides a solid method for determining invocation, because the constructed hierarchy ensures that method handling is decided at compile time and never at runtime.

Another benefit of linearization is that you can write traits to override the behavior of a shared parent class. Here's an example of a solid base class plus traits that add extra functionality when combined with a subclass. The example is rather lengthy so we'll cover it in two parts. First, here's the parent class and two traits that extend it:

```scala
scala> class RGBColor(val color: Int) { def hex = f"$color%06X" }
defined class RGBColor

scala> val green = new RGBColor(255 << 8).hex
green: String = 00FF00

scala> trait Opaque extends RGBColor { override def hex = s"${super.hex}FF" }
defined trait Opaque

scala> trait Sheer extends RGBColor { override def hex = s"${super.hex}33" }
defined trait Sheer
```

The two traits, `Opaque` and `Sheer`, extend the `RGBColor` class and add an opacity level to the red-green-blue color of its parent. The extra byte is often known as an alpha channel in computer graphics, so the traits are convering an RGB color value to an RGBA (a for alpha) color value, in hexadecimal format.

Now let's put these new traits to use. We'll extend both the parent class *and* one of the traits that extends the parent class. If we were just to extend the trait, there wouldn't be any way to pass a class parameter to `RGBColor`. Therefore, we'll extend both the parent class and functionality-adding trait:

```scala
scala> class Paint(color: Int) extends RGBColor(color) with Opaque
defined class Paint

scala> class Overlay(color: Int) extends RGBColor(color) with Sheer
defined class Overlay

scala> val red = new Paint(128 << 16).hex
red: String = 800000FF

scala> val blue = new Overlay(192).hex
blue: String = 0000C033
```

Because trait linearization is ordered from right to left, the hierarchy of "Paint" is "Paint" → "Opaque" → "RGBColor." The class parameter added to the `Paint` class is used to initialize the `RGBColor` class, while the `Opaque` trait between `Paint` and `RGBColor` overrides the hex method to add extra functionality.

In other words, our `Paint` class will output an opaque color value and our `Overlay` will output a sheer (i.e., translucent) color value. We were able to take advantage of trait linearization to insert extra functionality.

At this point you should know how to define traits and extend them with classes. Understanding where and when to use them, however, may take some time and experience. Traits look similar to abstract classes, and like an implementation-based version of Java's interfaces, but it's important to understand how linearization shapes the hierarchy of any class that extends them.

If you're still uncertain about using traits, the features we'll cover in the next two sections may bring you around. We'll look at a method to restrict traits to only be used with certain classes, in case you want to depend on the fields and methods of a class without directly extending it. We'll also see how traits can be used not only in class definitions but in class instantiations as well, providing built-in dependency injection.

Self Types

A *self type* is a trait annotation that asserts that the trait must be mixed in with a specific type, or its subtype, when it is added to a class. A trait with a self type cannot be added to a class that does not extend the specified type. In a way, it is a guarantee that the trait will always be extending that type, while not actually directly extending it.

A popular use of self types is to add functionality with traits to classes that require input parameters. A trait cannot easily extend a class that takes input parameters, because the trait itself cannot take input parameters. However, it can declare itself to be a subtype of that parent class with a self type and then add its functionality.

A self type is added immediately following the opening brace of the trait definition, and includes an identifier, the requested type, and an arrow (=>). A trait with a self type can access fields of that type as if it explicitly extended that type.

Syntax: Defining a Self Type

```
trait ..... { <identifier>: <type> => .... }
```

The standard identifier used in self types is "self," although any other identifier may be used. That is, except for a keyword like this. The benefit of using the common identifier "self" is that it can help to make your code more readable to other Scala developers.

Here is an example of a trait using a self type to ensure that it will always be a subtype of the specified type when mixed into a class:

```
scala> class A { def hi = "hi" }
defined class A

scala> trait B { self: A =>                                    ❶
     |    override def toString = "B: " + hi
     | }
defined trait B

scala> class C extends B
<console>:9: error: illegal inheritance;                       ❷
```

```
self-type C does not conform to B's selftype B with A
       class C extends B
                      ^
```

```
scala> class C extends A with B                                          ❸
defined class C
```

```
scala> new C()
res1: C = B: hi                                                          ❹
```

❶   Our trait B has a self type, adding the requirement that the trait can only ever be mixed into a subtype of the specified type, the A class.

❷   ... but just to prove it, let's try defining a class with trait B but without the requested class. No luck.

❸   This time, trait B is directly extending its requested type, A, so its self type requirement has been met.

❹   When our C class is instantiated, B.toString is invoked, which then invokes A.hi. The B trait is indeed used as a subtype of A here and can invoke one of its methods.

This example demonstrated the restrictions that self types add to traits. However, it didn't really distinguish self types as an important feature, because the trait B could have just extended A directly.

Let's try an example that demonstrates the benefit of self types. We'll define a class that requires parameters and then create a trait that should only be used to extend the class:

```
scala> class TestSuite(suiteName: String) { def start() {} }           ❶
defined class TestSuite

scala> trait RandomSeeded { self: TestSuite =>                          ❷
     |    def randomStart() {
     |      util.Random.setSeed(System.currentTimeMillis)
     |      self.start()
     |    }
     | }
defined trait RandomSeeded

scala> class IdSpec extends TestSuite("ID Tests") with RandomSeeded {   ❸
     |    def testId() { println(util.Random.nextInt != 1) }
     |    override def start() { testId() }
     |
     |    println("Starting...")
     |    randomStart()
     | }
defined class IdSpec
```

❶   Here is the base class, TestSuite, which takes an input parameter.

❷   Our trait needs to invoke `TestSuite.start()` but cannot extend `TestSuite` because it would require hardcoding the input parameter. By using a self type, the trait can expect to be a subtype of `TestSuite` without explicitly being declared as one.

❸   The test class `IdSpec` defines our self-typed trait as a subclass, allowing its `ran domStart()` to be invocable.

With self types, a trait can take advantage of extending a class without specifying its input parameters. It is also a safe way to add restrictions and/or requirements to your traits, ensuring they are only used in a specific context.

And now that we have studied a feature that can help to ensure safer and more stable type definitions, lets move on to something crazy: adding type definitions when you *instantiate* a class.

Instantiation with Traits

In this chapter we have used traits by having classes extend them, using the `extends` or `with` keyword in the class definition. The class that extends the trait will pick up the fields and methods of that trait, whether they are implemented by the trait or inherited from its own subtypes.

An alternate method for using traits is to add them to a class *when the class is instantiated*. A class defined without a dependency on, or even knowledge of, a given trait can take advantage of that trait's functionality. The only catch is that traits added at a class's instantiation extend the class, not the other way around. The left-to-right order of trait linearization includes the instantiated class in its ordering, so all of the traits extend the class and not the other way around.

You can add one or more traits to a class using the `with` keyword. The `extends` keyword cannot be used here, which is appropriate; your class is not actually *extending* the traits but instead *being* extended by them.

Let's verify that a class instantiated with a trait becomes the base class of that trait, by using the self types we learned about in the previous section. Here is an example of a class extended by a trait with a self type of that class, ensuring that the trait will extend the class:

```
scala> class A
defined class A

scala> trait B { self: A => }
defined trait B

scala> val a = new A with B
a: A with B = $anon$1@26a7b76d
```

Our new instance, a, is given the class name $anon$1, a numerically based shortened version of the word "anonymous." The instance's class is indeed anonymous, because it contains a combination of a class and trait that are not formally included in any named class definition. More to the point, we created an instance where trait B extended trait A.

The real value in instantiating with traits is in adding new functionality or configurations to existing classes. This feature is commonly known as *dependency injection*, because the actual functionality the parent class is dependent on isn't added until after the class definition, so the feature is "injected" into the class when instantiated. This also means that two instances of the class can operate under completely different configurations, because they may have had different configurable traits added during their instantiations.

Java developers may be familiar with the Spring (*http://spring.io/*) or Google Guice (*http://bit.ly/ls-googleguice*), which perform a similar function via custom Java annotations and initialization modules. Scala's traits, however, do not require any specific annotations or special packages to make dependency injection work. Just initialize a given class with another trait and you have a dependency-injected class that's ready to go.

Let's experiment with dependency injection by taking a data-oriented class common in most applications, User, and altering its output in new and mysterious ways:

```scala
scala> class User(val name: String) {
     |    def suffix = ""
     |    override def toString = s"$name$suffix"
     | }
defined class User

scala> trait Attorney { self: User => override def suffix = ", esq." }
defined trait Attorney

scala> trait Wizard { self: User => override def suffix = ", Wizard" }
defined trait Wizard

scala> trait Reverser { override def toString = super.toString.reverse }
defined trait Reverser

scala> val h = new User("Harry P") with Wizard
h: User with Wizard = Harry P, Wizard

scala> val g = new User("Ginny W") with Attorney
g: User with Attorney = Ginny W, esq.

scala> val l = new User("Luna L") with Wizard with Reverser
l: User with Wizard with Reverser = draziW ,L anuL
```

Our three new users, who are completely nonfictitious and whose resemblance to fictitious characters is purely coincidental, have acquired either magical new titles or new ways of printing their name. The suffixes of "Wizard" and "esq" were hardcoded in traits, but added to *separate* user instances at instantiation time.

Adding traits to classes at instantiation time is a kind of replacement shortcut for defining classes to perform the same job. In our example we could have defined three new individual classes that combined the class and traits and used them instead. However, we gained flexibility and simplicity with these instantiation traits, and avoided writing unnecessary code. By adding traits at instantiation time an infinite number of functional combinations becomes available.

Importing Instance Members

In "Accessing Packaged Classes" on page 152 we covered the use of the `import` keyword to add classes from external packages so they could be accessed without their package prefix. To wrap up this chapter on additional object-oriented features (notably objects, case classes, and traits), we'll look at an additional way to use namespace importing.

The `import` keyword can also be used to import *members* of classes and objects into the current namespace. This makes it possible to access them directly without specifying their enclosing instance (for classes) or name (for objects).

The syntax for importing class and object members is the same as importing packaged classes. You can import a single member of a class instance by name, or the entire set of fields and methods with the underscore character. Importing fields and methods does not override privacy controls, so only those that would be normally accessible can be imported.

Here is an example of a case class's members being imported for better accessibility:

```
scala> case class Receipt(id: Int, amount: Double, who: String, title: String)
defined class Receipt

scala> {
     |     val latteReceipt = Receipt(123, 4.12, "fred", "Medium Latte")
     |     import latteReceipt._
     |     println(s"Sold a $title for $amount to $who")
     | }
Sold a Medium Latte for 4.12 to fred
```

By importing the fields from a value with a lengthy name, `latteReceipt`, we could access them directly in our `println` statement with a much simpler line of code.

Importing class and case class instance members can be tricky, however, when you are working with multiple instances. Importing members from multiple classes would create a naming conflict, so keeping the import statements close to where they are being used is a good practice to follow.

The fields and methods of objects can be imported in the same manner. In fact, we have already seen examples of importing object members in previous chapters. The members of the collection.JavaConverters object were imported in "Java and Scala Collection Compatibility" on page 99 to demonstrate Java and Scala compatibility functions. Likewise, the global field of the concurrent.ExecutionContext.Implicits object was imported in "Future Collections" on page 125 to enable the creation of new futures.

As an example of object imports, let's add all of the methods from the util.Random object. This object extends the util.Random class, providing a single global instance that's useful to use when you don't need to set a new seed for random number generation:

```
scala> import util.Random._
import util.Random._

scala> val letters = alphanumeric.take(20).toList.mkString
letters: String = MwDR3EyHa1cr0JqsP9Tf

scala> val numbers = shuffle(1 to 20)
numbers: scala.collection.immutable.IndexedSeq[Int] = Vector(5, 10, 18, 1,
    16, 8, 20, 14, 19, 11, 17, 3, 15, 7, 4, 9, 6, 12, 13, 2)
```

The alphanumeric(): Stream and shuffle(Traversable) methods, members of the util.Random object (and parent class), are here made accessible without their object's prefix.

Importing instance members is a great way to streamline your code. Care must be taken to avoid naming conflicts, however, as well as any reductions in code readability. If readers of your code will get confused by the source of the imported members you are using, consider locating your import statement closer to the affected code.

Summary

While classes continue to be the core building block of Scala applications, they may be enhanced by traits and complemented or supplanted by objects. By supporting multiple inheritance by classes, traits extend the possibilities of highly reusable code. And based on the ordering of traits, in a class definition or at instantiation time, the possible varieties of functionality are staggering. Objects are less flexible than traits, but provide a built-in singleton mechanism with far less boilerplate than Java's singleton tricks or its static members and classes.

To be more precise, case classes should be included with classes as the core building block of Scala applications. In many applications case classes are used exclusively in place of classes, because the extra features they bring outweigh their subclassing limitations. To be even more precise, case classes aren't only classes. They also generate unseen companion objects. You may consider case class instances to be the same as class instances, but case classes overall are more than classes.

Every class instance and literal corresponds to a specific type. In this and the previous chapter you have learned how to create your own types with Scala. But a type is more than just a class. A class that takes a type parameter is a type, but every time it is instantiated with a type parameter, that too is a type. You can consider `List`, `List[Int]`, and `List[String]` to all correspond to the same class even though they have different types. The same is true with a given class, and that class mixed in with a trait at instantiation.

In the next chapter we will sort out the difference between classes and types. We'll also learn about new types that have been hidden by Scala's expressive syntax, and cover ways to improve the flexibility and specifications of your classes.

Break—Configuring Your First Scala Project

At this point we have covered the main body of content for this chapter. Before starting with the exercises, however, we'll need a short break to configure your first Scala project. The current approach of editing in the REPL and/or executing .scala files directly won't work for the applications you'll need to build.

With the introduction of objects as application entry points we now have a mechanism for executing our compiled code. We can compile classes in different files and packages and then access them from our application.

What we need now is a way to organize these dependencies and manage our project. Any code we run may have external dependencies such as Java and Scala libraries hosted in Maven repositories, local library dependencies, internal dependencies on our own code in other files and packages, and dependencies on the Scala libraries and runtimes. By using a dependency management and build tool, we can compile and execute against these dependencies while letting the tool handle library downloading and path configuration. We can also leverage dependency management to get our project imported into an Integrated Development Environment (or "IDE"), so we can edit and run code from the IDE or command line.

If you worked through the exercises in Chapter 7 (see "Exercises" on page 131) you'll know what tool I'm talking about. It is the Simple Build Tool (SBT), a Scala-based dependency management and build tool that you can use to configure, compile, and execute the Scala code in your project. If you haven't installed this tool yet, see Isn't SBT Hard to Learn? for the instructions.

Now that you have SBT installed, create an empty project directory. To avoid naming your project "MyProject" or "Project1," let's use the exciting phrase "HardyHeron" as the project name. You may want to use this as the directory name as well.

Inside this new directory, run the following commands in your shell to add a command-line application and execute it:

```
[HardyHeron] > mkdir -p src/main/scala

[HardyHeron] > cat > src/main/scala/Hello.scala

object Hello {
  def main(args: Array[String]) {
    println("Hello from SBT")
  }
}

[HardyHeron] > sbt run
[info] Set current project to hardyheron (in build file:~/HardyHeron/)
[info] Updating {file:~/HardyHeron/}hardyheron...
[info] Resolving org.fusesource.jansi#jansi;1.4 ...
[info] Done updating.
[info] Compiling 1 Scala source to ~/HardyHeron/target/scala-2.10/classes...
[info] Running Hello
Hello from SBT
[success] Total time: 3 s, completed June 6, 2014 10:38:08 PM

[HardyHeron] >
```

Did you notice that we were able to compile and run an application without a build script in place? SBT favors convention over configuration. Without a specific build script it will look for mainstream Scala code under *src/main/scala* and test-only Scala code under *src/test/scala*. The command `sbt run` invokes SBT with the "run" command, which executes any command-line application it can find in the code base.

Now let's add a build script. Although we clearly don't need one to compile and run an application, we will need it when we start adding external dependencies, i.e., external Java and Scala libraries. Let's add it now to simplify the process of adding dependencies later.

SBT supports writing a build script in its own Scala-like script language, stored in the file *build.sbt* at the root level of the project. It also supports writing a build script in Scala, stored in the "project" directory, containing an object that extends its `sbt.Build` parent class. Both types of SBT build scripts use some nonstandard Scala operators such as assignments (`:=`) and dependency grouping (%). Fortunately, when you see them in context they will likely make sense.

As of this writing in 2014, the SBT documentation recommends using the first approach, writing a *build.sbt* in your project's root directory. For this tutorial I'm going with the second approach, which may not be recommended but avoids the use of the SBT *.sbt* file format language in favor of the regular Scala syntax used in the second approach.

At the command line, run these commands to create a Scala-based build script and execute our "Hello" application. We'll start with one external dependency, the ScalaTest testing framework:

```
[HardyHeron] > cat > project/HardyHeronBuild.scala

import sbt._                                                              ❶
import sbt.Keys._

object HardyHeronBuild extends Build                                      ❷
{
  val hardyHeronDependencies = List(
    "org.scalatest" % "scalatest_2.11" % "2.2.1" % "test"                 ❸
  )

  val hardyHeronSettings = List(                                         ❹
    name := "HardyHeron",
    version := "1.0",
    scalaVersion := "2.11.2",
    libraryDependencies := hardyHeronDependencies
  )

  override lazy val settings = super.settings ++ hardyHeronSettings       ❺
}

[HardyHeron] >

[HardyHeron] > sbt compile
[info] Loading project definition from ~/HardyHeron/project
[info] Compiling 1 Scala source to ~/HardyHeron/project/target/scala-2.10/
  sbt-0.13/classes...
[info] Set current project to hardyheron (in build file:~/HardyHeron/)
[info] Updating {file:~/HardyHeron/}hardyheron...
[info] Resolving jline#jline;2.12 ...
[info] downloading http://repo1.maven.org/maven2/org/scalatest/           ❻
  scalatest_2.11/2.2.1/scalatest_2.11-2.2.1.jar ...
[info]   [SUCCESSFUL ] org.scalatest#scalatest_2.11;2.2.1!scalatest_2.11.jar
  (bundle) (5232ms)
[info] Done updating.
[success] Total time: 7 s, completed June 7, 2014 12:49:44 AM

[HardyHeron] > sbt "run Hello"                                            ❼
[info] Loading project definition from ~/HardyHeron/project
[info] Set current project to hardyheron (in build file:~/HardyHeron/)
[info] Running Hello
Hello from SBT
[success] Total time: 0 s, completed June 7, 2014 12:58:43 AM

[HardyHeron] >
```

❶ Import the contents of the sbt package and sbt.Keys at the top of Scala-based
   build files. This will pick up the Build base class, the property names (aka
   "settings") like name and version, and the special SBT operators like :=, %, and
   %%.

❷ The name of the object, and the filename, are up to you. SBT is just looking for subclasses of its `sbt.Build` class here.

❸ This is the standard format for defining Maven/Ivy library (aka "artifact") dependencies in SBT. The four components, in order, are the group, artifact, version, and the SBT component to which it applies, in this case to denote the library is for tests only. There are several public Maven repository search engines for finding libraries that include support for formatting the library as a dependency in SBT. The last component to note is the double-percent, `%%`, which instructs SBT to append `_2.11` (the major version of Scala we are using) to the artifact name. Scala libraries are generally compiled for specific major versions of Scala such as 2.10 and 2.11, and this format is a standard Scala addition that denotes the target version of the library.

❹ This is just a list of settings, using the operator `:=` to define settings based on keys in `sbt.Keys._`.

❺ The only field we're directly overriding is the lazy val settings, a regular `List` of SBT configurations. We'll start with the parent class's settings and then add in our project's settings.

❻ Our ScalaTest library is downloaded from the main public Maven repository, installed in a cache in your user directory, and added to the JVM "classpath" when you next execute your application.

❼ Let's run "Hello" to verify our build is successful. Because we'll be running this from the command line we'll use double quotes to surround `run-main Hello` so that SBT interprets it as a single argument.

Now that we have a working build script, let's import the project into an IDE. You'll gain instant compilation, code analysis, and discoverability in a modern IDE. If you are more familiar with text-editing environments like Sublime Text, Vim, or Emacs, you should spend some time becoming familiar with working in an IDE. Although these text editors have extensions to support Scala development, you'll likely find greater productivity gains with this statically typed language in an IDE that can anticipate and verify every line you write.

For this tutorial we'll be using the IntelliJ IDEA 13 (or later) IDE. You can download its excellent community edition (*http://bit.ly/ls-intellij*) for free. Make sure to install at least version 13 and also IntelliJ's Scala plug-in. You don't need any third-party SBT plug-ins, because IntelliJ IDEA 13 with Scala can open SBT projects directly.

To import the project, open IntelliJ IDEA and choose "Open Project," then select our "HardyHeron" project directory. In the "Import Project from SBT project" dialog, select all of the options and set the "Project SDK" to your installation of Java 1.8 (aka Java 8). If it doesn't appear you may need to click "New…" to configure IntelliJ IDEA to support your Java installation. Figure 9-1 shows how this dialog should appear after you have selected the options.

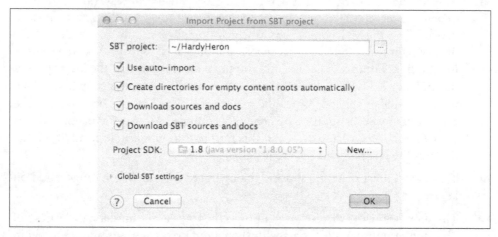

Figure 9-1. The Import Project dialog in IntelliJ IDEA 13

After importing the project, a project window should appear in IntelliJ IDEA. Navigate through the "Project" view (or select it from View → Tool Windows if it is not already open) until you find the *Hello.scala* file and open it up. You should see a view similar to Figure 9-2, with the project structure in the "Project" view and the source for the "Hello" class appearing with syntax highlighting to its right.

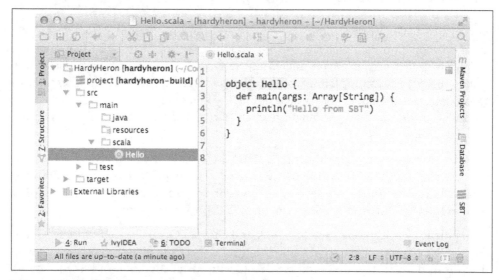

Figure 9-2. Viewing the project in IntelliJ IDEA

Now that we have the source loaded in the IDE, let's run it from here. Right-click in the "Hello.scala" source view and select Run Hello. You should see the output message from the "Hello" application appear in a new view, "Run," below the source.

At this point you should have a fully working SBT project up and running inside IntelliJ IDEA, and be able to add and edit your own classes, objects, and traits right here. If you haven't used this IDE before, you may want to read more about it by visiting the IntelliJ IDEA product website (*http://bit.ly/ls-idea*). It has screencasts, tutorials, and guides that will help to explain many of the features you'll encounter while working on the exercises in this chapter. We'll just be using the most basic features in the IDE, but understanding how to take advantage of core IDE features can help you to better experiment with and explore the Scala language.

Now that you have Scala running in the IDE, it's time to start some exercises.

Exercises

1. Let's cover how to write a unit test in Scala with the ScalaTest framework. This exercise will consist of adding a test to the IDE, executing it, and verifying its successful outcome. If you're already familiar with executing tests in an IDE this should be a fairly simple exercise. To better understand the ScalaTest framework, I recommend that you take a break from this exercise and browse the official documentation at the ScalaTest website (*http://www.scalatest.org/*).

   We'll start with the "HtmlUtils" object (see "Objects" on page 167). Create a new Scala class by right-clicking the *src/main/scala* directory in the IDE and selecting New → Scala Class. Type the name, **HtmlUtils**, and set the type to an object. Replace the skeleton object with the following source:

   ```scala
   object HtmlUtils {
     def removeMarkup(input: String) = {
       input
         .replaceAll("""</?\w[^>]*>""","")
         .replaceAll("<.*>","")
     }
   }
   ```

   The new *HtmlUtils.scala* file should be located in *src/main/scala*, the root directory for source code in our project. Now add a new "HtmlUtilsSpec" class under *src/test/scala*, creating the directory if necessary. Both SBT and IntelliJ will look for tests in this directory, a counterpart to the main *src/main/scala* directory. Add the following source to the *HtmlUtilsSpec.scala* file:

   ```scala
   import org.scalatest._

   class HtmlUtilsSpec extends FlatSpec with ShouldMatchers {

     "The Html Utils object" should "remove single elements" in {
   ```

```
      HtmlUtils.removeMarkup("<br/>") should equal("")
    }

    it should "remove paired elements" in {
      HtmlUtils.removeMarkup("<b>Hi</b>") should equal("Hi")
    }

    it should "have no effect on empty strings" in {
      val empty = true
      HtmlUtils.removeMarkup("").isEmpty should be(empty)
    }

  }
```

We're only using the `FlatSpec` and `ShouldMatchers` types from this package, but we will import everything so we can easily add additional test utilities in the future (such as "OptionValues," a favorite of mine). The class `FlatSpec` is one of several different test types you can choose from, modeled after Ruby's RSpec (*http:// rspec.info/*). `ShouldMatchers` adds the `should` and `be` operators to your test, creating a domain-specific language that can help make your tests more readable.

The first test starts off a bit differently from the other tests. With the `FlatSpec`, the first test in a file should start with a textual description of what you are testing in this file. Later tests will use the `it` keyword to refer to this description. This helps to create highly readable test reports.

In the test body, the `equal` operator ensures that the value preceding `should` is equal to its argument, here the empty string `""`. If not equal, it will cause the test to fail and exit immediately. Likewise, the `be` operator fails the test if the value before `should` isn't the same instance, useful for comparing global instances like `true`, `Nil`, and `None`.

Before running the test, open the IntelliJ Plugins preference panel under Preferences and ensure that the "jUnit" plug-in is installed. The plug-in will ensure that your test results will be easily viewable and browsable.

Once you have added the test to your project, go ahead and compile it in the IDE. If it doesn't compile, or it otherwise complains about the lack of a "ScalaTest" package, make sure your build script has the ScalaTest dependency and that you can view it in the "External Libraries" section of the "Project" view in IntelliJ.

Now we'll run it. Right-click the test class's name, `HtmlUtilsSpec`, and choose Run *HtmlUtilsSpec*. Executing the test will take no more than a few seconds, and if you entered the test and original application in correctly they will all be successful. Figure 9-3 shows how the test results should appear when the test completes.

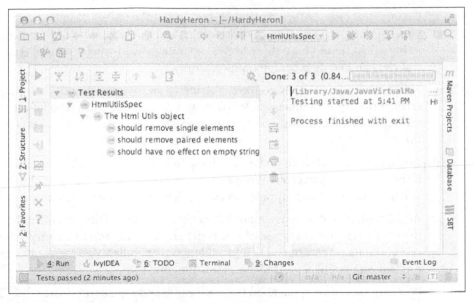

Figure 9-3. The Test Results view in IntelliJ IDEA

Let's conclude this exercise with an actual exercise for you to implement: add additional tests to our `HtmlUtilsSpec` test class. Are there there any feature areas that aren't yet tested? Are all valid HTML markup possibilities supported?

There's also the question of whether JavaScript contained within "script" tags should be stripped or appear along with the rest of the text. Consider this a bug in the original version of `HtmlUtils`. Add a test to verify that the JavaScript text will be stripped out and then run the test. When it fails, fix `HtmlUtils` and rerun the test to verify it has been fixed.

Congratulations, you are now writing tests in Scala! Remember to keep writing tests as you work through the rest of the exercises in this book, using them to assert how your solutions should work and to catch any (unforeseeable!) bugs in them.

2. Let's work on a different example from this chapter. Create a new Scala trait titled "SafeStringUtils" and add the following source:

```scala
trait SafeStringUtils {
  // Returns a trimmed version of the string wrapped in an Option,
  // or None if the trimmed string is empty.
  def trimToNone(s: String): Option[String] = {
    Option(s) map(_.trim) filterNot(_.isEmpty)
  }
}
```

Verify that the trait compiles in the IDE. If it all works, complete the following steps:

a. Create an object version of the trait.

b. Create a test class, `SafeStringUtilsSpec`, to test the `SafeStringUtils.trimTo None()` method. Verify that it trims strings and safely handles null and empty strings. You should have three to five separate tests in your test class. Run the test class and verify it completes successfully.

c. Add a method that safely converts a string to an integer, without throwing an error if the string is unparseable. Write and execute tests for valid and invalid input. What are the most appropriate monadic collections to use in this function?

d. Add a method that safely converts a string to a long, without throwing an error if the string is unparseable. Write and execute tests for valid and invalid input. What are the most appropriate monadic collections to use in this function?

e. Add a method that returns a randomly generated string of the given size, limited to only upper- and lowercase letters. Write and execute tests that verify the correct contents are return and that invalid input is handled. Are there any appropriate monadic collections to use in this function?

3. Write a command-line application that will search and replace text inside files. The input arguments are a search pattern, a regular expression, the replacement text, and one or more files to search.

a. Start by writing a skeleton command-line application that parses the input arguments: the search pattern, the replacement text arguments, and the files to process as a list of strings. Print these out to verify you have captured them correctly.

b. Execute this skeleton application by running it from the command line with `sbt "run-main <object name> <input arguments>"`. The input arguments must be in the same double quotes as the "run-main" argument so that the SBT tool reads it all as a single command. You can also run it from the IDE by selecting Run → Run... and creating a runtime configuration. Runtime configurations allow you to specify the input arguments once, or else to show the entire configuration every time it is executed. Verify that your search pattern, replacement text, and list of files is successfully parsed.

c. Implement the core of the application by reading each input file, searching for and replacing the specified pattern, and then printing the result out to the console. Try this with a few input files to verify your pattern gets replaced.

d. Now write the modified text back to the file it was read from. Here is an example of using the Java library to write a string to a file:

```
import java.io._
val writer = new PrintWriter(new File("out.txt"))
writer.write("Hello, World!\nHere I am!")
writer.close()
```

e. Make your application safer to use by having it create a backup of its input files before modifying them. You can create a backup by first writing the unmodified contents out to a file with the input's name plus *.bak*. Use `new java.io.File(<file name>).exists()` to ensure that the backup file's name does *not* exist before creating it. You can try incremental numbers such as *.bak1* and *.bak2"* to find unique backup filenames.

f. Create a test class and write tests to verify that your application will work as expected. The core functionality of your application should be invocable as methods without actually launching the application. Make sure the functionality is broken down into methods of a readable and manageable size, and then write individual tests for the core methods as well as the `main` method. To end the exercise, run your tests and verify they all succeed, then run your application from the command line with a test file.

4. Write an application that summarizes a file. It will take a single text file as input and print an overall summary including the number of characters, words, and paragraphs as well as a list of the top 20 words by usage.

   The application should be smart enough to filter out nonwords. Parsing a Scala file should reveal words, for example, and not special characters such as "{" or "//". It should also be able to count paragraphs that have real content versus empty space.

   Write tests that use your own multiline strings to verify the output. Your application should be modularized into discrete methods for easier testing. You should be able to write a test that gives the string "this is is not a test" and receives an instance that will reveal the word "is" as the top used word.

   To really test out your knowledge of this chapter's contents, make sure to use objects, traits, and case classes in your solution.

5. Write an application that reports on the most recently closed issues in a given Git-Hub project. The input arguments should include the repository name, project name, and an optional number of issues to report with a default value of 10. The output will have a report header and display each issue's number, title, username, number of comments, and label names. The output should be well-formatted, with fixed-width columns delimited with pipes (|) and a header delimited with equals signs (=).

   You'll need to read in the issues from the GitHub API (see exercise 7 in "Exercises" on page 102 for information on reading a URL's contents), parse the JSON values, and then print a detailed format. Here is an example URL for returning the 10 most recent closed issues from the official Scala project on GitHub:

   ```
   https://api.github.com/repos/scala/scala/issues?state=closed&per_page=10
   ```

We'll use the Json4s (*http://json4s.org/*) library to parse the JSON response into a list of our own case classes. First, add this dependency to your build script and rebuild the project:

```
"org.json4s" %% "json4s-native" % "3.2.10"
```

This can go either before or after the ScalaTest dependency. IntelliJ should pick up the change, download the library, and rebuild your project. If it is not doing so, open the SBT view in IntelliJ and refresh the project, or run `sbt clean compile` from the command line.

The JSON response from the API is rather large, but you don't need to parse all of the fields. You should design a case class that contains the exact fields you want to parse from the JSON, using the `Option` type for nullable or optional fields. When you parse the JSON response, Json4s will insert only the fields you have defined in your case class and ignore the rest.

Here is an example of using Json4s to parse the "labels" array from the larger GitHub issue document. If you study the output from the API for a single record, you should be able to design a series of case classes that will only contain the information you need. Note that the JSON document returned by the API is an array, so you will probably need to invoke the `extract` method with a `List` (e.g., `extract[List[GithubIssue]]`):

```
import org.json4s.DefaultFormats                                          ❶
import org.json4s.native.JsonMethods                                      ❷

val jsonText = """
{
  "labels": [
    {
      "url": "https://api.github.com/repos/scala/scala/labels/tested",
      "name": "tested",
      "color": "d7e102"
    }
  ]
}
"""

case class Label(url: String, name: String)                              ❸
case class LabelDocument(labels: List[Label])                           ❹

implicit val formats = DefaultFormats                                    ❺
val labelDoc = JsonMethods.parse(jsonText).extract[LabelDocument]        ❻

val labels = labelDoc.labels
val firstLabel = labels.headOption.map(_.name)
```

❶ `DefaultFormats` has support for common date formats as well as numbers and strings.

❷ We're using the "native" JSON parser in JsonMethods to parse JSON documents and extract them into case class instances.

❸ A "Label" is what I'm calling an item in the "labels" JSON array. Note that I didn't need to specify the "color" field.

❹ The total JSON document has a single field, "labels," so we need a case class that represents the document.

❺ The implicit keyword is one we'll study in Chapter 10. I'm sorry to spring this on you before we have had a chance to cover it, but you'll need this line to ensure that Json4s can parse your JSON document.

❻ JsonMethods parses the JSON text to its own intermediate format, which can then be extracted with a given case class.

6. This exercise depends on the previous exercise being finished. Once you have the completed GitHub report application, let's work on refactoring it for better reusability and reliability.

   a. Start by writing tests for the GitHub report to verify the correct behavior of each component. How much of the logic in the application can you test if your computer lacked an Internet connection? You should be able to test most of the logic without being able to actually connect to the GitHub site.

   b. Refactor the JSON handling code out to its own trait, e.g., "JsonSupport." Write tests to verify that it parses JSON code correctly, and handles exceptions that may be thrown by the Json4s library. Would it be useful to provide an object version of this trait?

   c. Do the same for the web handling code. Create your own "HtmlClient" trait and object that can take a URL and return the content as a list of strings. Can you include the server's status response in a class along with the content? Make sure to write tests to verify the web handling code can prevent any exceptions from being thrown.

   d. Finally, refactor your report generation code, the part that handles the clean fixed-width columns, into a reusable trait. Can it take a tuple of any size and print out its contents? Is there a more appropriate data type that it should take, one that supports variable numbers of columns but knows how to print out strings versus double values? Make sure your report generation code takes the maximum line width as an argument.

CHAPTER 10

Advanced Typing

By this point in the book you should have a pretty good understanding of the Scala language. If you have read the chapters and pursued the exercises, then you are already pretty good at defining classes, writing functions, and working with collections. You know everything you need to in order to go out and start building your own Scala applications.

However, if you want to be able to read other developers' Scala code, read and understand the Scala API, or understand how Scala works, you will want to read this chapter. In it we will cover many of the type features that make the language possible.

One interesting feature is how the apparently high-level tuples and function literals are built with regular classes. Their fancy syntax belies their humble foundation, which you can validate by creating them as class instances:

```scala
scala> val t1: (Int, Char) = (1, 'a')
t1: (Int, Char) = (1,a)

scala> val t2: (Int, Char) = Tuple2[Int, Char](1, 'a')
t2: (Int, Char) = (1,a)

scala> val f1: Int=>Int = _ + 2
f1: Int => Int = <function1>

scala> val f2: Int=>Int = new Function1[Int, Int] { def apply(x: Int) = x * 2 }
f2: Int => Int = <function1>
```

Another interesting type feature is implicit classes. Implicit classes provide a type-safe way to "monkey-patch" new methods and fields onto existing classes. Through automatic conversion from the original class to the new class, methods and fields in the implicit class can be invoked directly on the original class without any changes to the class's structure:

```scala
scala> object ImplicitClasses {
     |   implicit class Hello(s: String) { def hello = s"Hello, $s" }
     |   def test = {
     |     println( "World".hello )
     |   }
     | }
defined object ImplicitClasses

scala> ImplicitClasses.test
Hello, World
```

Implicit parameters share a similar behavior to implicit classes, providing parameters in the local namespace that may be added to implicit-ready methods. A method that defines some of its parameters as being "implicit" can be invoked by code that has a local implicit value, but can also be invoked with an explicit parameter:

```scala
scala> object ImplicitParams {
     |   def greet(name: String)(implicit greeting: String) = s"$greeting, $name"
     |   implicit val hi = "Hello"
     |   def test = {
     |     println( greet("Developers") )
     |   }
     | }
defined object ImplicitParams

scala> ImplicitParams.test
Hello, Developers
```

Finally, we'll get down to types themselves. The type parameters we have used for classes, traits, and functions are actually quite flexible. Instead of allowing any type to be used as a type parameter, you can specify that one meet an upper bound (with <:) or a lower bound (with >:):

```scala
scala> class Base { var i = 10 }; class Sub extends Base
defined class Base
defined class Sub

scala> def increment[B <: Base](b: Base) = { b.i += 1; b }
increment: [B <: Base](b: Base)Base
```

Type parameters can also morph into compatible types, even when bound in a new instance. When a type parameter is specified as covariant (with +), it can change into a compatible base type. The List collection is covariant, so a list of a subclass can be converted to a list of a base class:

```scala
scala> val l: List[Base] = List[Sub]()
l: List[Base] = List()
```

Learning these advanced type features will give you extra tools for writing better Scala code. You will also be better able to understand the official Scala library documentation, as the library makes heavy use of advanced type features. Finally, they will help you to see and understand the machinery that installs many Scala features in place.

In the next section, we'll take a closer look at the foundation of tuples and functions as regular classes, and how you can start taking advantage of their methods.

Tuple and Function Value Classes

If you have already read the previous chapters in this book there will be no need to introduce tuples and function values to you. They were well covered in "Tuples" on page 25 and "Function Types and Values" on page 66, respectively. What we *haven't* yet covered about them is that behind their special syntax is a set of regular classes.

That's right, the special sauce that makes tuples like (1, 2, true)) and function literals like (n: String) => s"Hello, $n" possible is just... sauce. The syntax shortcuts to create these instances are short and expressive, but the actual implementation is plain old classes that you could have written yourself. Don't be disappointed by this discovery, however. The good news is it means these high-level constructs are backed by safe, type-parameterized classes.

Tuples are implemented as instances of the TupleX[Y] case class, where "X" is a number from 1 to 22 signifying its *arity* (the number of input parameters). The type parameter "Y" varies from a single type parameters for Tuple1 to 22 type parameters for Tuple22. Tuple1[A] has the single field _1, Tuple2[A,B] has the fields _1 and _2, and so on. When you create a tuple with the parentheses syntax (e.g., (1, 2, true), a tuple class with the same number of parameters gets instantiated with the values. In other words, the expressive syntax of tuples is simply a shortcut to a case class you could have written yourself.

The TupleX[Y] case classes each extend a ProductX trait with the same number. These traits offer operations such as productArity, returning the arity of the tuple, and productElement, a nontype-safe way to access the nth element of a tuple. They also provide companion objects that implement unapply (see Table 9-1) to enable pattern matching on tuples.

Let's try an example of creating a tuple not with the parentheses syntax but by instantiating the Tuple2 case class:

```
scala> val x: (Int, Int) = Tuple2(10, 20)
x: (Int, Int) = (10,20)

scala> println("Does the arity - 2? " + (x.productArity == 2))
Does the arity = 2? true
```

Tuple case classes are just a data-centric implementation of an expressive syntax. Function value classes are similar but provide a logic-centric implementation.

Function values are implemented as instances of the FunctionX[Y] trait, numbered from 0 to 22 based on the arity of the function. The type parameter "Y" varies from a single type parameter for Function0 (because the return value needs a parameter) to 23 type parameters for Function22. The actual logic for the function, whether an invocation of an existing function or a new function literal, is implemented in the class's apply() method.

In other words, when you write a function literal, the Scala compiler converts it to the body of the apply() method in a new class extending FunctionX. This forcing mechanism makes Scala's function values compatible with the JVM, which restricts all functions to being implemented as class methods.

Let's try out FunctionX types by writing a function literal with the regular syntax we have used thus far, and then as the body of a FunctionX.apply() method. We'll create an anonymous class that extends the Function1[A,B] trait:

```scala
scala> val hello1 = (n: String) => s"Hello, $n"
hello1: String => String = <function1>

scala> val h1 = hello1("Function Literals")
h1: String = Hello, Function Literals

scala> val hello2 = new Function1[String,String] {
     |    def apply(n: String) = s"Hello, $n"
     | }
hello2: String => String = <function1>

scala> val h2 = hello2("Function1 Instances")
h2: String = Hello, Function1 Instances

scala> println(s"hello1 = $hello1, hello2 = $hello2")
hello1 = <function1>, hello2 = <function1>
```

The function values stored in hello1 and hello2 are essentially equivalent. And the Function1 class, along with all of the other FunctionX classes, overrides toString with its name in lowercase surrounded by angle brackets. Therefore, when you print out hello1 and hello2 you get the same output, <function1>. If this looks familiar to you, it's probably because you've seen this in every single code sample in the book where we have stored function values. Except, of course, where we have seen <function2> emitted by values of Function2 and so on.

The Function1 trait contains two special methods not available in Function0 or any of the other FunctionX traits. You can use them to combine two or more Function1 instances into a new Function1 instance that will execute all of the functions in order when invoked. The only restriction is that the return type of the first function must match the input type of the second function, and so on.

The method andThen creates a new function value from two function values, executing the instance on the left followed by the instance on the right. The method compose works the same way but in opposite order.

Let's try them out with regular function literals:

```
scala> val doubler = (i: Int) => i*2
doubler: Int => Int = <function1>

scala> val plus3 = (i: Int) => i+3
plus3: Int => Int = <function1>

scala> val prepend = (doubler compose plus3)(1)
prepend: Int = 8

scala> val append = (doubler andThen plus3)(1)
append: Int = 5
```

Understanding how first-class functions are implemented as FunctionX classes is an important first step to learning Scala's type model. The language provides a concise and expressive syntax while the compiler takes care of supporting the JVM's less-expressive runtime model, all while supporting type-safety for more stable applications.

Implicit Parameters

In "Partially Applied Functions and Currying" on page 74 we studied partially applied functions, where a function could be invoked without its full set of parameters. The result was a function value that could be invoked with the remaining set of unspecified parameters, invoking the original function.

What if you could invoke a function without specifying all of the parameters, but the function would actually be executed? The missing, unspecified parameters would have to come from *somewhere* to ensure the function would operate correctly. One approach would be to define default parameters for your function, but this would require having the function know what the correct values for the missing parameters should be.

Another approach is to use *implicit* parameters, where the caller provides the default value in its own namespace. Functions can define an implicit parameter, often as a separate parameter group from the other nonimplicit parameters. Invokers can then denote a local value as implicit so it can be used to fill in as the implicit parameter. When the function is invoked without specifying a value for the implicit parameter, the local implicit value is then picked up and added to the function invocation.

Use the implicit keyword to mark a value, variable, or function parameter as being implicit. An implicit value or variable, if available in the current namespace, may be used to fill in for an implicit parameter in a function invocation.

Here's one example of a function defined with an implicit parameter. The function is defined as a method in an object to keep its namespace separate from the invoker's namespace:

```scala
scala> object Doubly {
     |    def print(num: Double)(implicit fmt: String) = {
     |      println(fmt format num)
     |    }
     | }
defined object Doubly

scala> Doubly.print(3.724)
<console>:9: error: could not find implicit value for parameter fmt: String
              Doubly.print(3.724)

scala> Doubly.print(3.724)("%.1f")
3.7
```

Our new `print` method has an implicit parameter, so we'll either need to specify an implicit value/variable in our namespace or add the parameter explicitly. Fortunately, adding the explicit parameter works fine.

This time we'll add an implicit local value to invoke the `print` method without explicitly passing the implicit parameter:

```scala
scala> case class USD(amount: Double) {
     |    implicit val printFmt = "%.2f"
     |    def print = Doubly.print(amount)
     | }
defined class USD

scala> new USD(81.924).print
81.92
```

Our implicit value was picked up as the second parameter group for the `Doubly.print` method, without the need to explicitly pass it.

Implicit parameters are heavily used in Scala's library. They mostly provide functionality that callers can choose to override but otherwise may ignore, such as collection builders or default collection ordering.

If you use implicit parameters, keep in mind that excessive use can make your code hard to read and understand. Developers usually like to know what's being passed to a function they are invoking. Finding out that their function invocation included implicit parameters without their knowledge may be an unwelcome surprise. You can avoid this by limiting your implicit parameters to circumstances that support a function's implementation without changing its expected logic or data.

Implicit Classes

Another implicit feature in Scala, similar only in nature to implicit parameters, is implicit conversions with classes. An *implicit class* is a type of class that provides an automatic conversion from another class. By providing an automatic conversion from instances of type A to type B, an instance of type A can appear to have fields and methods as if it were an instance of type B.

What About Implicit Defs?

Until Scala 2.10, implicit conversion was handled by *implicit def* methods that took the original instance and returned a new instance of the desired type. Implicit methods have been supplanted by implicit classes, which provide a safer and more limited scope for converting existing instances. If you want to use implicit defs in your own code, see the `scala.language.implicitConversions()` method in the Scaladocs for instructions on how to fully enable this feature.

The Scala compiler uses implicit conversions when it finds an unknown field or method being accessed on an instance. It checks the current namespace for any implicit conversion that (1) takes the instance as an argument and (2) implements that missing field or method. If it finds a match it will add an automatic conversion to the implicit class, supporting the field or method access on the implicit type. Of course if a match isn't found, you will get a compilation error, which is the normal course of action for invoking unknown fields or methods on your instances.

Here is an example of an implicit class that adds a "fishes" method to any integer value. The implicit class takes an integer and defines the "fishes" method it wants to add to integers:

```
scala> object IntUtils {
     |   implicit class Fishies(val x: Int) {               ❶
     |     def fishes = "Fish" * x                          ❷
     |   }
     | }
defined object IntUtils

scala> import IntUtils._                                    ❸
import IntUtils._

scala> println(3.fishes)                                    ❹
FishFishFish
```

❶　Fishies, defined inside an object, implicitly converts integers to itself ...

❷　... so that the fishes() method will be defined for all integers.

❸　Before using it, the implicit class must be added to the namespace ...

❹ ... and then the `fishes()` method can be invoked on any integer.

Implicit classes make this kind of field and method grafting possible, but there are some restrictions about how you can define and use them:

1. An implicit class must be defined within another object, class, or trait. Fortunately, implicit classes defined within objects can be easily imported to the current namespace.

2. They must take a single nonimplicit class argument. In the preceding example, the `Int` parameter was sufficient to convert an `Int` to a `Fishies` class in order to access the `fishes` method.

3. The implicit class's name must not conflict with another object, class, or trait in the current namespace. Thus, a case class could not be used as an implicit class because its automatically generated companion object would break this rule.

The preceding example follows all of these rules. It is implemented inside an object ("IntUtils"), takes a single argument with the instance to be converted, and has no name conflicts with other types. Although you can implement your implicit classes in objects, classes, or traits, I find it works better to implement them in objects. Objects aren't subclassable, so you will never automatically pick up an implicit conversion from them. Also, you can easily add an object's implicit classes to your namespace by importing some or all of the object's members.

To be precise, you will never automatically pick up an implicit conversion *other than the ones in the* `scala.Predef` *object*. The members of this object, a part of the Scala library, are automatically added to the namespace. It includes, among other type features, implicit conversions that enable some of Scala's expressive syntax. Among them is the arrow operator (`->`) that you have already used (see "Tuples" on page 25) to generate 2-sized tuples from any two values.

Here's a simplified version of the implicit class that makes the arrow operator possible:

```scala
implicit class ArrowAssoc[A](x: A) {
  def ->[B](y: B) = Tuple2(x, y)
}
```

As an example, take the expression `1 → "a"`, which generates a tuple with an integer and a string. What's really occurring is an implicit conversion of an integer to an instance of `ArrowAssoc` followed by an invocation of the "→" method, which finally returns a new `Tuple2`. But because the implicit conversion was added to the namespace... implicitly... the expression is no greater than two values separated by an arrow.

Implicit classes are a great way to add useful methods to existing classes. Used carefully, they can help to make your code more expressive. Take care to avoid hurting readability, however. You wouldn't want developers who hadn't seen the `Fishies` implicit class be forced to wonder, "What the heck is a *fishes* method and where is it implemented?"

Types

We just devoted several sections in this chapter to type-related features such as implicit conversions and function classes. In this section we'll move on from type-related features to focus on the core subject of types themselves.

A *class* is an entity that may include data and methods, and has a single, specific definition. A *type* is a class specification, which may match a single class that conforms to its requirements or a range of classes. The `Option` class, for example, is a type, but so is `Option[Int]`. A type could be a relation, specifying "class A or any of its descendants," or "class B or any of its parent classes." It could also be more abstract, specifying "any class that defines this method."

The same can be said for traits, being entities that can include data and methods and have single, specific definitions. Types are class specifications but work equally well with traits. Objects, however, are not considered to be types. They are singletons, and while they may extend types they are not types themselves.

The examples I have used to describe the concept of types in Scala all pertain to some wonderful features we'll explore in this section. They can help you to write stricter, safer, stabler, and better-documented code, which is the entire point of having a strong type system.

We'll start with the ability to define your own types without creating a single class.

Type Aliases

A *type alias* creates a new named type for a specific, existing type (or class). This new type alias is treated by the compiler as if it were defined in a regular class. You can create a new instance from a type alias, use it in place of classes for type parameters, and specify it in value, variable, and function return types. If the class being aliased has type parameters, you can either add the type parameters to your type alias or fix them with specific types.

Like implicit conversions, however, type aliases can only be defined inside objects, classes, or traits. They only work on types, also, so objects cannot be used to create type aliases.

You can use the `type` keyword to define a new type alias.

Syntax: Defining a Type Alias

```
type <identifier>[type parameters] = <type name>[type parameters]
```

Okay, this is the type section, so let's create some types!

```scala
scala> object TypeFun {
     |     type Whole = Int
     |     val x: Whole = 5
     |
     |     type UserInfo = Tuple2[Int,String]
     |     val u: UserInfo = new UserInfo(123, "George")
     |
     |     type T3[A,B,C] = Tuple3[A,B,C]
     |     val things = new T3(1, 'a', true)
     | }
defined object TypeFun

scala> val x = TypeFun.x
x: TypeFun.Whole = 5

scala> val u = TypeFun.u
u: TypeFun.UserInfo = (123,George)

scala> val things = TypeFun.things
things: (Int, Char, Boolean) = (1,a,true)
```

In this example, the type `Whole` is now an alias for the abstract class `Int`. Also, the type `UserInfo` is an alias for a tuple with an integer in the first position and a string in the second. Because a `Tuple2` is an instantiable case class, we were able to instantiate it directly from the type alias `UserInfo`. Finally, our `T3` type doesn't fix its type parameters, and so can be instantiated with any types.

Type aliases are a useful way to refer to existing types with a local, specific name. A `Tuple2[Int,String]` used regularly inside a class may be more useful if it were named `UserInfo`. However, as with other advanced type features, type aliases should not replace careful object-oriented design. A real class named `UserInfo` will be more stable and intuitive in the long term than using type aliases.

Abstract Types

Whereas type aliases resolve to a single class, *abstract types* are specifications that may resolve to zero, one, or many classes. They work in a similar way to type aliases, but being specifications they are abstract and cannot be used to create instances. Abstract types are popularly used for type parameters to specify a range of acceptable types that may be passed. They can also be used to create *type declarations* in abstract classes, which declare types that concrete (nonabstract) subclasses must implement.

As an example of the latter, a trait may contain a type alias with an unspecified type. That type declaration can be reused in method signatures, and must be filled in by a subclass.

Let's create such a trait:

```scala
scala> class User(val name: String)
defined class User

scala> trait Factory { type A; def create: A }
defined trait Factory

scala> trait UserFactory extends Factory {
     |     type A = User
     |     def create = new User("")
     | }
defined trait UserFactory
```

The abstract type A in Factory is used as the return type from the create method. In a concrete subclass the type is redefined with a type alias to a specific class.

Another way of writing this trait and class would be to use type parameters. Here's an example of implementing the preceding trait and class with them:

```scala
scala> trait Factory[A] { def create: A }
defined trait Factory

scala> trait UserFactory extends Factory[User] { def create = new User("") }
defined trait UserFactory
```

Abstract types are an alternative to type parameters when designing generic classes. If you want a parameterizable type, then type parameters work great. Otherwise, abstract types may be more suitable. The UserFactory example class works just as well with a parameterizable type versus defining its own type alias.

In this example there were no restrictions on the type allowed for subclasses of the Factory trait. However, it is often more useful to be able to specify *bounds* for the type, an upper or lower bound that ensures that any type implementation meets a certain standard.

Bounded Types

A bounded type is restricted to being either a specific class or else its subtype or base type. An *upper bound* restricts a type to only that type or one of its subtypes. Another way of saying this is that an upper bound defines what a type must be, and through polymorphism accepts subtypes. A *lower bound* restricts a type to only that type or else one of the base types it extends.

You can use the upper-bound relation operator (<:) to specify an upper bound for a type.

Syntax: Upper Bounded Types

```
<identifier> <: <upper bound type>
```

Before trying out a bounded type, let's define a few classes for testing:

```
scala> class BaseUser(val name: String)
defined class BaseUser

scala> class Admin(name: String, val level: String) extends BaseUser(name)
defined class Admin

scala> class Customer(name: String) extends BaseUser(name)
defined class Customer

scala> class PreferredCustomer(name: String) extends Customer(name)
defined class PreferredCustomer
```

Now we'll define a function that takes a parameter with an upper bound:

```
scala> def check[A <: BaseUser](u: A) { if (u.name.isEmpty) println("Fail!") }
check: [A <: BaseUser](u: A)Unit

scala> check(new Customer("Fred"))

scala> check(new Admin("", "strict"))
Fail!
```

Our type parameter A is limited to only types that are equal to or extend the BaseUser type. This makes it possible for our parameter u to access the "name" field. Without the upper-bound restriction, accessing the "name" field on an unknown type would have led to a compilation error. The exact type of the u parameter is preserved, so a future version of this check function could safely return it with the correct type if necessary.

A less restrictive form of the upper-bound operator is available using the view-bound operator (<%). While an upper bound requires a type (and is compatible with subtypes), a view bound also supports anything that can be treated as that type. Thus view bounds are open to implicit conversion, allowing types that are not the requested type but can be converted to it. An upper bound is more restrictive, because implicit conversions are not considered as part of the type requirements.

The opposite of upper bounds are lower bounds, which specify the lowest acceptable class. Use the lower-bound relation operator (>:) to specify a lower bound for a type:

Syntax: Lower Bounded Types

```
<identifier> >: <lower bound type>
```

Let's create a function that returns no lower than a Customer type, although the actual implmentation may be lower.

```
scala> def recruit[A >: Customer](u: Customer): A = u match {
     |    case p: PreferredCustomer => new PreferredCustomer(u.name)
     |    case c: Customer => new Customer(u.name)
     | }
recruit: [A >: Customer](u: Customer)A

scala> val customer = recruit(new Customer("Fred"))
customer: Customer = Customer@4746fb8c

scala> val preferred = recruit(new PreferredCustomer("George"))
preferred: Customer = PreferredCustomer@4cd8db31
```

Although a new PreferredCustomer instance was returned, the type of the prefer
red value is set by the return type, which guarantees no lower than a Customer.

Bounded types can also be used to declare abstract types. Here is an example of an
abstract class declaring an abstract type and using it in a declared method. The concrete
(nonabstract) subclasses then implement the type declaration as a type alias and use the
type alias in the defined method. The result is that implementations of the class implement the method but assure that only a compatible type is used:

```
scala> abstract class Card {
     |    type UserType <: BaseUser
     |    def verify(u: UserType): Boolean
     |
     | }
defined class Card

scala> class SecurityCard extends Card {
     |    type UserType = Admin
     |    def verify(u: Admin) = true
     | }
defined class SecurityCard

scala> val v1 = new SecurityCard().verify(new Admin("George", "high"))
v1: Boolean = true

scala> class GiftCard extends Card {
     |    type UserType = Customer
     |    def verify(u: Customer) = true
     | }
defined class GiftCard

scala> val v2 = new GiftCard().verify(new Customer("Fred"))
v2: Boolean = true
```

As with nonbounded types, the choice of using abstract types defined inside base classes
versus type parameters isn't always clear. Many developers prefer type parameters for
their more expressive syntax. However, using bounded types is often preferred over
nonbounded types. They not only restrict invalid type usage in the subclasses but also

work as a kind of self-documentation. They make it clear which types are *expected* to be used with a set of classes.

Type Variance

Whereas adding upper or lower bounds will make type parameters more restrictive, adding type variance makes type parameters *less* restrictive. *Type variance* specifies how a type parameter may adapt to meet a base type or subtype.

By default, type parameters are *invariant*. An instance of a type-parameterized class is only compatible with that class and parameterized type. It could not be stored in a value where the type parameter is a base type.

This behavior often surprises developers, who are familiar with Scala's support for polymorphism. With polymorphism, a value with a given type may take the shape of one of its base types. For example, an instance of a type can be assigned to a value with the explicit type of its base type.

Here's an example of Scala's polymorphism, allowing lower types to be stored in values with higher types. We'll use this two-part vehicular class hierarchy for the rest of the examples in this section:

```scala
scala> class Car { override def toString = "Car()" }
defined class Car

scala> class Volvo extends Car { override def toString = "Volvo()" }
defined class Volvo

scala> val c: Car = new Volvo()
c: Car = Volvo()
```

The same polymorphic adaptation doesn't hold for type parameters, however:

```scala
scala> case class Item[A](a: A) { def get: A = a }
defined class Item

scala> val c: Item[Car] = new Item[Volvo](new Volvo)
<console>:12: error: type mismatch;
 found    : Item[Volvo]
 required: Item[Car]
Note: Volvo <: Car, but class Item is invariant in type A.
You may wish to define A as +A instead. (SLS 4.5)
       val c: Item[Car] = new Item[Volvo](new Volvo)
```

While a Volvo instance may be assigned to a value of type Car, an Item[Volvo] instance may *not* be assigned to a value of type Item[Car]. Type parameters, being invariant by default, cannot adapt to alternate types even if they are compatible.

To fix this, you'll need to make the type parameter in Item *covariant*. Covariant type parameters can automatically morph into one of their base types when necessary. You can mark a type parameter as being covariant by adding a plus sign (+) in front of the type parameter.

Let's redefine the Item class with a covariant type parameter so that the Item[Volvo] type can change into Item[Car]:

```scala
scala> case class Item[+A](a: A) { def get: A = a }
defined class Item

scala> val c: Item[Car] = new Item[Volvo](new Volvo)
c: Item[Car] = Item(Volvo())

scala> val auto = c.get
auto: Car = Volvo()
```

The type parameter "A" is now covariant and can morph from a subtype to a base type. In other words, an instance of Item[Volvo] can be assigned to a value with the type Item[Car].

The Item.get() method likewise supports the type parameter's covariance. While the instance is a Item[Volvo] and contains an actual Volvo, the value's type is Item[Car] and so the return type of c.get is Car.

Covariance is a great tool for morphing type parameters into their base types. However, it is not always applicable. For example, an input parameter to a method cannot be covariant, for the same reasons that a base type cannot be converted to a subtype.

An input parameter being covariant means that it would be bound to a subtype but be invokable with a base type. This is an impossible conversion, because a base type cannot be converted to a subtype.

Let's see what the Scala compiler says when we try to use a covariant type parameter as an input parameter type for a method:

```scala
scala> class Check[+A] { def check(a: A) = {} }
<console>:7: error: covariant type A occurs in contravariant position in
    type A of value a
         class Check[+A] { def check(a: A) = {} }
```

As the error from the Scala compiler explains, a type parameter used in a method parameter is contravariant, not covariant. *Contravariance* is where a type parameter may morph into a subtype, in the opposite direction of a polymorphic transition from subtype to base type.

Contravariant type parameters are marked with a minus sign (–) in front of the type parameter. They can be used for input parameters to methods but not as their return types. Return types are covariant, because their result may be a subtype that is polymorphically converted to a base type.

Let's redefine this example with a contravariant type parameter so it can compile:

```scala
scala> class Check[-A] { def check(a: A) = {} }
defined class Check
```

Alternatively, you could also leave the type parameter invariant. Then the check() method could only be invoked with an input parameter of the exact same type as its class's type parameter:

```scala
scala> class Check[A] { def check(a: A) = {} }
defined class Check
```

This demonstrates how to solve the "covariant parameter in contravariant position" error, but we'll need a better example to demonstrate contravariance versus covariance. Let's run through the experience of defining covariant and contravariant type parameters with a more comprehensive example.

In the first of two parts we'll define the classes and methods to use. We'll use the Car class, its subclass Volvo, and a new subclass of Volvo called VolvoWagon. With this three-level class hierarchy we can pick a middle class, Volvo, and try to replace it with either its subclass or base class. Then we'll use Item to test covariance and Check to test contravariance. Finally we'll define methods that require Item and Check with the middle class Volvo. This way we'll be able to experiment with its subclass and base class to find out what works:

```scala
scala> class Car; class Volvo extends Car; class VolvoWagon extends Volvo
defined class Car
defined class Volvo
defined class VolvoWagon

scala> class Item[+A](a: A) { def get: A = a }
defined class Item

scala> class Check[-A] { def check(a: A) = {} }
defined class Check

scala> def item(v: Item[Volvo]) { val c: Car = v.get }
item: (v: Item[Volvo])Unit

scala> def check(v: Check[Volvo]) { v.check(new VolvoWagon()) }
check: (v: Check[Volvo])Unit
```

The Item class clearly needs a covariant type parameter. When bound to type Volvo its get() method will return a Volvo, which we should be able to store in a value with the type Car. This follows the standard rules of polymorphism where a base class value can store an instance of its subclass.

Likewise, the Check class clearly needs a contravariant type parameter. When bound to type Volvo its check() method takes a Volvo, so we should be able to pass it an instance of VolvoWagon. This also follows the standard rules of polymorphism, where an instance of a subclass can be passed to a method that expects its base class.

In the second of two parts we'll invoke the methods with the base class, exact class, and subclass:

```
scala> item( new Item[Car](new Car()) )                                    ❶
<console>:14: error: type mismatch;
 found    : Item[Car]
 required: Item[Volvo]
              item( new Item[Car](new Car()) )
               ^

scala> item( new Item[Volvo](new Volvo) )

scala> item( new Item[VolvoWagon](new VolvoWagon()) )                       ❷

scala> check( new Check[Car]() )                                            ❸

scala> check( new Check[Volvo]() )

scala> check( new Check[VolvoWagon]() )                                     ❹
<console>:14: error: type mismatch;
 found    : Check[VolvoWagon]
 required: Check[Volvo]
              check( new Check[VolvoWagon]() )
```

❶ The Item class has a covariant type parameter, which can morph from a subclass to a base class but not the other way around.

❷ Here we see covariance in action, as Item[VolvoWagon] becomes Item[Volvo].

❸ Here is contravariance in action, as Check[Car] becomes Check[Volvo].

❹ But not the other way around, because a contravariant type parameter cannot move from a base class to a subclass.

Covariance and contravariance can make type parameters less restrictive, but have their own restrictions about how they may be used. If you are unsure whether to use them, consider leaving your type parameters invariant. This is the default state for type parameters, and you may find it safer to keep all type parameters invariant unless a need arises to change them.

Package Objects

Most of the advanced types we have covered in this chapter, such as implicit parameters, implicit conversions, and type aliases, can only be defined within other types. This restriction helps to corral these entities, ensuring that in most cases they are only added to the namespace explicitly through imports.

One exception is the scala.Predef object, whose contents are added automatically to the namespace in Scala. Another exception is through package objects, a unique object for each package that also gets imported into the namespace of any code in that package.

Package objects are defined in their own file, *package.scala*, located in the package they will be affecting. You can define a package object by adding the package keyword before the object in the definition.

Here is an example package object that defines a new type alias, *Mappy*:

```
// located on com/oreilly/package.scala
package object oreilly {
  type Mappy[A,B] = collection.mutable.HashMap[A,B]
}
```

Any class, trait, or object defined in this package will pick up the Mappy[A,B] type alias and be able to use it directly.

The core "scala" package in the Scala library includes a package object like this one, adding many popular immutable collections to the namespace (albeit without fun names like "Mappy").

Package objects are a good solution for defining type aliases, implicit conversions, and other advanced types. They extend the range of these features, removing the need to manually import a class, trait, or object just to pick them up.

Summary

Scala combines the paradigms of functional programming and object-oriented programming, supporting both first-class functions and class definitions. What we know now is that its first-class functions *are* class definitions.

The type features in Scala can make your classes and methods safer and more restrictive. By specifying bounds to acceptable type parameters, your code can declare its requirements and ensure type safety.

They can also make them less restrictive, while also providing the same amount of type-safety. Covariant and contravariant type parameters give your types flexibility in how they accept and return compatible types. And implicit classes and parameters free your code from the restrictions of fixed methods and explicit parameters, while preventing unexpected type violations.

At this point you should have no limitations on the Scala code you can understand. This would be a good time to review the Scala API in depth, becuase its frequent use of variance annotation and implicit parameters will be understandable now. You could go even further by reading through the source of the Scala library itself. I suggest starting with collections you're well familiar with such as Option and Future.

In addition to working through the exercises in this chapter, you may want to start getting familiar with some of Scala's excellent open source libraries. We have covered only a fraction of the SBT build system, but you'll need to know it well to build more than a beginning application. Apache Spark (*https://spark.apache.org/*) is a popular way to do data analysis and other calculations with Scala. Typesafe (*https://typesafe.com/*), the company that manages the Scala code base, also provides the Play (*https://www.play framework.com/*) web framework and the Akka distributed computing framework (*http://akka.io/*). The Spray (*http://spray.io/*) and Finagle (*http://bit.ly/ls-finagle*) libraries are great for building networked applications, but if all you need is a REST API, the Scalatra (*http://www.scalatra.org/*) framework may be more suitable for you.

Finally, if you really enjoyed this section on Scala's type system and want to explore more Haskell-like type safety features, check out the Scalaz (*http://bit.ly/ls-scalaz*) library. Pronounced "Scala-Zed," the library will help you write safer and more expressive code than we could have covered in this book. Learning the Scalaz library, as well as other projects by the Typelevel group, may also help you to become a better developer.

Questions

While this is an important chapter to read and comprehend, its techniques are rather advanced. You may not find some of them to be useful until you start writing your own libraries or advanced applications in Scala.

In this chapter I'll depart from the standard exercises section followed in previous chapters. If you have completed all of the previous exercises then you should be familiar with developing concise classes and functions in the REPL, and larger applications in an IDE. Instead, let me ask you some questions about the advanced typing features and capabilities you have read about in this chapter.

You may want to find solutions to the questions by experimenting in the REPL or an IDE. It may also be useful to consider the questions a thought experiment to be completed when you have more experience using the language.

1. How would you extend a function? What are some of the applications for a class or trait that extends Function1[A,B]? If you are writing such a class or trait, would you extend Function1[A,B] or choose to extend A => B ?

2. How would you write a function type for a function that has two parameter lists, each with a single integer, and returns a single integer? If you wrote it as a Func tionX class, what would the exact class and type parameters contain?

3. A popular use for implicit parameters is for a default setting that works most of the time but may be overridden in special cases. Assume you are writing a sorting function that takes lines of text, and the lines may start with a right-aligned number. If you want to sort using the numbers, which may be prefixed by spaces, how would you encode this ability in an implicit parameter? How would you allow users to override this behavior and ignore the numbers for sorting?

4. Assume you wrote your own version of Option[A], calling it Perhaps[A], and implemented one or two methods to access its contents. What kind of implicit con-

version would you need to provide in order to allow it to be treated as a collection? How would you be able to invoke `flatMap` and `filter` on your instance without implementing those methods?

5. How would you implement your own string class named `Characters` that supports all of the JVM's `java.lang.String` methods but can also be treated as a Scala collection? Would a combination of types and conversions do most of the work for you? I suggest perusing the source code for `scala.Predef` to find some hints.

6. How would you add a "sum" method on all tuples, which returns the sum of all numeric values in a tuple? For example, (*a*, "hi", 2.5, 1, true).sum should return 3.5.

7. A `Function1` type takes type parameters, one for the input value and one for the output value. Which one should be covariant? Which one should be contravariant?

Reserved Words

Table A-1 displays the reserved words in Scala. Reserved words are part of the Scala language definition, and cannot be used as identifiers. To keep the definitions concise, I have used "class" where "class, object, and trait" may be more accurate.

Table A-1. Scala's reserved words

Name	Description
_	The wildcard operator, representing an expected value.
:	Delimits a value, variable, or function from its type.
@	Defines an annotation for a class or its member. Annotations are a JVM feature but are seldomly used in Scala, with @annotation.tailrec being a popular exception.
#	A type projection, which delimits a type from its subtype.
<-	Delimits a generator from its identifier in a for-loop.
←	A single-character (\u2190) alternative to <-.
<:	The upper-bound operator, restricting types to those that are equal to or extend the given type.
<%	The view-bound operator, allowing any type that may be treated as the given type.
=	The assignment operator.
=>	Used in match expressions and partial functions to indicate a conditional expression, in function types to indicate a return type, and in function literals to define the function body.
⇒	A single-character (\u21D2) alternative to =>.
>:	The lower-bound operator, restricting types to those that are equal to or are extended by the given type.
abstract	Marks a class or trait as being abstract and uninstantiable.
case	Defines a matching pattern in match expressions and partial functions.
catch	Catches an exception. An alternate syntax that predates the util.Try monadic collection.
class	Defines a new class.
def	Defines a new method.

Name	Description
do	Part of the `do..while` loop definition.
else	The second part of an `if..else` conditional expression.
extends	Defines a base type for a class.
false	One of the two `Boolean` values.
final	Marks a class or trait as being nonextendable.
finally	Executes an expression following a `try` block. An alternate syntax that predates the `util.Try` monadic collection.
for	Begins a for-loop.
forSome	Defines an existential type. Existential types are a flexible method for specifying type requirements, but are discouraged in general Scala development. See SIP-18 (*http://docs.scala-lang.org/sips/completed/modularizing-language-features.html*) (Scala Improvement Process #18) for details on why existential types are considered an "opt-in" feature in Scala.
if	The first part of an `if..else` conditional expression, or the main part of an `if` conditional statement.
implicit	Defines an implicit conversion or parameter.
import	Imports a package, class, or members of a class to the current namespace.
lazy	Defines a value as being lazy, only defined the first time it is accessed.
match	Begins a match expression.
new	Creates a new instance of a class.
null	A value that indicates the lack of an instance. Has the type `Null`.
object	Defines a new object.
override	Marks a value or method as replacing the member of the same name in a base type.
package	Defines the current package, an incremental package name, or a package object.
private	Marks a class member as being inaccessible outside the class definition.
protected	Marks a class member as being inaccessible outside the class definition or its subclasses.
return	Explicitly states the return value for a method. By default, the last expression in a method is used as the return value.
sealed	Marks a class as only allowing subclasses within the current file.
super	Marks a class member reference as one in the base type, versus one overridden in the current class.
this	Marks a class member reference as one in the current class, versus a parameter with the same name.
throw	Raises an error condition that breaks the current flow of operation and only resumes if the error is *caught* elsewhere.
trait	Defines a new trait.
true	One of the two `Boolean` values.
try	Marks a range of code for catching an exception. An alternate syntax that predates the `util.Try` monadic collection.
type	Defines a new type alias.

Name	Description
val	Defines a new, immutable value.
var	Defines a new, mutable variable.
while	Part of the do..while loop definition.
with	Defines a base trait for a class.
yield	Yields the return value from a for-loop.

Where Are My Favorite :: and ++ Operators?

The :: and ++ operators are valid method identifiers, not reserved words. The Scala collections library defines methods with these identifiers, which means you can also use them for your own methods.

Index

Symbols

" (quotation marks, double)
    enclosing string literals, 17
    """" (triple quotes), for multiline strings, 18
$ (dollar sign)
    referencing external data in string interpolation, 18
& (ampersand)
    & (Boolean and) operator, 23
    && versus & operator, 23
' (quotation marks, single)
    enclosing Char literals, 23
( ) (parentheses)
    defining capture group in regular expressions, 20
    denoting a Unit literal, 24
    enclosing Boolean expression in if expression, 36
    enclosing tuples, 25
    grouping function parameters, 55
    in for-loops, 38
    in functions, 48, 50
        leaving out for single-parameter functions, 67
* (asterisk)
    in vararg parameters, 54
    multiplication operator, 13
-> relation operator, 86
. (period), member access operator, 13

. dot notation, 57, 91
    accessing class fields and methods, 143
/ (slash)
    division operator, 118
: (colon)
    :: (cons) operator, 89
<% view-bound operator, 210
<: upper-bound relation operator, 209
<< (left shift operator), 40
= (equals sign)
    == (equals) operator, string comparisons, 18
    before procedure body, 48
>: lower-bound relation operator, 210
@annotation.tailrec, 51
@param keyword in Scaladoc, 61
[ ] (square brackets), for type parameterization, 13
\ (backslash)
    escaping special characters in string literals, 17
_ (underscore)
    wildcard operator, 154
`` (backquotes), names enclosed in, 14
{ } (curly braces)
    enclosing expression blocks, 27, 28
    in for-loops, 38
    in if expressions, 31
    in references to external data, 18

We'd like to hear your suggestions for improving our indexes. Send email to index@oreilly.com.

K

key-value pairs
    in maps, 85

L

lambda expressions (or lambdas), 69
    (see also function literals)
lazy collections, 115
lazy values, 150
left shift operator (<<), 40
left-associative notation, 89
line comments, 61
linearization, 177
    benefits of, 178
    multiple inheritance ordering and, 178
list-folding operations, 97
listener class (example), 148
lists, 83
    accessing elements, 84
    arithmetic operations on, 90
        adding items to end of list, 92
    constructing with cons operator, 89
    converting buffer of 2-sized tuples to, 110
    converting mutable collections to, 109
    converting other collection types to and from, 98
    covariant type parameters of List, 200
    creating and manipulating, 86
        checking for end of a list, 88
        creating a List iterator, 87
    empty, head element wrapped in an Option, 118
    higher-order functions available in List, 85
    iterating over, using for-loops, 84
    List type, official documentation, 90
    mapping, 92
    matching on head and tail elements, 101
    reducing, 93
        Boolean reduction operations, 94
        creating your own reduction operation, 95
        list-folding operations, 97
    retrieving an element by its index, using List.apply(), 150
    Seq as root type, 113
    type parameters, 84
    using User class with (example), 139

literals, 16
    assigning to new values without stating type, 17
    case-insensitive characters in, 17
    Char, 23
    defined, 9
logical operators
    obtaining Boolean values from, 23
Long type, 15
    converting to Int, using toInt method, 16
loops, 37–41
    for-loops, 37
    iterator guards in, 39
    nested iterators in, 39
    value binding in, 40
    while and do/while, 40
lower bounds, 209
lower-bound relation operator (>:), 210

M

map function
    using with Option collection, 119
map operations
    for-loop as, 38
map() function, 65
    in List, 85
mapping, defined, 92
maps, 85
    building, 109
    converting mutable collections to, 109
    converting other collection types to, 98
    immutable, converting to and from buffers, 110
    mutable and immutable versions of Map, 155
        adding both to current namespace, 156
match expressions, 31–37
    failing to provide matching pattern for input expression, 34
    in partial functions, 77
    matching types with pattern variables, 36
    matching with pattern guards, 36
    matching with wildcard patterns, 34
    pattern alternative in, 33
    syntax, 32
    taking integer status code and returning appropriate messsage, 32
    using with collections, 100
    versus if .. else blocks, 32

MatchError type, 34, 77
methods, 57
   and operator notation, 59
      methods with more than one parameter,
         60
   apply methods, 150
   chaining method calls, 60
   defined, 57
   for case classes and companion objects
      automatically generated methods, 174
   implementing abstract method with a value,
      147
   implicit parameters in, 200
   in abstract classes, 146
   in case classes and companion objects, 173
   inherited, overriding methods in parent
      class, 140
   object, 168
   overloaded, 149
   private, 159
   protected, 158
mkString method, 173
monadic collections, 117
   Future, 125–130
   Option, 117–121
   Try, 121–125
mutable collections, 107
   converting to immutable, 109
   creating from immutable ones, 109
   creating new, 108
   importing all into current namespace, 154
   using collection builders, 111

N

named parameters, 53
   in classes, 143
   placeholders for, 72
namespaces
   duplicate class names in, 155
   importing class into current namespace, 153
   importing instance members into current
      namespace, 184
   resetting namespace in REPL, 154
   scala.Predef object automatically added to,
      216
naming conventions, 13
   for packages, 152
   for pattern variables, 36
nested classes, 142

nested functions, 52
nested iterators, 39
Nil type
   lists ending with instance of, 88
None type, 117
Nothing type, 22
   lists and, 88
null keyword, 22
Null type, 22
null values
   avoiding a method call on null, 68
   creating Option object with, 117
   using a pattern guard to differentiate be-
      tween nonnull and null response, 36
numeric data types, 15
   automatic type conversions, 15
numeric literals, 16

O

Object class, 138
object-oriented Scala
   classes, 137
      abstract, 146
      anonymous, 148
      apply methods, 150
      defining, 142
      final and sealed, 161
      lazy values in fields, 150
      more class types, 146
      more field and method types, 149
      overloaded methods in, 149
      packaging, 151
      privacy controls, 158
objects, 167–173, 207
   advantages of using, 173
   and case classes, 173
   apply methods and companion objects, 169
   classes and, 168
   command-line applications with, 172
   defining, 168
   importing members into current namespace,
      184
   pure functions as utilities, 168
   types having AnyRef as root, 22
   using for writing functions, 175
operator notation, 59
   benefits and drawbacks of, 60
   versus dot notation in list methods, 91

About the Author

Jason Swartz is a Software Engineer in the San Francisco Bay Area, developing Scala applications at Loyal3 and Netflix. Before making the switch to functional programming he managed the developer docs and support team at eBay, wrote advertising and merchandising platforms in Java, and built tools and UI prototypes at Apple.

Colophon

The animal on the cover of *Learning Scala* is the American Ostrich, or the greater rhea (*Rhea americana*), a tall, flightless bird found in eastern South America. Known locally as the ñandú, it is one of the two birds that comprise the rhea species, along with its smaller, more uncommon counterpart, the lesser rhea (*rhea pennata*).

Endemic to Argentina, Bolivia, Brazil, Paraguay, and Uruguay, the greater rhea inhabits open areas with tall vegetation, such as grasslands, savanna, and grassy wetlands. Curiously, a small nonindigenous population also exists in rural northwest Germany, established in 2000 after several escaped from a farm. These birds have prospered in the wild, defying all expectations.

While markedly similar to the African ostrich, the greater rhea has three toes rather than two and is about half the size; adult rheas stand at about five feet tall and weigh between 44 and 60 pounds. Its fluffy plumage is gray, with dark patches on the crown, neck, and upper back. The bird's long, powerful legs make it a fast runner, capable of reaching speeds of over 35 miles per hour. Its large wings, which help maintain balance while running, are also flaunted in elaborate courtship displays.

The American Ostrich typically nests near water. Rheas are polygamous, and so each male may mate with up to twelve females during the spring and summer, its breeding season. Males become extremely territorial during this period, behaving aggressively toward one another. After mating, the female will deposit her eggs into the nest and often move on to a new partner. The male alone will incubate the eggs of all of its mates, typically in the same nest. Later, he will forcefully guard and care for the young.

Apart from breeding rituals, they are communal birds, amassing flocks of 10 to 100 and even mixing with other large animals, such as deer. The greater rhea enjoys a diet of plants, seeds, and fruit but also has been known to consume insects, small rodents, reptiles, and small birds. It also swallows pebbles to aid digestion.

Many of the animals on O'Reilly covers are endangered; all of them are important to the world. To learn more about how you can help, go to animals.oreilly.com.

The cover image is from Cassell's Natural History. The cover fonts are URW Typewriter and Guardian Sans. The text font is Adobe Minion Pro; the heading font is Adobe Myriad Condensed; and the code font is Dalton Maag's Ubuntu Mono.

Have it your way.

Get even more for your money.

Join the O'Reilly Community, and register the O'Reilly books you own. It's free, and you'll get:

- $4.99 ebook upgrade offer
- 40% upgrade offer on O'Reilly print books
- Membership discounts on books and events
- Free lifetime updates to ebooks and videos
- Multiple ebook formats, DRM FREE
- Participation in the O'Reilly community
- Newsletters
- Account management
- 100% Satisfaction Guarantee

Signing up is easy:

1. Go to: oreilly.com/go/register
2. Create an O'Reilly login.
3. Provide your address.
4. Register your books.

Note: English-language books only

To order books online:
oreilly.com/store

For questions about products or an order:
orders@oreilly.com

To sign up to get topic-specific email announcements and/or news about upcoming books, conferences, special offers, and new technologies:
elists@oreilly.com

For technical questions about book content:
booktech@oreilly.com

To submit new book proposals to our editors:
proposals@oreilly.com

O'Reilly books are available in multiple DRM-free ebook formats. For more information:
oreilly.com/ebooks

O'REILLY ®

9 781449 367930